D1807189

THE UNRELENTING CONFLICT

By the same author

A Garland of Legends
'Lawrence of Arabia' and 'The Arab Revolt'
1992

A Bibliography of the Printed Works of James Parkes
with selected quotations
1977
(together with Diana Bailey)

THE UNRELENTING CONFLICT
Britain, Balfour, & Betrayal

SIDNEY SUGARMAN

The Book Guild Ltd
Sussex, England

This book is sold subject to the condition that it shall not, by way of
trade or otherwise, be lent, re-sold, hired out, photocopied or held in
any retrieval system or otherwise circulated without the publisher's prior
consent in any form of binding or cover other than that in which this is
published and without a similar condition including this condition being
imposed on the subsequent purchaser.

The Book Guild Ltd
25 High Street,
Lewes, Sussex

First published 2000
© Sidney Sugarman 2000

Set in Perpetua
Typesetting by Acorn Bookwork, Salisbury, Wiltshire
Printed in Great Britain by
Antony Rowe Ltd, Chippenham, Wiltshire

A catalogue record for this book is available from the British Library
ISBN 1 85776 462 5

In memory of James Parkes

'Now, there is the breach; there is the violation of the pledge; there is the abandonment of the Balfour Declaration; there is the end of the vision, of the hope, of the dream.'

Winston Churchill in the House of Commons
23 May 1939

INTRODUCTION

Towards the end of his account of the British Mandate in Palestine John Marlowe wrote:

'During the years 1945–7 the British Government, or rather the Foreign and Colonial and Middle East and War Office officials advising the British Government, had become convinced that the obligations incurred by Great Britain under the Palestine Mandate represented the principal if not the only obstacle to that policy of friendship and co-operation with the Arab League which had become the cornerstone of British Middle East policy. The 1939 White Paper policy, the maintenance of which was regarded as the only possible interpretation of the Mandate consistent with Arab friendship, had been whittled away as the result of American support for Zionism and as the result of Zionist resistance in Palestine. In these circumstances, and in view of the fact that the continued British military occupation of Palestine was no longer regarded as strategically vital, the U.N. Assembly Resolution provided H.M.G. with the opportunity of ridding themselves of a troublesome burden and at the same time made it possible for them, once relieved of their Mandatory obligations, to attempt to provide for an Arab solution in Palestine and so, as it seemed, to remove a cause of misunderstanding between Great Britain and the Arab League.' (*The Seat of Pilate*, London, 1959, p.240)

In short, in Marlowe's view, Britain had decided by 1947 that if the responsibilities imposed by the terms of the Mandate impeded

1

her prospects of Arab friendship, her interests, certainly in the Middle East, would best be served by surrender of the Mandate. The consequences of such a step had been weighed by the British.

'The validity of the policy which had begun to emerge', wrote Marlowe, 'was dependent on the correctness of the British estimate of the ability of the Arab League to impose an Arab solution on Palestine once the British had withdrawn.' (op.cit.)

The nature of the 'Arab solution' envisaged by the British is revealed in Marlowe's statement that

'H.M.G. continued to pin their faith on the Arab League armies which, with the connivance and indeed encouragement of H.M.G., were poised to invade Palestine as soon as the Mandate had terminated.'

'Connivance' and 'encouragement' indicate both collusion and association. The Arab Legion of Transjordan, while not the largest of the Arab League armies, was known to be the most efficient and to all intents and purposes a British force.

'It was maintained by means of a two-and-a-half million pounds subsidy from the British Treasury, it was British-trained and British-armed, and there were thirty-seven British officers, including the Commanding Officer, serving with the Legion. During the weeks before the invasion, it received heavy reinforcements of arms and ammunition from British military stores in Palestine. The military conversations in Amman, which lasted five days (from 25 April to 29 April 1948), produced a paper plan – which was apparently communicated to the British Military Command in Palestine – by which (a) Transjordan and Iraqi forces in the north would cross the Jordan just south of the Sea of Galilee and capture Haifa by means of a converging movement by two columns advancing through Lower Galilee and the Emek, and (b) Transjordan and Egyptian forces in the south would join up near Hebron and jointly capture Jerusalem.' (Marlowe, p.247)

In London the Foreign Secretary, Ernest Bevin, was involved in preparations for the proposed conflict. At the end of February 1948 King Abdullah of Jordan had sent his Prime Minister, Taufiq Pasha Abul Huda, and his Foreign Minister, Fawzi Pasha al-Mulqi, to London to negotiate an agreement with Bevin. Glubb Pasha, the British Commander of the Arab Legion, who attended this meeting as military adviser and Arabic interpreter, reported the agreement reached at this meeting, writing:

'The Transjordan Government proposed to send the Arab Legion across the Jordan when the Mandate ended, and to occupy that part of Palestine awarded to the Arabs which was contiguous with the frontier of Transjordan. I can to this day almost see Mr. Bevin sitting at his table in that splendid room. When I had finished my translation thus far, he interrupted Taufiq Pasha's statement by saying: ''It seems the obvious thing to do.''

Some four weeks prior to this meeting – on 16 January – Nuri Said, Iraq's 'elder statesman', had joined Bevin at a private dinner meeting and had relayed to the British Foreign Secretary the decisions of the Arab League meetings. Bevin's response to his requests encouraged Nuri to report to the Iraqi Parliament

'Britain viewed with favour the Arab aims regarding Palestine. Talks about arms for the Iraqi army were most satisfactory.'

Corroboration came from Reuter's Baghdad correspondent on 14 March:

'The Iraqi Army received today its first batch of warplanes from Britain. War equipment and other essential materials to equip the army on a modern scale would be arriving continuously from Britain from now on.'

Six weeks later the 2nd Motorised Brigade of the Iraqi army, presumably by that time satisfactorily equipped, left Baghdad to participate in the invasion of Palestine.

The Anglo-Egyptian Treaty of 1936 placed the British under an obligation to defend Egyptian territory but provided no restraint on Egyptian preparation to invade Palestine. Indeed, Brigadier Clayton of the British Middle East Office had attended the Arab League meeting at Aley in the Lebanon in October 1947, when the decision was made that the states of the Arab League would invade Palestine in the event of the partition proposal being approved by the Assembly of the United Nations. Marlowe has ventured that:

'It seems probable that the British attitude in the *ad-hoc* Committee was dictated (a) by knowledge of and, possibly, connivance in the Arab League plan to invade Palestine; (b) by a belief that this invasion would succeed; and (c) by a desire to adopt such an attitude towards that invasion as would ensure reasonable Arab friendliness towards Great Britain.' (op.cit. p. 234)

Marlowe's reference (see above) to the need 'to remove a cause of misunderstanding between Great Britain and the Arab League' may call for an explanation of the relationship between the two parties. The Arab League was first publicly mentioned by Anthony Eden, then Foreign Secretary, in 1941. Four years later he presided over the necessary diplomatic exchanges and negotiations which brought about the formal establishment of the League in March 1945 by Egypt, Iraq, Saudi Arabia, Yemen, Transjordan, Syria and Lebanon. In his memoirs (*Full Circle*, London, 1960) Eden records his delight:

> 'to hear at the end of 1954 that Nuri-es-Said, the Prime Minister of Iraq, was working on a plan to strengthen the Arab League pact by the inclusion of Turkey and with the help of the United Kingdom and the United States. . . . This agreement was signed on February 24.'

The member states of the League met at Inchass, one of King Farouk's country palaces, on 2 June 1946, and called for an end to all Jewish immigration into Palestine and the prevention of all further land sales to Jews. They also undertook to support the resistance of the Palestine Arabs 'with all the means at our disposal'. Seven days later they met again, at Bludan in Syria: this meeting was attended by the Damascus correspondent of the London *Times* together with Brigadier Clayton from the British Embassy in Cairo. They discussed their territorial claims to the Negev, the 'Arab Triangle' ('West Bank') and the Haifa Port Enclave. The Syrians claimed the Galilee: the ex-Mufti demanded the expulsion of the entire Jewish population and the re-establishment of his own authority.

In 1964 the Arab League established the P.L.O. Its Secretary-General from 1945 to 1952, Azzam Pasha, will long be remembered for his declaration, even before the Partition Plan vote was taken at the United Nations in 1947, that 'this will be a war of annihilation and dreadful slaughter, reminiscent of the Mongol slaughter and the Crusades'. While the Chief of the Imperial General Staff, Montgomery, appeared in the course of a lecture delivered about the same time to the Imperial Defence College to endorse Azzam Pasha's view of the likely outcome of the threatened conflict he refrained from employing the Egyptian's lurid language, contenting himself with informing his listeners that in his opinion 'the Jews had bought it'. A more professional assessment of the situation was offered by General Macmillan, the G.O.C. British troops in Palestine, in the month before the Arab invasion, when he concluded that 'in terms of troops, equipment and geography, the combined Arab armies would have no difficulty in taking over the whole country'.

In the light of the information now available it would have been difficult for any observer to have then arrived at any other conclusion. When Ben Gurion checked the armouries of the Haganah in April 1947 he found its stock of weapons to be as follows:

> 10,073 rifles (of which only 1,353 were stored in the central armouries or were in the hands of the Haganah or Palmach units: the remaining 8,720 were scattered in 'penny packets' under the control of the settlements and kept there for local defence), 1,900 sub-machine guns, 444 light machine guns and 186 medium machine guns, 672 2-inch mortars and 96 3-inch mortars. (Figures given by Ben Gurion to Jewish leaders in Israel in July 1948.)

When fighting started on 30 November 1947, the Palmach establishment was 3,000, including about 1,000 girls, but the existence of a partly-trained reserve of nearly 3,000 enabled the Palmach to mobilise quickly a total of five battalions numbering about 5,000, including 1,200 girls. There were no heavy machine guns, no artillery, no anti-tank or anti-aircraft weapons, no real armoured cars nor any vestige of air or naval strength.

When Glubb's Arab Legion crossed the river Jordan by the Allenby Bridge at dawn on 15 May 1948, his forces amounted to

'two brigades, each consisting of two semi-mechanised regiments, one battery of eight 25-pounders and one engineer squadron still in process of formation. Each regiment had one squadron of twelve armoured cars, three motorised rifle squadrons and one headquarter squadron.' (Godfrey Lias, *Glubb's Legion*, 1956, p. 180)

On the same day the 2nd Egyptian Brigade, under Colonel Neguib, crossed the opposite border into Palestine and advanced along the coastal road through Gaza towards Tel Aviv without meeting any opposition, for the local Arabs were friendly and enthusiastic, and the route was guarded by local guerrilla leaders and their followers. Israeli scouts watched the advance from their observation posts in the hills, reporting a total of 1,500 vehicles in addition to armour and field guns. The Egyptians proceeded unhindered until they reached Isdud (Ashdod) at the northern end of the Gaza Strip, where Neguib assembled his force of 2,500 men, 10 tanks, six field guns and a few mounted 2-pounder guns. Against this force, whose eastern flank was guarded by the 4th Egyptian Brigade, Shimon Avidan deployed the remnants of the Givati Brigade, which had been in continuous action since the previous December and had already suffered 950 casualties. The gaps had been filled with raw recruits from Tel Aviv and Rehovot, enabling him to count 1,800 'bayonets' supported by a mobile unit of eight lorries and three horses.

In her admirable *Britain's Moment in the Middle East 1914–1956* (London, 1963) Elizabeth Monroe recalled that 1917 was 'the year in which the British climbed on to the shoulders of the Zionists in order to get a British Palestine' (p. 38). On the morning of 15 May 1948, it seemed that they would finally be able to achieve 'a British Palestine' over the prone bodies of the Zionist defenders. We have to look beyond the Balfour Declaration of 1917 and Britain's acceptance of the League of Nations Mandate for Palestine in order to comprehend the full nature and purpose of the British connection in that embattled country.

1

Drang nach Osten

Over the past centuries a number of Western nations have turned towards the East – in search of trade, in search of treasure, in search of adventure, and, following the early years of commercial development, in a bid for territory. English writers have spoken of 'the Lure of the East' and the 'Push to the East', but perhaps the most felicitous phrase has come from the Germans, among the last in the processions Eastward, for *Drang* has the meanings of 'pressure', 'distress' and 'impulse' as well as 'intense desire'.

England's *Drang nach Osten* may be dated back to the middle of the fifteenth century. In 1458 Robert Sturmy of Bristol made the first trading voyage in a British ship to the Levant. He was followed during the first half of the sixteenth century by a procession of tall ships from London, Southampton and Bristol, which succeeded in establishing trading with Sicily, Candia, Chios and Cyprus and eventually reached Beyrout and Tripoli. Efforts were made to establish amicable relations with Constantinople and Teheran, and in 1553 Sultan Suleiman granted English merchants permission to trade within the area of his territories on the same terms that he had granted to the French and the Venetians.

In 1566 Shah Tahmas conferred on English merchants the privileges necessary to live and trade in Persia. In 1578 the first British Ambassador presented his credentials to the Sublime Porte, and in the same year two London merchants, Sir Edward Osborne and Richard Staper, sent William Harborne overland to Constantinople and through him obtained a grant of safe conduct and trading privileges from the Sultan. In recognition of their enterprise the Queen issued, in 1581, a charter constituting both gentlemen together with others a corporation with monopoly rights, under the name of the Turkey Company.

The Turkey Company with its 19 vessels conducted a lucrative trade, successfully forcing its way through the Straits of Gibraltar in the face of armed Spanish opposition. In 1592 it amalgamated with another English syndicate, the Venice Company, to form the Levant Company, with Aleppo as its chief mart: the new company continued its activities for more than two centuries, but failed in its efforts to establish an overland trade with India. In 1583 Ralph Fitch and John Newberry had jointly made an attempt to traffic with the East by a land route, penetrating through Syria to Ormuz and thence to Goa, the Portuguese headquarters in India. Only Fitch survived their eight years of wandering in Southern Asia: his reports revealed much detailed information concerning all the lands between Palestine and Siam but proved fairly conclusively that the obstacles to an overland route were at that time insuperable.

In 1599 the sum of £30,000 was subscribed to finance a voyage to India by the eastern route. In the following year this capital sum was doubled, and on 31 December 1600, a charter was granted, and the East India Company, the greatest corporation in English history, entered on its long career.

The first expedition of the East India Company, in 1601, sailed under the command of Sir James Lancaster, who had ten years earlier doubled the Cape of Good Hope and traversed the Indian Ocean in order to establish a sea route to the east. The venture was brilliantly successful and opened up a new era in English expansion. The first English factories on the mainland of India were planted in the years 1610–11. From the beginning of the seventeenth century to the middle of the nineteenth the famous 'East Indiamen' held unquestioned pre-eminence in the world.

From a simple trading company it grew in the reign of Charles II into a great chartered company, with the right to acquire territory, coin money, and command fortresses and troops.

Other European nations were contending for trading rights in the peninsula. Portugal had been among the earliest: the Dutch and the French were to follow hard on the heels of the English. In 1612 a pair of English ships under Captain Best drove a Portuguese squadron from the mouth of the Tapti, and by so doing secured the concession of a factory at Surat. In 1620 the English appeared in the Persian Gulf, and two years later captured the island fortress of Ormuz. From then on the East India Company extended its sway by the successive acquisition of factories in all parts of the Indian peninsula. Sir Thomas Roe spent the years 1615–18 at Agra, with the full rank of Ambassador from the King. Madras, which ultimately became the chief English port on the Coromandel Coast, was founded by Francis Day in 1639. He built Fort St George there, and Madras became the head factory of the eastern coast.

In 1665 the English commenced their tenure of Bombay, increasing its population through public works from 10,000 to 60,000 in twelve years. In 1686 Joe Charnock, who, after thirty years in India became head of the Bengal council, founded the city of Calcutta: its Fort William was built by his successor in 1697–8. In the meantime the French were endeavouring to establish their own East India Company in the area, first occupying the islands of Reunion and Mauritius, where they built a naval base before founding the first French factory at Surat, in 1668, and another on the Bay of Bengal in the following year. Their first clashes came, not with the English, despite their recent conflict in the West Indies, but with the Dutch, who defeated them in battles off Ceylon and the Coromandel Coast, finally driving them to Pondicherry.

Meanwhile the United East India Company progressed from

strength to strength. In 1715 it opened a regular trade with China. By 1737 its subscribed capital amounted to £4,200,000. The war which broke out between England and France in 1744 served to hasten the inevitable conflict which must sooner or later have begun independently between the two rivals on Indian territory. In the following two years both parties increased their naval power in the area, Britain sending out four warships while the French increased their fleet at Pondicherry to ten vessels. The first blood went to France with their capture of Madras in September, 1746.

The British counter-attack came in the following year, and the conflict continued until 16 January 1761, when Pondicherry surrendered to the British, notwithstanding the reinforcements of 2,000 troops and nine ships sent from France in 1758. Two years later Pondicherry was restored to the French by the Treaty of Paris, but taken again by Madras forces in 1778 after a 70 days' siege.

In 1784 William Pitt the Younger passed his India Bill into law, creating a Board of Control, to take charge of all civil, military and revenue affairs, consisting of a Secretary of State with a seat in the Cabinet, Chancellor of the Exchequer, and four privy councillors, with provision for the appointment of a Governor-general by the King's ministers. Until 1857 this board, in association with the East India Company, functioned virtually as the effective Government of India, but the Indian Mutiny which broke out in that year led to the transference of the Government of India from the Company to the Crown.

2

'The practice of politics in the East may be defined by one word: dissimulation.' Benjamin Disraeli (Contarini Fleming, pt. V, ch. 10)

In the year 1858, the year in which the Government of India passed to the British Crown, the shares of the Suez Canal Company (the Compagnie Universelle du Canal Maritime de Suez) were placed on the market. The British Government, from its fear of French pretensions in Egypt, and its anxiety about the safety of communications with its Indian Empire, set itself to oppose the construction of the canal by every means within its power.

A block of 80,000 shares, representing one-fifth of the entire issue, had been set aside for Great Britain, but were not taken up. The United States also had refused a block of 20,000 shares, and the Egyptian Government, initially allotted 64,000 shares, was thus enabled to subscribe to 177,642 shares. The man who led the fierce antagonism to the project in England was the Prime Minister, Lord Palmerston. His long-standing hostility to the French adventure in the Middle East − particularly in Egypt − blinded him to the advantages which could be derived by Britain from the completion of a project which would virtually halve the length of the existing 10,000-mile sea journey from England to India, where her most valuable interests then lay.

One aspect of the rivalry between the two powers emerged from their competition for the control of Palestine. They had already clashed at the time of Napoleon's invasion of that country in

1798, which was defeated in the next year by the intervention of the British. When Mehemet Ali, with the connivance of the French, invaded Syria in 1840, Palmerston went into action and ensured his expulsion from the country.

It was in that same year that Palmerston attempted to interest the Sublime Porte in the restoration of the Jews to Palestine, a project which at that time, though possibly with motives which differed from his, was engaging certain religious circles in England. On the very day (August 11th) that Mehemet Ali was expelled from Syria, Palmerston wrote to the British Ambassador in Constantinople (Lord Ponsonby): 'There exists at present among the Jews dispersed over Europe a strong notion that the time is approaching when their nation is to return to Palestine', an obscure speculation (for at that time there was no organised movement among European Jews seeking return to that impoverished and inhospitable land) which was succeeded by the revelation of what might be regarded as a more empirical motive:

> 'The Jewish people, if returning under the sanction and protection of the Sultan, would be a check upon any future evil designs of Mehemet Ali or his successor ... the promulgation of some law in their favour would spread a friendly disposition towards the Sultan among the Jews in Europe, and the Turkish Government must at once see how advantageous it would be to the Sultan's cause thus to create useful friends in many countries by a single edict'.

Some months later (on 17 February 1841) he expanded on this theme, writing to Ponsonby 'that the Jews who are scattered throughout other countries should be induced to go and settle in Palestine.' But, he pointed out, possibly revealing his motive, the Jews would require 'some real and tangible security' and should be able to count on British protection and be allowed to transmit any complaints through British authorities.

It is conceivable that Palmerston's solicitude may have been inspired by his desire to establish a role within the Turkish Empire comparable to that of France, who had long represented Catholic interests in the Levant, or Russia, who claimed to protect all Orthodox Christians in the Ottoman Empire. His idea of a similar status for Protestants received the support of Prussia, and in 1841 the two Protestant Powers agreed to establish a Protestant Bishopric in Jerusalem.

In 1838 Britain had made overtures towards opening a consulate in Jerusalem, the first in the city after the abolition of the French consulate more than 100 years previously, and on 31 January 1839, the consul, W.T. Young, received the following message: 'Viscount Palmerston has instructed me to signify that part of your function as British vice-consul in Jerusalem will be to offer protection to the Jews in general.' By a strange coincidence a leading member of the London Society for Promoting Christianity Among the Jews, Lord Ashley (later to become the seventh Earl of Shaftesbury), happened to be married to Palmerston's step-daughter. The Society had since 1820 maintained a mission in Jerusalem, and at a meeting of 'The Jews' Society' in 1845 Lord Ashley declared: 'Our Church and our nation have been called to the glorious service of making known the Gospel of Christ to the many thousands of Israel.' It would appear that between Palmerston and his son-in-law both the political and spiritual needs of the Jews would be receiving the most earnest attention.

3

'The Suez Canal came to complete Egypt's introduction to world strategy, commerce, diplomacy and thought. The Canal made Egyptian territory the object of fierce rivalries by opening it to the world.' Jean and Simonne Lacroutre: Egypt in Transition, London, 1958.

Palmerston, who had so vigorously opposed the Suez Canal project, died six years after the work of its construction had begun; four years before its ceremonial opening on 17 November 1869. In 1875 Disraeli purchased on behalf of the British Government the Khedive's shares (44 per cent of the total share issue) in the Suez Canal Company, for £4,000,000, and in 1882 the British commenced their occupation of Egypt, thus ensuring the control of the entire canal zone.

The Mediterranean routes eastward towards the Levant and the northern approaches to the Suez Canal had during the previous hundred years been secured by a succession of British conquests, commencing with the capture in 1783 of Gibraltar, which controlled the western approach to the Mediterranean; in 1830 it became a Crown Colony. Cyprus was occupied in 1878, while Malta, almost exactly midway between Gibraltar and Cyprus, had been in British occupation since 1799. In Sicily, lying to the north of Malta, a British garrison had been established in 1806; the island came fully under British control between 1811 and 1814. Thus staging-posts along the short sea route to India were established even before the completion of the British occupation of Egypt.

With the exception of Cyprus, which had passed into British occupation by a negotiated arrangement with Turkey (though in 1914 it was annexed by Britain), these British successes in the Mediterranean had all been achieved at the expense of the French, who had at Gibraltar participated in the battles for its possession on the side of the Spaniards and had shared their defeat. From the fall of Pondicherry in 1761 until the British occupation of Egypt in 1882, the history of the region is a record of Franco-British rivalry and conflict.

The French, a Mediterranean power, saw the British as intruders into their territories. Throughout the seventeenth century France had assumed the role of ally and protector of the Ottoman Empire, where her involvement had been recognised since the treaty in 1535 between François I and the Ottoman Suleiman I, which conferred on France the privileges of the capitulations and acknowledgement of her position as the protector of Latin Christianity in the Ottoman Empire. The capitulations had been extended in 1740 and again in 1802. France suffered a setback, as we have seen, in the defeat, through the intervention of the British, of her attempts to install Mehemet Ali in the area, but in 1842 came back to afford protection to the Maronites of Lebanon at a time when they were suffering persecution at the hands of the Druzes and other Moslem elements.

Although Palmerston had failed in his efforts to establish a parallel role in the area, but with the Jews as his protégés, the British could claim some compensation for this failure in their achievements on the far side of the Peninsula, where in 1820 they had signed agreements with the various amirs and sheikhs of the Gulf coasts and islands for the cessation of piracy in the Persian Gulf. These agreements subsequently resulted in the establishment of British protection for the various rulers. Thus the entire Gulf became an area of British influence; and in 1853 the existing agreements were expanded into a perpetual maritime truce embracing the seven sheikhdoms and principalities extending along the

Arabian coast of the Gulf, and the area became known as the Trucial Coast (or Trucial Oman), with Britain undertaking to provide both protection and financial support for the sheikhdoms and their rulers. At the western end of the southern coast of the Peninsula the British had in 1839 acquired the town and harbour of Aden, developing it as a coal depot, supply station and base for ships on the long sea route to India.

These developments in the Persian Gulf and the Arabian coast areas to the south can be related to the British interests in India – for the Gulf waters reached out to the Indian Ocean – and also to the prospect of an overland route which would reach from the Mediterranean to the Indian Ocean: conceivably from Palestine to Mesopotamia. Curzon (Curzon of Kedleston, Governor-General of India from 1899 to 1905) had earlier displayed an interest in Persia, writing in 1892 *Persia and the Persian Question*; later he exerted himself to encourage British trading with that country, paying a visit to the Persian Gulf in 1903, following the granting in 1901 of an oil concession to W.K. D'Arcy. Oil in commercial quantities was discovered in 1908, and the Anglo-Persian Oil Co. was formed in the following year. An oil refinery was built in Abadan on the eastern shores of the Shatt-el-Arab at the northern end of the Persian Gulf in 1912; eventually it covered four acres, at that time the largest oil refinery in the world.

These developments brought Britain into renewed conflict with the Russians, who had twice in the nineteenth century (1804–13, and 1826–28) failed in their attempts to establish a corridor to a warm-water port in the Gulf on the route to India by forcing a passage through Persian territory. In 1907 Russia and Great Britain agreed to make up their differences in Asia and to divide Persia into three zones: the whole of Northern Persia, down to Isfahan and Yazd and including Teheran, to come under direct Russian influence, while southern Persia would be under British control, implying recognition of a British hegemony over the Persian Gulf.

The achievement of British predominance over Egypt, the Red Sea and the Persian Gulf drew Britain's interests also towards the region in which land communications between those areas might be developed. At the heart of this region lay Palestine, the only country from which a land attack could be launched against the Suez Canal. Evidence of the British awareness of the strategic significance of Palestine in relation to their Middle East interests can be found in the survey of that country conducted as far back as 1878 by two young lieutenants of the Royal Engineers. It was published as a one-inch map in 26 sheets, followed in 1882 by a 'special edition' on a smaller scale, 'Illustrating The Old Testament / The Apocrypha and Josephus / For the Committee of the Palestine Exploration Fund.'

Headed 'Map of Western Palestine from surveys conducted by Lieuts. C.R. Condor and H.H. Kitchener, R.E.' it was frankly a military survey, despite the 'Palestine Exploration Fund' camouflage. Fifty years later it was remarked by Field Marshal Lord Wavell in his *The Palestine Campaigns* (Constable, 1928), when commenting on 'the lack of good maps' in the Palestine Campaign in the First World War, that: 'The best map available was the survey made by Lord Kitchener in 1878 when a subaltern in the Royal Engineers. It was excellent as far as it went, but the detail was not always sufficiently accurate for tactical purposes.'

4

'England is determined not only to keep Egypt, but also, according to our latest reports, to lay a strategic railway from Port Said to the Persian Gulf, thus gradually drawing into her sphere of influence the great stretches of territory between those two termini.' Hohenlohe, 1895 (Prince of Hohenlohe-Schillingsfurst, 1819–1901), Chancellor of the German Empire and Prime Minister of Prussia.

A few years before the two young Royal Engineers lieutenants were diligently marking on their map of Palestine the hypothetical territories of the legendary ten tribes of Israel another group of ten tribes in northern Europe (Baden, Bavaria, Brunswick, Hanover, Mecklenburg Schwerin, Mecklenburg Strelitz, Oldenburg, Prussia, Saxony and Schleswig Holstein) were federating to emerge in 1870 as the German Empire, and on 18 January 1871, King William of Prussia was proclaimed German Emperor at Versailles.

Bismarck, in control of the foreign policies of Prussia, had always avoided involvement in the 'Eastern Question', but his removal by Kaiser Wilhelm II heralded the move by the new Germany towards fresh imperialist ventures. Soon the German companies were building railroads in Anatolia, with dreams of a 'Berlin-Baghdad axis' that would lead through Austria and Anatolia to the Persian Gulf, where oil-prospecting had recently commenced. The political contest with Britain for markets and investment opportunities became intensified at the end of the century with the appearance of a powerful German Navy, and the Kaiser's visit in 1898 to the Holy Land, when the walls of Jerusalem were breached at the Jaffa Gate to permit his triumphal entry in a mounted procession. (Contrasting with this pageantry, when Allenby, 19 years later, entered Jerusalem as a conqueror, he left his car outside the Jaffa Gate and entered the city humbly, on foot.)

Soon after the Kaiser's visit a German Lutheran church was built near to the Church of the Holy Sepulchre, and the German Benedictine Abbey of the Dormition was erected on Mount Zion. In 1910 the Kaiser built on the Mount of Olives a German Hospice named after the Empress Augusta Victoria, housing a palace, a hostel and hospital. After the British occupation at the end of the First World War it served the victors as their 'Government House'.

The Kaiser's visit promptly bore fruit. In 1899 the Ottoman Sultan Abdulhamid II awarded the concession for the extension of the Anatolian Railway to Baghdad and the Persian Gulf to the Deutsche Bank and the German-Anatolian Railway Company. A further full and definite concession was granted in 1903 to the newly-formed Baghdad Railway Company, in which German interests predominated. To this project Britain was the principal objector and negotiated an agreement which provided that the line would not extend beyond Basra in the direction of the Persian Gulf. In the event, the progress of the undertaking was checked because of the First World War, and the railway did not reach Baghdad until 1940.

A full account of the struggle between the European powers for the control of communications throughout the Ottoman Empire, and more especially those from the Mediterranean to the Persian Gulf, is beyond the scope of the present work, but some salient factors require emphasis. Possibly the most important is the development of the manifest conviction on the part of Britain

21

that the most significant strategic position in the area was that of Palestine, which stood at the crossroads of the routes from Arabic-speaking North Africa to the Asiatic parts of the Arab world and from the 'Fertile Crescent' of Syria and Iraq to the Holy Cities of the Arabian Peninsula.

The French were equally aware of these factors. In 1903, for instance, well over half of the French capital in Turkey, excluding loans to the Ottoman Treasury, was invested in railways. The division of Turkey into financial spheres of influence controlled variously by Britain, France and Germany was based almost entirely on the railway ambitions of each of these powers. As early as the 1830s British circles had drafted a plan for the creation of a land route in the form of a railway connecting Syria and Mesopotamia, the Mediterranean Sea and the Persian Gulf. Half a century later British railway ambitions in the area centred on a scheme for a line from Haifa to Baghdad which became known, after its originator, Sir William Willcocks, as the Willcocks project. Ultimately agreement was reached between Britain and Germany that British interests were to be in control from the south of a line drawn from Beirut to Ma'an and from there across Arabia to Basra: the area to the north of this line to be left at the disposal of the Germans. Their diplomats commented that the agreement 'permits the British one day to build a railway connection from the Suez Canal to the Persian Gulf. Such a connection, however, would not harm the Baghdad Railway.'

However this agreement may have satisfied German and British aspirations, it failed to take into account the French designs. France had hoped to extend her railway system via Galilee, Samaria and Judea towards the Egyptian frontier and via Trans-jordan towards the Red Sea. She wanted to secure the ports from Beirut to Jaffa and to gain the exclusive protectorate over the holy places of Galilee and Jerusalem. Britain, on the other hand, was determined to convert Palestine into a buffer zone to guard the eastern approaches to the Suez Canal. She saw the Negev as the area through which she planned the line of the Suez-Kuwait railway and a protective zone against possible approaches from the Red Sea. Kitchener wished to secure Haifa for a naval base as well as the starting point of the railway line to Baghdad. The question was: how could all this be achieved? The entry of Turkey into the First World War on the side of Germany could provide the opportunity, if she were to be defeated, for the victors to occupy those areas which had for nearly a century provoked their rivalries.

5

*'It was easier to conquer the East than to know what to do
with it'. Horace Walpole, Fourth Earl of Orford, to
Horace Mann, 27 March 1772*

The vulnerability of the Suez Canal to attack from the direction
of Palestine was demonstrated at the very commencement of the
war when, early in November 1914, the Turkish 8th Corps,
supported by a vanguard of some 2,000 Bedouin irregulars,
crossed the Egyptian border and established itself in the area
between El Arish, on the Mediterranean coast, and Katia, east of
Kantara and within 25 miles of the Canal. Katia was garrisoned
by the Bikanir Camel Corps, who were, on 21 November,
engaged in a skirmish with the invaders. The action appears to
have been of the nature of an exploration of the British defences,
and it was followed two months later by an attack mounted by a
force of 20,000 men, with nine batteries of field artillery and a
battery of 5.9-inch howitzers. This force reached the Canal area
on 1 February and delivered its attack at 3 a.m. on 3 February. It
was repulsed, and after several hours of fighting the Turkish force
withdrew.

Despite its failure, this attempt, according to Wavell,

'showed the Turks that there was every hope of immobilis-
ing large numbers of British troops in Egypt by the mere
threat of blocking the Canal. Accordingly, while their main
force withdrew to Beersheba, Kress [Colonel Kress von
Kressenstein, Chief of Staff to the VIII Corps] was left in the

desert with a force of three battalions, two mountain batteries and a squadron of camelry, to keep British anxieties alive by minor enterprises and raids against the Canal, a task he carried out with considerable ingenuity and energy.' (op. cit., p. 33)

An impressive aspect of this venture, bearing on the British concern about the constant threat to the Canal from the east, was that it revealed that the Turks were able to bring a large force with heavy guns and a bridging train across more than 100 miles of desert.

Von Kressenstein kept the British on the defensive until the Battle of Rumani in the early part of August 1916. Earlier that year, in the middle of April, he had advanced towards Katia with a force of approximately 3,500 men, six guns and four machine guns. At 4.30 a.m. on 23 August his raiding force fell on the two squadrons of the Worcestershire Yeomanry at Oghratina, four miles east of Katia, and overwhelmed them after three hours of fighting. The Turks then pressed on to Katia, which was defended by a squadron of Gloucesters and a squadron of Worcesters. These were unable to repel the attackers, and the remnant of the brigade was withdrawn to the Canal.

Despite this series of military reverses the British and the French continued with their discussions on the subject of their conflicting claims to a Syria (understood at that time to include Palestine) then being strongly held by the enemy. The French were uncompromising. At a meeting in London on 23 November 1915, at the very moment that the Allied defeat at Gallipoli was casting its shadow over the Middle East campaign, the French representative, Francois Georges-Picot, a former Consul-General in Beirut, had insisted that Syria was a purely French possession and had defined Syria in this context as the area reaching from the Taurus ridges in the north down to the Egyptian frontier, and from the Mediterranean to Mosul and the Euphrates. He

25

conceded that Jerusalem and Bethlehem might be formed into a separate enclave under an international regime, but insisted that the whole of Palestine and Syria must be regarded as French.

In these discussions the British War Office was represented by Sir Mark Sykes, who in the course of the negotiations elicited that, in view of the British position in Mesopotamia, France would be prepared to give up the coastal strip to the south of Acre. He proposed that Britain be granted the status of a titular power over Palestine, together with the territory east of the Jordan and Mesopotamia, while France would enjoy a similar status in Syria. When Asquith asked him what he thought of the military value of the Arabs he replied that

> 'They have a negative value, they are bad if they are against us, because they add to the enemy's forces, but I do not count on them as a positive force; even when they are armed they do not fight to win.'

When Balfour asked him what sort of arrangement with France he had in mind, he replied that he favoured a French sphere extending from Acre northwards to Alexandretta, British control over a strip of land extending from the coast of Haifa-Acre bay eastward to Kirkuk in Mesopotamia, and an international enclave in Jerusalem.

The negotiations continued into the new year. At times the two parties appeared to be approaching agreement, but in March 1916 Picot told Sykes: 'The French would never consent to England having temporary or provisional charge of Palestine.' This was of course the main issue between them. Although Sykes was willing to give every consideration to the French demands, he felt that he could not compromise on his concept of a British-controlled Palestine which could counter the German threat to dominate the Middle East. He feared that a Teutonised Turkey would give Germany military bases that would threaten both Egypt and India, and that German control of Palestine would give Berlin a lever for exerting pressure on the religious bodies.

The Sykes-Picot Agreement was ratified in March 1916. It provided for the division of the area between the Mediterranean and the Persian border into four zones: a Blue (French) Zone to the west and the north of Aleppo, Hama, Homs and Damascus, and south to a point immediately to the east of Acre; a Red (British) Zone covering Kuwait and Lower Mesopotamia up to the Persian frontier; and French ('A') and British ('B') Zones of Influence divided from each other by a line reaching from Haifa to the Persian frontier after passing through a point between Mosul (in the French Zone) and Kirkuk. The southern demarcation line of the British 'B' Zone stretched eastward from Aqaba towards Kuwait. An International ('Brown') Zone covered the coastal area between Haifa and the Egyptian frontier, running to the south of Hebron to the Dead Sea and including Tiberias, Nablus and Jerusalem.

On the face of it this may have appeared to be an equitable arrangement, giving the French the same measure of authority in Lebanon and the coastal areas of Syria as the British would be enjoying in Lower Mesopotamia, but the creation of an international zone which covered most of historic Palestine manoeuvred the British out of the prospect of that control of the Palestinian hinterland which she required in order to protect the projected trans-Arabian railway in its passage through international and French-controlled areas, and to cover the eastern approaches to Egypt.

Although Sykes was a party to this arrangement he was not oblivious to the need for some formula which would validate British or pro-British control of Palestine. Leopold Amery, his closest colleague in the War Cabinet Secretariat, wrote that

'Sykes soon persuaded me that, from the purely British view, a prosperous Jewish population in Palestine, owing its

27

inception and its opportunity of development to British policy, might be an invaluable asset as a defence of the Suez Canal against attack from the North and as a station on the future air-routes to the East.' (*Chaim Weizmann*, London, Gollancz, 1945, p. 11)

'It is difficult to suppose' wrote Leonard Stein, 'that Sykes and Amery did not ask themselves ... how Great Britain was to extricate herself from the "unfortunate engagements" to the French' (i.e. the agreement to incorporate the greater part of Palestine in the 'Brown' (International) Zone). The idea of a special relationship between Great Britain and the Jews in Palestine, with the same underlying assumption that the French interest in Palestine was not an insuperable obstacle, was introduced in veiled language in a discussion on the future of Turkey in the June 1917 issue of *The Round Table*.

The Editor of *The Round Table* was Philip Kerr, a specialist adviser in foreign and Imperial affairs to Lloyd George, who had become Prime Minister following his period in the War Office as Secretary of State. The presiding genius of *The Round Table* was Lord Milner, who had served in Egypt from 1889 to 1892 and later became Colonial Secretary. Together with Leopold Amery they formed a group which represented a point of view on the fringe of the inner circle of Government. Another member of *The Round Table* was Geoffrey Dawson, then Editor of *The Times*, who contributed from May 1917 onwards to the growing support for an aggressive policy in Palestine in line with Lloyd George's views on the future of that country.

On 3 April Lloyd George had impressed on Mark Sykes the importance of securing the addition of Palestine to the British area, and had also expressed his opposition to 'a condominium with France.' On the following day Sykes, according to C.P. Scott of the *Manchester Guardian*, confirmed that 'George was against any concession and thought we could take care of the

Holy Places better than anybody else.' In Lloyd George's view the object of the Palestine campaign was not merely to inflict a military defeat on the Turks but to bring Palestine permanently under British control. If all went well the war would end with Great Britain in possession, and Palestine, liberated from the Turks by her exertions, would, on a realistic view, be at her disposal. The French would clearly be difficult, but if at the end they were compelled to recognise a British title to Palestine by right of conquest and actual possession, moral right might be added to the British claim if it could be shown that there was a world-wide desire for Britain to become a protecting power for a Jewish Commonwealth in Palestine.

But throughout these discussions and negotiations the Palestine whose possession was being so strongly disputed was yet firmly in the hands of the Turks. A strong effort, from 24 March to 19 April 1917, on the part of the British to penetrate the Gaza defences had been decisively defeated, with heavy British casualties. Nevertheless the War Cabinet decided that the Palestine campaign should continue to be vigorously prosecuted, and General Murray, who commanded the Egyptian Expeditionary Force, was instructed to proceed with the capture and occupation of Jerusalem. Reinforcements were sent to the area from Salonika, India and Aden, and the War Office decided on a change of leadership. General Sir Edmund Allenby arrived in Egypt on 27 June 1917, to take over Murray's command, and preparations were made for a renewed attack on the Gaza defences.

Before his departure for Egypt Allenby had been informed by Lloyd George that 'he wanted Jerusalem as a Christmas present for the British nation'. Allenby launched his offensive on 27 October, and by 16 November the British forces had advanced approximately 50 miles, and the Gaza–Beersheba line had been broken.

The road to Jerusalem was now open.

6

2 November 1917 was the day that the British forces broke through the Turkish defences at Gaza, capturing Sheikh Hasan, their furthest objective on this front, and also the day that Arthur Balfour wrote his historic letter to Lord Rothschild, informing him that the British Government 'view with favour the establishment in Palestine of a national home for the Jewish people . . .'

The momentous text of this declaration was the result of four months of deliberation. Balfour's draft in August had stated that 'His Majesty's Government accept the principle that Palestine should be reconstituted as the national home of the Jewish people and will use their best endeavours to secure the achievement of this object . . .'

A full account of the genesis of the Declaration has been given by Leonard Stein in his 675-page *The Balfour Declaration*, published in London by Vallentine-Mitchell in 1961, and the reader who seeks a comprehensive history of its background is strongly recommended to seek a copy of this admirable and well-researched book. In this present work we must be content with an account of the reception in the British press of the Declaration as finally published.

On 9 November the *Daily Chronicle* described it as 'Epoch-making' and the *Manchester Guardian* saw in it 'at once the fulfilment of an aspiration and the sign-post of a destiny', while on the following day the *Daily News* ventured its belief that the Declaration 'may prove to be an event of the first importance in the history of the world'. The belief that the Declaration paved the way for the emergence of a Jewish State was widespread.

The London newspaper headlines declared: 'A State for the Jews' (*Daily Express*); 'Palestine for the Jews' (*The Times*, *Morning Post*, *Daily News*), while the *Spectator* wrote of 'the proposal for the establishment of a Jewish State in Palestine'. The *Manchester Guardian* saw the Declaration as leading to 'the ultimate establishment of a Jewish State', while the *Observer* wrote: 'It is no idle dream that by the close of another generation the new Zion may become a state.' The *Daily Chronicle* wrote of 'the return of one of its oldest and most gifted members to a normal place within the circle'; the *Nation* referred to the Declaration as 'the simple and humane act of reparation'; the *Spectator* perceived a Jewish state in Palestine as a rallying point for Jews all over the world, and the *Observer* visualised 'a unique link between east and west'.

This almost universal euphoria was exalted on 11 December by Bonar Law's announcement to the House of Commons that Allenby would that day be making the official entry into Jerusalem, following the surrender of the city to the British. The Chief Rabbi wrote to the King:

'On behalf of the Jewish communities of the Empire, whose ecclesiastical chief I have the honour to be, I humbly congratulate your Majesty on the world historic victories of your Majesty's army in the Holy Land. The occupation of Jerusalem following so closely upon the epoch-making declaration of your Majesty's Government on Palestine as the National Home for the Jewish people, causes the hearts of millions of my brethren throughout the world to throb with deepest gratitude to Almighty God, who alone doeth wondrous things.'

And the leading article in the *Daily Telegraph* of that historic day concluded:

'And now, in the cycle of the ages, we note with a wondering surprise that once more Jerusalem may become the actual as it has long been the spiritual centre of Jewry.

'It is a marvellous reversal of fortune; one of the most wonderful of all the wonderful things that are happening in this extraordinary period. It is almost a source of deepest pride that it should be British troops that have led the way and a British commander who is to plant the standard of St. George on the site of the great House which Solomon built in honour of Jahveh.'

Who then could have known that 30 years later the Arab Legion, led by British officers, would replace this flag with the standard of Jordan?

In the midst of all this rapture the *Observer* ventured a shrewder note, writing: 'There could not have been at this juncture a stroke of statesmanship more just or wise', and one has only to glance at the simple manipulation involved in the rearrangement by Milner of Balfour's wording: 'Palestine should be reconstituted as the national home of the Jewish people' (in his August 1917 draft) into the 'principle that every opportunity should be afforded for the establishment of a home for the Jewish people in Palestine', Milner's August 1917 draft which finally emerged in the published Declaration as 'the establishment in Palestine of a national home for the Jewish people', to see how the prospect of 'Palestine as a national home for the Jewish people' – an explicit term – could have been so adroitly annihilated by the offer of a 'national home *in* Palestine', which might mean anything – or, perhaps, nothing at all.

At least one political observer failed to share the common euphoria. Low's cartoon in the *Evening Standard* depicted a bewildered Jewish settler hesitantly perched near the edge of a Palestinian landscape. Ormsby-Gore, crouching beside him, traces in the sand a boundary line which closely circumscribes the pioneer's feet. Within this tiny orbit a notice board proclaims

'THE JEWISH NATIONAL HOME', while Ormsby-Gore reassuringly tells him: 'After all, it does give you a national standing.'

STANDING ROOM ONLY.

But even in the United States the American Zionists joined in the exuberance. Their Provisional Executive Committee for General Zionist Affairs issued a statement on 14 November declaiming: 'British Declaration favouring Jewish State' – 'Not only a Jewish homeland in Palestine but protection of the status of Jews throughout the world guaranteed by Great Britain.' In Germany members of the Berlin Zionist Executive and other Jewish leaders were summoned to the Foreign Office on 5 January to hear a prepared statement by von der Bussche-Haddenhausen, Under-Secretary of State, declaring the German Government's benevolent intentions towards the Jews and continuing:

'As regards the aspirations in Palestine of Jewry, especially Zionists, we welcome the recent statement expressing the Turkish Government's intention ... to promote a flourishing Jewish settlement within the limits of the capacity of the country, local self-government corresponding to the country's laws, and free development of their civilisation.'

7

After the Armistice General Sir Arthur Money was appointed chief Administrator of O.E.T.A. (Occupied Enemy Territorial Organisation) South, covering the greater part of historic Palestine. Allenby had announced that the military administration of the territory would be conducted in accordance with the Laws and Usages of War, virtually providing for the maintenance of the status quo in that territory. But the terms of the Balfour Declaration carried a promise of departure from the status quo, and it soon became apparent that, in the first place, such a departure would not be permitted by the Administration, and, secondly, that in any case the Balfour Declaration did not meet with the approval of the Administration.

Weizmann recorded in his autobiographical *Trial and Error* that

'General Money had on his staff several advisers and officials who, from the first moment, felt it to be their duty to impress upon the Jewish communities under their charge that, whatever the politicians in London might have been fools enough to say or do, *here* we were in a quite different world.'

Indeed, members of the Administration did not hesitate to convey to the Government in London their comments or advice on matters of policy. Money called at the Foreign Office on 16 January 1919, on the occasion of a visit to London, and saw Curzon, who later that day wrote to Balfour, informing him of Money's view that 'a Jewish Government in any form would mean an Arab rising, and the nine-tenths of the population who are not Jews would make short shrift with the Hebrews.' (India Office Library, Curzon Papers)

Curzon did not hesitate to remind Balfour that: 'As you know, I share these views, and have long felt that the pretensions of Weizmann & Company are extravagant and ought to be checked.' In no wise discouraged by Curzon, Money continued his campaign, advising the Government on 2 May to drop the Balfour Declaration, writing that

'No mandatory Power can carry through the Zionist programme except by force ... If a Mandate for Great Britain is desired by His Majesty's Government, it will be necessary to make an authoritative announcement that the Zionist programme will not be enforced in opposition to the majority.'

When this memorandum had been communicated to Herbert Samuel, with an invitation to put forward any suggestions he might have to offer 'as to how the present hostility to Zionism in Palestine can best be allayed by the administrative authorities on the spot' , he merely acknowledged what must have by then become evident to most people, replying that 'the attitude of the administrative authorities in Palestine does not appear to be in harmony with the Government.'

Allenby could hardly have failed to be aware of this situation and asked Weizmann, whom he had invited to dinner, 'for a more detailed report on the relations between the Jewish population and his administration.' Weizmann replied that

'while we understood that matters of high policy could not at the moment be implemented, and that the Balfour Declaration could not find practical application till after the war, the continuance of strained relations between the Jewish population and the British military authorities was doing no good to anyone at present, and might seriously prejudice the future. It was not simply a matter of relations between the Jews and the British, nor was it the immediate question of the particular rebuffs or setbacks. It was rather the effect on the Arab mind. But it seemed as though the local administration was bent on ignoring the Home Government's attitude towards our aspirations in Palestine, or, what was worse, was going out of its way to show definite hostility to the policy initiated in London. The outlook for later relations between Jews and Arabs was, in these circumstances, not a promising one.' (*Trial and Error*, pp. 279–80)

Allenby's own views were in fact that Palestine *had* no future for the Jews, but his natural courtesy prevented him from expressing those views in the language of Curzon, with his references to 'Weizmann & Company', or Sir Henry Wilson, the Chief of the Imperial General Staff, who described Weizmann in his diary on 21 January as 'the Jew who is running the Zionist movement – a clever rogue but a bad face', and who a few days later (on 4 February), when Weizmann had protested to him that the British officers in Palestine were both pro-Arab and anti-Zionist, noted in his diary 'which is very likely, & quite right.' (Imperial War Museum archive)

This attitude was revealed, as we shall see, from time to time in the Foreign Office records. On 4 February a Foreign Office senior official, J.D. Gregory, had minuted:

'The Jews deserve all they get. Their whole influence in Eastern Europe during the war was against us and our allies: nearly all the German and Austrian spies were Jews: and now they are busy undermining the foundations of European civilisation. It is little wonder that the two races which have suffered most, first from Jewish espionage and then from Jewish Bolshevism, should take a truculent revenge on them.' (Foreign Office papers, 371/13749)

It is unlikely that Gregory would have been rebuked by Curzon, who had taken over the Foreign Office from Balfour, for writing in this vein. On 25 March Curzon warned Balfour of 'the consequences of inviting the Jews to return to Palestine' (India Office Library: Curzon papers), while on 1 June the British Ambassador in Paris, Lord Bertie of Thame, wrote that

'a Jew State in Palestine would be the gathering together there of all the scum of the Jewish populations of Russia, Poland, Germany, Hungary and what has been the Austrian Empire.'

Curzon continued his campaign against Weizmann, to whom he referred in a letter written on 9 August to Balfour as 'that astute but aspiring person' who criticises 'sharply the conduct of such officers who do not fall on the neck of the Zionists (a most unattractive resting place).' (India Office Library: Curzon Papers). Even T.E. Lawrence ('Lawrence of Arabia'), who had once informed the Anglican Bishop of Jerusalem that Weizmann was 'a great man whose boots neither you nor I, my dear Bishop, are fit to black' (*Letters of T.E. Lawrence*, Spring Books, 1964, pp. 342–3), was now caught up in this campaign of contempt and denigration, writing to Curzon on 27 September:

'Zionists are not a Government, and not British, and their action does not infringe the Sykes-Picot agreement. They are also Semites and Palestinian, and the Arab Govt. is not afraid of them (can cut their throats, or better pull all their teeth out, when it wishes). They will finance the whole East, I hope, Syria and Mesopotamia alike. High Jews are unwilling to put much cash into Palestine only, since that country offers nothing but a sentimental return. They want 6%.' (Lawrence to Curzon, Lawrence Papers)

Curzon continued to receive support from many quarters,

including a telegram on 12 October from John Wardrop, the British Government's representative in Georgia:

> 'I cannot too strongly insist as I have been doing for last two years that nearly all the present misery of world is due to Jewish intrigues ... In England and America as well as in this part of the world a diabolical plot is being carried out for (?ruin) and enslavement of Christendom.' (Wardrop to Curzon: Foreign Office papers, 371/3663)

From eastern Poland a Foreign Office representative, P. Wright, sent a full report on 'Jewish Bolshevism' and the eastern Jews in general, writing; 'The village Jew lives in barbarous filth. ... The Jew claims a right to all the profits, and the Pole to kick the Jew whenever he feels the inclination', and then giving an account of the murder of a Polish soldier by a Jew who had performed one of 'those horrible mutilations practised by Jewish Chassidim murderers' (and without doubt personally witnessed by Mr Wright) 'and which is one of the many ways in which they do not seem to be European.' (Wright to Foreign Office, 18 December 1919: Rumbold papers)

C.R. Ashbee, the British Civic Adviser in Jerusalem from 1918 to 1922, immortalised his own views on these matters in his outspoken *Palestine Notebook*, published by Heinemann in 1923, the year following his retirement. In a July 1918 entry he writes of 'the modern Haluca (*sic*) Jew, the type that wails on Friday evenings' who will sell

> 'even his most cherished convictions ... An English officer the other day, one of the red and efficient sort that gets things done, turned up at the wailing place, but on the wrong day, and found nothing doing. Quickly drawing a shilling from his pocket he seized on the nearest Haluca and shouted: ''Here – WAIL, you blighter!'' And he wailed.'

Fortunately he was able to find relief from such pitiful and contemptible types in different company. On 3 July he attended an Arab 'recruiting meeting. There were some fifty of us. We smoked, talked, drank coffee. They were beautiful people. They sat around in their silk *abayehs*, black-and-gold *argals*, and fingered their rosaries.' Three days later he accompanied General Money to view the installation of the new water supply, and recalled that when

> 'the much-abused Pontius Pilate (on whom be peace!) constructed his noble water supply the Jews rose in revolt. They thought it an unnecessary innovation. When you see the filth in which the Haluca Jew lives, and observe his arrogant obscurantism, you understand why.'

In a September 1918 entry he writes despairingly of the state of the British Government's mind in respect of the problem of keeping – or not keeping – Palestine.

> 'Mind? What mind is there to make up? If there should be some reflective Jew at the council table the decision will probably go in favour of England, for the Jews want us here, and it will not be the first time in history that English instinct has been like wax in their hands.' (pp. 35–36)

In December he records a visit to 'the Meascheorim Market' (a most peculiar version of the widely-used Mea She'arim), which he was

> 'trying to get cleaned up . . . and had to give a building permit to the adjoining Synagogue. Apparently it needed a pagan to appreciate the squalor, the foulness, the meanness, the lying, the sneaking furtiveness of this purely Jewish Society, its phthisis, its ophthalmia, its hereditary disease. I think these Jews of the Holy City are even worse than their brethren of Whitechapel of whom I saw so much in my Toynbee Hall days . . .'

Ashbee loses no opportunity to vent his bitterness. In a passage on page 184 he ventures:

> 'It will be a queer day for them (the Zionists) when England gives up being exploited at a high cost in money and reputation for the sake of Jewish Nationalism. ... The Arabs ... are learning much the same lesson, i.e. to rely on themselves. They are learning quicker than the Jew Nationalists. But then they have not lived on others so long, and so have not the habit of exploitation and blood sucking – habits hard, doubtless, to throw off.'

Inevitably this accumulating rancour had to explode into a final hymn of hate. This flowed from his fluent pen when, in the early part of 1922:

> 'The best Moslem residential area in the city has now been flooded with the drainage of Meoscheorim, and a pool of liquid sewage lies, at the moment of writing, in the lovely valley between the Grand Mufti's house and ours. For us it will mean that we shall probably not be able to return to our house. ... Had the situation been reversed and the drains of a Moslem slum voided into the best Jewish quarter there would have been such an outcry in Israel as would have moved Wall Street and Park Lane:
>
> Benjamin, and Levy, Cohen, and Sassoon,
> Lewis, Mond, and Meinertzhagen moaning all in tune,
> Franklin, Montefiore, and Harrari in between,
> Isaac, Fels, and Israeli baying at the moon,
> Ladenburg, and Schlezinger, and Trier, and Duveen,
> All the tribes in harmony from counter, pale, and dune –
> Was such a sorrow ever known, or such a scandal seen!
> Samuel, Schiff, and Rothschild twined in richer cords,
> Mourning all together in a cry that is the Lord's'

Poor Meinertzhagen. In the *Preface* to his *Middle East Diary* (Cresset Press, 1959) he wrote:

'With my foreign-sounding name it is inevitable that the ignorant and offensive should, when roused to anger, apply German nationality to me and a Jewish origin: "German Jew". The name is, in fact, of Danish origin and, so far as I can trace, there is no Jewish blood in my veins, nor has there ever been; for some 400 years ago, a direct ancestor of mine was Archbishop of Cologne. But on three occasions I have been dubbed, in malice, a Jew. The first occasion was in Kenya in 1905, when I reported a member of the administration for gross dishonesty. He lost his job and referred to me as a "bloody Jew", the worst abuse he could produce.'

Ashbee's jibe was not included in the other two occasions referred to by Meinertzhagen.

8

Ashbee recorded in his *Palestine Notebook* that in May 1918, when he was working for the Egyptian Government, he 'was invited by the Military Administration of Palestine (O.E.T.A.) to help in the new plans for the reconstruction of the City of Jerusalem. This led to my appointment as Civic Advisor'.

In his autobiography, *Orientations*, Sir Ronald Storrs revealed that he was the spirit behind that appointment.

> 'In my search for a Technical Assistant something more than Architect and Town Planner, I remembered that almost the only good "Entertainment" lecture I had heard at Charterhouse had been delivered by one C.R. Ashbee, a disciple of William Morris. . . . I at least look back upon our mutual relations with gratitude and pleasure.' (Op. cit. Definitive Edition, 1945, p. 312)

Storrs, formerly the Oriental Secretary in Cairo, had been appointed Military Governor of Jerusalem, with the local rank of Lieutenant-Colonel, at the end of December 1917. His book reveals an attitude towards Jews which would in no way inhibit 'the gratitude and pleasure' which, he wrote, resulted from his 'mutual relations' with Ashbee. In a letter written in June 1916, referring to the capture of Mecca from the Turks, he remarks that 'the loss of the two Holy Places they have so long exploited should prove in the end mortal to the Jews now reigning on the Bosphorus', explaining in a footnote that 'The Committee of Union and Progress was largely under *Donme* – Crypto-Jew – influence'. (p. 162)

In the previous month he had visited Baghdad, where he met 'the Grand Rabbi Eleazer', and on 16 May noted in his diary that 'Persecutions here took the milder but (considering the martyrs) more agonizing form of insistence upon gold in exchange for miserably depreciated Ottoman paper.' (p. 227) Arriving in Jerusalem on 20 December he lost no time in recording in his diary on that day that 'As usual the Jews have cornered the small change, for which they extort a commission of 5 or 6 per cent. Surely here is a chance for the Zionists to stop these filthinesses.' (p. 277)

His diary three days later records an encounter with an

'Assembly of the Ashkenazi Jews ... I taxed them with cornering small change, and was met with mixed defences and denials. ''They had not cornered, but if the Muslim wheat and sesame dealers refused to accept Egyptian paper (now 6 per cent depreciated), and, while paying in bank-notes, would only accept hard coin, who would blame them if they did corner?'' ... I left this remarkable and powerful Synod after about an hour, and seemed to breathe an easier atmosphere' (but only after he 'was forced in answer to toasts for the liberating army to raise my glass to the health and prosperity of the Jewish Community in Jerusalem'). (p. 281)

Likewise 'powerful' was the 'colony of Sephardim originally from Italy, Damascus and Salonika', which he met in Egypt (p. 339). He finds space in his book for anti-Jewish and anti-Zionist gibes. 'At a time when Jews all over the world are pouring their money into Palestine without hope of material returns or even of beholding the country, wiseacres knew that ''there must be money in it somewhere, or the Jews would not be going there''. The Army riddle — ''What is a Zionist?'' ''A Zionist is a Jew who is prepared to pay another Jew to go and live in Palestine''' (p. 348)

His cynical comment on the League of Nations Palestine Mandate, finalised on 24 July 1922, was that

> 'none of the fifty-two signatories were going to quarrel with their Jews over so remote an objective an issue – to say the least were not going to retain them against their will: "Let My People go?" "Yes verily, and by God's help so I will!"'
> (p. 350)

Storrs expresses a sympathetic understanding of Syrian nationalist aspirations.

> 'For four centuries the Arabs, Moslems as well as Christian, of Syria and Palestine (one community though administratively divided into two (though Palestine and Syria were one military command)) had groaned under the heavy empty hand of Ottoman misrule. . . . With the British liberation of their country they found their hopes not accomplished but extinguished. Throughout history the conqueror had kept for himself the territory he conquered (save in those rare instances where he returned it to the inhabitants); and that Britain should take and keep Palestine would have been understood and welcomed. Instead she proposed to hand it, without consulting the occupants, to a third party; and what sort of third party! To the lowest and (in Arab eyes) the least desirable specimens of a people reputed parasitic by nature, heavily subsidized, and supported by the might of the British Empire. If the Jews were "not coming but returning" to Palestine – the distinction seemed but verbal – on the strength of a book written two thousand years ago; if there were no international statute of limitations and the pages of history could be turned back indefinitely, then let the Arabs "return" to Spain*, which they had held quite as long and at least as effectively as the Jews had held Palestine.' '*or the Welsh to England'. (p. 351)

The opening paragraph of the previous chapter in the present work refers to the hostility to the Balfour Declaration freely displayed by members of the Palestine Administration. 'But what was O.E.T.A.?' poses Storrs.

'It was the remnant of the small staff originally chosen for the purpose, with the accretions of the officers placed by the Army in charge of newly conquered areas: without expectation of long continuance, still less of permanency. And who were these officers? What had they been before the War? There were a few professional soldiers. Apart from these our administrative and technical staff, necessarily from military material available on the spot, included a cashier from a Bank in Rangoon, an actor-manager, two assistants from Thos. Cook, a picture-dealer, an Army coach, a clown, a land valuer, a bo'sun from the Niger, a Glasgow distiller, an organist, an Alexandria cotton-broker, an architect (not in the Public Works but in the Secretariat), a Junior Service London postal official (not in the Post Office but as Controller of Labour), a taxi-driver from Egypt, two school-masters and a missionary.' (p. 360)

If this was an accurate picture – if the fate of the promised Jewish National Home was indeed in the hands of this motley assembly – it becomes less difficult to understand the conflict which developed between the administration and the Yishuv. Storrs parted company from them when he left Palestine in 1926 to go to Cyprus as the island's Governor, but after he was permanently invalided from further government service in 1934 he felt able to express his views with greater freedom.

The *News of the World* of 16 May 1948, two days after the establishment of the Independent Republic of Israel, afforded him three full-length columns to write on 'Palestine: The Dream that Turned Nightmare', enabling him to attribute President Truman's decision to recognise Israel to 'Zionist electoral

46

pressure' (i.e. the 'Jewish vote'). 'The strongest power in the United Nations has suddenly become its weakest link. . . . What the Arabs will not endure is the slicing away of soil which has been their home for 1,300 years and the planting in it of a foreign State. (What country in the world *would* endure it that could prevent it?)'

To Truman's proposal that 100,000 displaced Jews should be immediately admitted to Palestine he retorted that: 'The economic absorptive capacity of Vermont (the smallest State in the United States of America) would alone account for the 100,000 souls. . . . On the same basis, the province of Natal alone could account for a further 350,000, and so on'. In short, anywhere except Palestine: 'For such a proof of comprehension and practical good will would relieve the Arabs of the humiliation of being treated as a mere involuntary dumping ground for people unacceptable elsewhere.'

Until his death in 1955 Storrs continued to express these views, drawing freely from diaries and correspondence covering the preceding half-century. There was, however, one incident during his term of office in Jerusalem – an event which sent waves of horror around the world – which he seemed to be reluctant to recall, writing in *Orientations* that: 'The days that followed have been described by most of those concerned with a bitterness which it is no purpose of mine to increase, nor would I renew grief unspeakable'.

On Easter Day 1920, he had attended Matins at St George's Cathedral in the company of his father, the Dean of Rochester, and his mother, while the Arab mobs from Nablus and Hebron swarmed into the city, where the police force had been left in the charge of a young Lieutenant. 'The Police', Storrs wrote, 'were but partially trained and wholly without tradition. There was no British Gendarmerie: we had not one single British Constable.' (p. 331)

Of the resulting carnage it was left to others to report the gruesome details.

9

Hierosolyma est Perdita

Before the Jerusalem pogrom of April 1920 there had been no massacre of Jews in that city since 15 July 1099, when it was stormed by the Crusaders and its Moslem and Jewish defenders and their families were mercilessly slaughtered.

After Saladin's reconquest in 1187 Jews began to return to the city, and before the end of the nineteenth century had formed the majority of its inhabitants. Thus the 1920 pogrom, coming as it did after four centuries of Turkish rule, so shocked Weizmann that when, a few days later, he met Philip Kerr at the San Remo Conference, his 'mood was such', he wrote, 'that I started on him straight away with congratulations on the first pogrom under the British flag.'

Much has been written about the atrocity. Although Churchill the same month reported to the House of Commons: 'I regret to say that about 250 casualties occurred, of which nine-tenths were Jewish', Philip Graves (who had been *The Times* correspondent at Constantinople for several years before 1914, staff officer in Eastern theatres of the Great War, member of the 'Arab Bureau' and of the Arab section of the Headquarters Staff in Palestine) wrote in 1923 that: 'The Zionists have made too much of this "pogrom" and too little of the difficulties of the military', but conceded that 'At the same time mistakes were made by some members of the Military Administration. The Chief of Staff to the Chief Military Administrator appears to have left Jerusalem for a trip to Jericho by motor-car at a moment when crowds were already gathering in ominous fashion near the Jaffa Gate.' Other writers have commented on the behaviour of Lt. Col. L.R.E. Waters-Taylor, the Chief of Staff referred to, both before and following the outrage.

Horace B. Samuel was at the time a Military Magistrate in the service of the O.E.T.A., and gave his account of the affair in his *Unholy Memories of the Holy Land*, published by the Hogarth Press in 1930. In Chapter IV ('The Reign Of Terror') he describes the attitude of the authorities, with which, because of his position, he soon became familiar, in their dealings with the Arabs: an attitude which left these with the impression that, as between themselves and the Jews, the Government was with them. Further,

> 'The bulk of the police was Arab, and many of them were quite naturally members of various nationalist clubs. Was it to be expected that in the event of any racial disturbance the Arab police could reasonably maintain an attitude of Olympian objectivity, or indeed do anything else but act, strike, and shoot true blue? In fact, a report had been officially made to the Higher authorities that in the event of any disturbance the police could not be relied upon. Further, Arab agitators from outside Palestine came to Jerusalem, where they devoted themselves without let or hindrance to inflaming popular opinion.'

It was the *Nebi Moussa* Festival which provided the opportunity for the military junta to give full scope to their benevolent passivity. 'Had the Administration been particularly zealous to suppress disorder, it would have been simple to have taken such elementary precautions as the utilization of British soldiers to patrol the streets.' (When, before the approach of the festival, Weizmann had communicated his apprehensions to the Military Governor, General Bols had replied: 'There *can* be no trouble, the town is stiff with troops.') 'In point of fact', continued

Samuel, 'the only deviation from normal routine was the transference, by the orders of an Arab officer, of those Jewish policemen who were usually on duty inside the Old City to other beats outside the walls. The Jews in the Old City were consequently left to be protected against Arabs by Arabs.' It was within the Old City, of course, that the ensuing carnage was confined.

As the hour before the commencement of the celebration approached it became evident that there was some portent in the wind. Although it was not normal for Arab shops to close on the occasion of this festivity, some local Arab shops in the Old City began to close. Moslem shops in the Jewish quarter bore signs that they were Moslems, and the Christians marked their houses with crosses. The thousands of pilgrims were led by a British Military Band to the Municipality, where they were greeted by the Mayor and then harangued by rabble-rousers. From the balcony of the Arab Club two young men produced a large photograph of Feisul (Pretender at that time to the non-existent throne of Syria plus Palestine) and shouted: 'Long live our King – King Feisul! In the name of our King we urge you to fight the Jews.'

According to Samuel this proved to be the signal for a simultaneous attack in all four quarters of the Old City. He wrote:

'It would have been ridiculous and unreasonable to have expected the Arab police forcibly to interfere with these pious efforts of their own brethren to obtain their political liberties. Nor did they. According to the Zionists, they joined in the good patriotic work, just as they were to do a year later on the occasion of the Jaffa riots, while the euphemistic British account, given to me by one of the officials, was that their attitude was one of "passive resistance".' (op. cit., p. 57)

Among other eyewitness accounts of the pogrom, two have been published by Lieut. Col. J.H. Patterson, D.S.O., who had commanded the 38th–42nd Royal Fusiliers in the Palestine Campaign. He was a Dublin-born Protestant who had commanded the 33rd Battalion of the Imperial Yeomanry in the Boer War, and the Zionist Mule Corps in the Gallipoli campaign. Originally an engineer by profession, he was also a successful writer, the author of *The Man-Eaters of Tsavo*, *In the Grip of the Nyika*, *With the Zionists in Gallipoli*, and *With the Judaeans in the Palestine-Campaign*. In April 1920, having in the previous year returned to England, he received two letters from Palestine, the first, dated 10 April 1920, from a 'Senior British Officer', who wrote:

My Dear Colonel,

We are passing through terrible and unprecedented times. Who could ever have thought that a pogrom 'a la Russe', with all its horrors, could take place in Jerusalem under British rule! Who could ever have conceived that it should be possible, in the Holy City of Jerusalem, that for three days Jews, old and young, women and children could be slaughtered; that rape should be perpetrated, Synagogues burnt, scrolls of the Law defiled, and property plundered right and left, under the banner of England!

The anti-Jewish feeling of the Administration here you, of course, know all about, as you have experienced it yourself, but latterly the notorious *Syria Genuba* (an Arab daily in Jerusalem) printed day after day inflammatory articles against the Jews. Anti-Jewish demonstrations were allowed to take place and inflammatory speeches were allowed to be made against the Jews. The evil men amongst the Arabs openly declared that they would slaughter the Jews at the Festival of Nebi Musa. The Government was warned by the Jewish press, and by Jewish responsible leaders, but these were not listened to, and as a matter of fact the Feast was proclaimed with great pomp, Lord Allenby and Major-General Louis Jean Bols, the Chief Administrator, being present.

(Signed) XX.

The other letter was dated 11 April 1920.

My Dear Colonel,

With my wife I went up to Jerusalem to spend the Easter week-end, and a very nice week-end it surely was! Long before this letter reaches you, you will have learned something of the happenings in the Holy City, but as my wife and I saw the first blow struck, and had very personal experiences of the immediately ensuing bother, you may be interested.

The happenings here have raised all sorts of questions, and while for the moment the trouble is over, I fear the end is not yet. On the morning of Easter Sunday we were standing on the balcony of the New Grand Hotel watching the progress of an Arab procession just arrived from Hebron. As the procession reached the entrance to the Jaffa Gate it just had the appearance of the usual show of this kind — a bit noisy, but apparently well-behaved. It was escorted by two officers of the Military Administration and a few of the Arab police. All at once the members of the procession formed themselves into a square, just inside the gate, and the first thing we saw then was an old Jew, about 70 years of age, get his head split open with an Arab's sword, and as soon as he was down he was stoned; within a few more minutes a lot more Jews got like treatment. By this time the crowd was well out of hand and rushed quickly into the Old City looting and killing, and a few hours afterwards there was a steady evacuation of battered Jews. There was no military present. The following day the trouble started again, and a lot more were injured, and the third morning there was more looting and more casualties, and then at last the military took strong steps and the trouble was at an end . . .

Yours sincerely,
(Signed) E.N.

One of the 'strong steps' taken by the military was the arrest of Lieutenant Jabotinsky, of the Jewish Self-Defence Corps, with some score of its members.

'In less than half an hour from the beginning of the outbreak', wrote Patterson, 'two companies of the Self-Defence Corps marched to the Jaffa and Damascus Gates to assist in quelling the disturbance within the walls, but they found the gates closed to them and held by British troops. It is very significant that within a few minutes of the commencement of the pogrom, British troops held all the gates of the city, with explicit orders to allow no one in and *no one* out – not even helpless women, fleeing from the horrors that were being enacted in the Jewish quarter, unless they held special permits. For nearly three days the work of murder, rape, sacrilege, and pillage went on practically unchecked – all under British rule. A very significant fact that all through this Jerusalem pogrom the hooligans' cry was *"El dowleh ma ana"*, which means "The Government is with us".' (op. cit. pp. 269–70)

Meinertzhagen has provided evidence of this confidence displayed by the rioters in his *Middle East Diary*, writing that 'On the day of the rioting the following notice was displayed all over Jerusalem: "The government is with us, Allenby is with us, kill the Jews; there is no punishment for killing Jews"', while following the riots he reported 'a meeting of notables in Jerusalem' where a speaker, Aref el Aref, claimed that 'fortunately the British Administration is on our side and we shall not be hurt. My advice then is to continue the assault on the Jews.' Another speaker, Kamal il Budsiri, said: 'We shall deliver our country by the sword. We are glad the massacre of the Jews took place and that we have looted them. And in consequences many Jews have been arrested and we are free', while Fahry il Husseini told his audience: 'We have to thank the police who are on our side.' On 13 April, the Mufti of Jerusalem sent the following

54

message to the Moslems of Hebron:

'We are proud of our great victory and of the murder of Jews whom we have killed and the booty we have taken. Do your best through the Chief Secretary to assure that the Government does not oppose us.' (op. cit., p. 85)

The Mufti at that time would have been Kamel Effendi, the brother (and predecessor) of the notorious Haj Amin al-Husseini. The Chief Secretary was the Lieut. Col. L.R.E. Waters-Taylor whom Meinertzhagen accused of conspiracy and collaboration with Haj Amin, and with frequent and secret contacts with Feisal. On the morning of the Jerusalem pogrom Waters-Taylor had left the city and spent the day in Jericho. Two days after the rioting he sent for the Mayor of Jerusalem – Moussa Kasim Pasha – and said 'I gave you a fine opportunity; for five hours Jerusalem was without military protection; I had hoped you would avail yourself of the opportunity but you have failed.' Meinertzhagen had reported these facts to both Bols and Allenby, and later in a despatch dated 14 April to Lord Curzon. Allenby took issue with the War Office on Meinertzhagen's actions, threatening resignation as Commander-in-Chief if one of his staff was permitted to write in this way, with the result that Meinertzhagen lost his appointment and was recalled to London.

On his way thence, at Port Said he recorded in his diary on 2 June 1920: '. . . I have achieved my object. My offending despatch found Lord Curzon, Lloyd George and Herbert Samuel at San Remo. They acted on my advice within twenty-four hours of its receipt. The military administration fell and with it Bols and Waters-Taylor.'

Before its ultimate disappearance the Administration endeavoured to strike a final blow. At the end of the first day's rioting British troops had detained between 300 and 400 Arabs in a mosque. The next morning these were released, and the attacks on the

Jews promptly recommenced, while at the same time the authorities arrested Jabotinsky, 'on the quite plausible ground', wrote Horace Samuel, 'that it was their duty to prevent civil war among the population.' At the same time the Administration caused intensive searches to be made among the Jews, found a certain number of rifles, and caused numerous arrests.

Jabotinsky was tried on a charge of 'banditism, instigating the people of the Ottoman Empire to mutual hatred, pillage, rapine, devastation of the country, and homicide in divers places' and was sentenced to 15 years penal servitude. Presumably to counter any possible criticism of this sentence on the grounds of harshness, the Court passed the same sentence on two Arabs caught raping Jewish girls during the pogrom. With his hair cropped, and clothed in prison garb, he was marched with these two Arabs through Jerusalem and Kantara, places where he was well-known as a British officer.

The storm of protest aroused by this sentence reached the House of Commons. Following a statement by Mr Churchill, who was then Secretary of State for War, the War Office took action and the sentence was annulled. It is of interest to note that the same indulgence was eventually extended to Haj Amin el Husseini, who had responded to a five-year sentence for his part in organising the disturbances by discreetly slipping out of the country while on bail, but was recalled in the following year and appointed Mufti of Jerusalem at the same time that Aref el Aref, who had been accused on inciting to riot during the disturbances, was rewarded with the Governorship of Jenin, thus justifying the confidence he had earlier expressed (see above) in the policies of the British Administration.

10

'By the mandate swindle England and France got the lot.'
(T.E. Lawrence to William Yale, 22 October 1929)

The League of Nations was established in 1919–20 as a permanent international organisation 'to promote international co-operation and to achieve international peace and security.' Article 22 of the League's Covenant was concerned with 'peoples not yet able to stand by themselves', whose 'well-being and development . . . form a sacred trust of civilisation', and recommended that 'tutelage of such peoples should be entrusted to advanced nations . . . as Mandatories on behalf of the League.'

'After scenes that President Wilson once described as "the whole disgusting scramble" for the Middle East, the mandates for former Turkish territories were allotted at the San Remo Conference of April 1920 – Syria and Lebanon to France, Palestine and Mesopotamia (Iraq) to Britain. The decisions accorded neither with the wishes of the inhabitants nor with the unqualified end-of-war undertakings about freedom of choice. They were pieces of unabashed self-interest, suggesting to many onlookers that all talk of liberating small nations from oppression was so much cant. Yet extension of the British Empire on these terms was accepted by the British Government and people, though both were on the whole adverse to taking on more territory. The explanation of this anomaly lies in the magic word "mandate". It was sufficiently elastic to suggest to the British left that here was a fitting job for the new League of Nations, and to the British right that the essentials of imperial defence would remain safely in British hands.' (Monroe, op. cit., p. 66)

The Mandate for Palestine gave recognition to the 'historical connection of the Jewish people with Palestine' and directed the Mandatory to assist in the establishment of a Jewish National Home in Palestine, but in September 1922 the Council of the League of Nations approved the proposal of the British to exclude the eastern part of the mandated territory, comprising more than three-quarters of the total area of Palestine, from the Mandate's provisions concerning the Jewish National Home. The adoption of this measure resulted in the first partition of the country into two areas, the larger of which designed to become exclusively Arab and to be denied to Jewish residence or settlement.

It might appear that destiny had played a hand in this development, for in January 1921 Abdullah, the second son of Sharif Hussein, King of the Hejaz, fortuitously appeared in Amman and announced his intention of invading Syria and after expelling the French, 'take over the kingdom . . . Having told the world of his plans, which involved the armed invasion of territory which was under British Mandate, the Amir sat back and waited to see what His Britannic Majesty's Government would do.' (Sir Alec Seath Kirkbride: *A Crackle of Thorns*, John Murray, 1956, p. 25)

Although, writing over thirty years after the event, Kirkbride, who had been posted to the area 'with the task of setting up local autonomous administrations', describes the territory as being 'under British Mandate' at the time, the distribution of the Mandates was not formalized by the League of Nations until July 1922, some 15 months after the Amir actually took over the control of the whole country, and in the circumstances one may be forgiven for suspicions of an attitude of *laissez faire* on the part of the British, if not something more disquieting.

In his *Arab Command* (Hutchinson, 1942), Major C.S. Jarvis has given a fuller description of Abdullah's venture than is to be found elsewhere, writing:

'Early in 1921 the Emir Abdullah, the son of King Hussein of the Hedjaz, came to Maan from Mecca by the derelict railway, which had not been functioning since 1918. No coal was available, and the engine was stoked the whole of the five-hundred mile journey by sawing up the poles of the disused telegraph line. The various cuts in the line, made by Lawrence and Peake during the war, were repaired roughly by a small breakdown gang which accompanied the party, and eventually the train wheezed and bumped its way into Maan. Abdullah, who was accompanied by the Sherif Ali Ibn Hussein, had come north, so bazaar rumour said, under orders from his father to raise a force of Arabs in Trans-Jordan for operations against the French in Syria, and all the ex-Syrian officials and politicians flocked to Maan to see him. Abdullah, however, had arrived without a force, or money to raise one, and he therefore remained at Maan, which at that time was outside Trans-Jordan territory . . .'
(Op. cit., p. 80)

Kirkbride, who questioned Abdullah's real intentions, writing: 'Whether his bellicose intentions towards Syria had ever existed was a moot point', was released from military service to a post in the Secretariat of the High Commissioner in Jerusalem, and the Amir Abdullah was left, undisturbed, to take over control of the whole country in March 1921. The British took no action until the July, when they announced that they were prepared to recognize the Amir's rule over that part of the mandated territory which lay east of the river Jordan, and in the following month they contrived the election of Abdullah's younger brother, the Emir Feisal, to the throne of Iraq,* thus ensuring Hashemite rule

---

* See Philby's *Arabian Days*, pp. 203–05

over 180,000 square miles of Arabian territories with the support of British 'advisers' and British military and financial assistance. From its inception the Arab Legion of Transjordan (later Jordan) was under the command of a British officer: F.G. Peake Pasha from 1921 to 1939, and thereafter J.B. Glubb Pasha until 1956.

The suggestion that Abdullah may have been prepared to launch an attack on the French army in Syria, with its fighter aircraft and tanks, is hilarious, especially in view of his known martial record. Readers of Lawrence's *Seven Pillars* can follow that undistinguished military progress during the Desert Campaign in its pages, while his last-known venture has been recorded by H.St.J. Philby, who had, in the middle of March 1919, been summoned to attend a meeting of the Middle East Departmental Conference at the Foreign Office.

'In an ante-room I found an imposing array of generals, admirals, Under-Secretaries of State and Hubert Young as Secretary. We were ushered into Lord Curzon's presence . . . The great man opened the proceedings with his inimitable urbanity. The trouble was Khurma' (an oasis whose possession had for some time been disputed by Ibn Sa'ud and Abdullah's father, the Sharif Hussein). 'Curzon supported Hussein: ''Now in all these Arabian problems our policy is a Husain policy, and . . . we must be satisfied that our man, if we decide in his favour as we would like to do, will win if it comes to a fight. Otherwise the consequences may be very serious indeed.'' Curzon then 'asked the opinion of the admirals and generals, who with one accord scouted the very idea that a rabble of Wahabi fanatics could make any serious stand against the British-trained and British-equipped and British-armed regulars of the Hijaz.'

Philby a few weeks later received an urgent summons to the Foreign Office, where Curzon reported:

'. . . Husain, as authorized by us, sent up his army under his son Abdullah to occupy Khurma. Reconnaissance failed to show any signs of Wahhabi concentrations or counter-measures. But in the small hours of 19 May the Wahhabis in force attacked the camp from all sides. Abdullah and his staff fled on horseback to Taif; the rest of his army was annihilated.' (*Arabian Days*, Robert Hale, 1948, pp. 176 and 178)

It was less than two years after this lesson that the Foreign Office were presented with the prospect of Abdullah proposing to lead yet another batch of warriors, this time against a trained and fully-equipped European army. How fortunate for all concerned that Churchill's swift action in April 1921, resulting in the creation of the Amirate of Transjordan under Abdullah, preserved the French forces in Syria from the threat of annihilation.

The Mandate for Palestine included in its preamble a paragraph which supplemented the original succinct wording of the Balfour Declaration by adding that: 'whereas recognition has thereby been given to the historical connection of the Jewish People with Palestine and to the grounds for reconstituting their national home in that country', but omitted the promise of independence and constitution which was included in the other Middle East mandates.

The areas of Lebanon and Syria, placed under a French Mandate endorsed by the League of Nations in July 1922, amounted to some 76,000 square miles. Thus the five territories designed to achieve ultimate Arab independence (for under the terms of the Mandates other than the Palestine Mandate the Mandatories were committed to 'facilitate the progressive development' of these territories 'as independent states') together covered over 250,000 square miles, or roughly 25 times the size of the 10,000 square-mile area which was to include the site of a Jewish National Home, but despite these figures the Arabs and their supporters have never ceased to complain that the British reneged on wartime promises that the Arabs would be given their full independence in the territories recovered from the Turks.

The arguments which have been used to support this contention are too well-known to require their repetition in these pages. It should suffice to look at a current map of the Arabian Peninsula and then add the 810,000 square miles of Saudi Arabia and the 116,000 square miles of South Yemen (formerly the British Colony of Aden together with the Aden Protectorates) to the 250,000 square miles of the Arab mandates in order to realise the extent of the territories which in this century have been placed under Arab rule, at a cost to the British in the Great War of tens of thousands of lives and mountains of gold.

There can be no questioning of the sacrifices which were thus made in the bitter four-year battle to drive the Turk out of the Arabia which he had occupied for 400 years: they were Allied sacrifices. The Arabs of Syria and Palestine and Mesopotamia did not participate in the fighting against the Turks; on the contrary, all the evidence of our official war historians and the many writers who have left records of their experiences in those theatres of war is that when the Arabs did take up arms in that conflict it was against the Allies.

It would not be possible in this present work to give more than a representative selection from their authoritative pens. Arnold Wilson, who served through the Mesopotamian campaign, has left a sad and detailed record of the horrors and the treachery British soldiers were forced to endure during a campaign that cost the British 60,000 lives. Major Jarvis, in a different vein, wrote of his experiences in the Palestine campaign.

'Great Britain is held responsible for "letting the Arabs down" because at the Treaty of Versailles they were not given all that they were promised, i.e. to hold all the terri- tory they captured, but looking at the matter from an

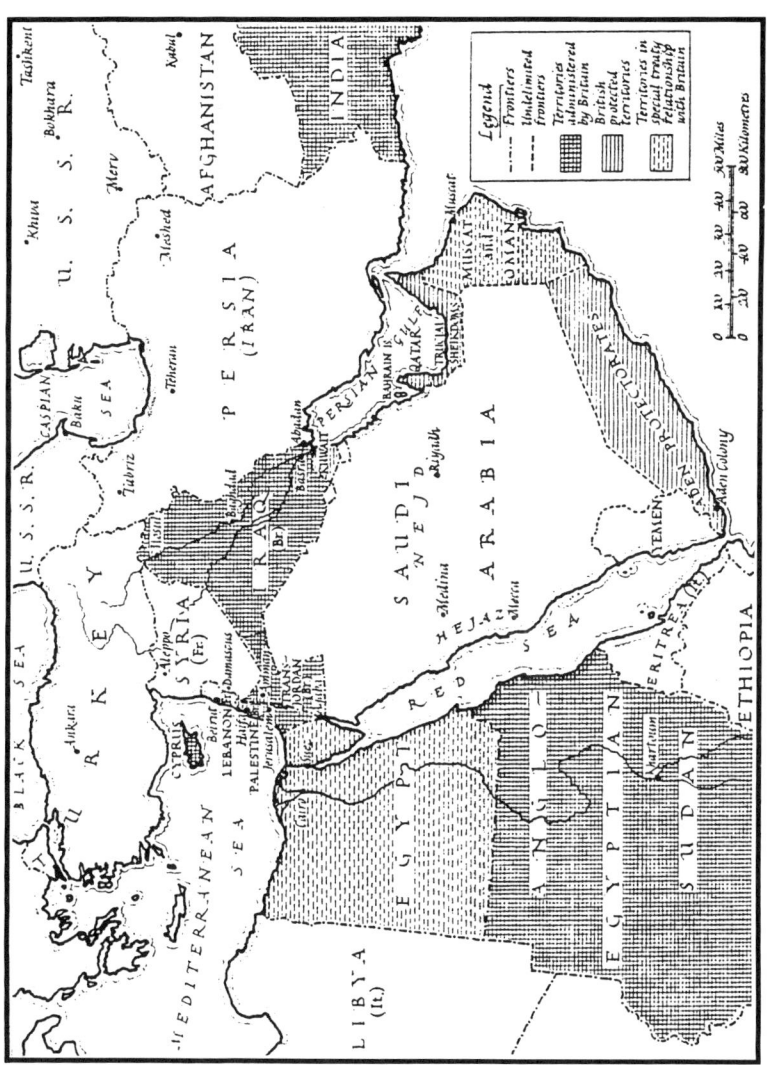

THE MIDDLE EAST IN 1926

Legend

Frontiers

Undelimited frontiers

Territories administered by Britain

British protected territories

Territories in special treaty relationship with Britain

unbiased standpoint I cannot see, considering all things, that we have failed to honour our bond to any great extent. The Iraqians who took no part in the War have their independence, and the Hedjaz or Saudi Arabia has it also. Trans-Jordan has a very modified form of British Mandate which practically amounts to independence. Syria is a French Mandate, and the difference between a French Mandate and a French colony may not be very easy to define, but it must be remembered that the Syrians as a people did nothing whatsoever towards assisting the Arab cause except for the isolated action of some eastern Bedouin in the very last stages of the campaign and the services of a few Syrian officers who deserted from the Turkish Army. The great mass of the Syrian people did absolutely nothing beyond hold secret meetings and talk. The inhabitants of Palestine did rather less than this, and yet it is from the educated *effendiyah* of the Syrian and Palestinian towns that one hears all this talk of Arab independence and Great Britain's perfidy. In the first place these people took no part whatsoever in assisting the Allies to drive out the Turk from their country, and secondly they are not Arabs. I have lived and worked with Arabs for eighteen years and know the race, and no amount of oily food and cloying sweetmeats could turn this hardy desert stock into the effete and languid creatures that now claim kinship with the nomads of Arabia and talk so loudly of the Arab independence for which they fought.' (*Three Deserts*, Murray, 1951, pp. 182–83)

11

The period of the granting of the Mandates had also witnessed the first awakening of a national consciousness in the history of the Palestine Arabs. During the 400 years they had lived under the Turks they were recognized by their rulers only as Syrians. The area west of the Jordan had under the Ottomans been divided into four Sanjaks: Beirut, Acre, Baloa (Nablus) and the Independent Sanjak of Jerusalem; 'Palestine' was not to be found in the Turkish maps. Their country dismembered in this manner, their numbers reduced to a tiny fraction of the former population and their land denuded, it was small wonder that thus debilitated the spirit had been lacking to inspire even the faintest stirring of nationalism.

In the words of the Palestine Royal Commission Report of July 1937:

'In the twelve centuries and more that had passed since the Arab conquest Palestine had virtually dropped out of history. One chapter only is remembered – the not very noble romance of the Crusades. In economics as in politics Palestine lay outside the main stream of the world's life. In the realm of thought, in science or in letters, it made no contribution to modern civilization. Its last state was worse than its first. In 1914 the condition of the country was an outstanding example of the lethargy and maladministration of the pre-war Ottoman regime. The population, still overwhelmingly Arab in character, eked out a precarious existence mainly in the hills. On the plains, where life and property was less secure, such irrigation-works as had existed in ancient times had long disappeared. Oranges were grown round Jaffa, but most of the maritime belt was only sparsely populated and only thinly cultivated. Esdraelon for the most part was marshy and malarious. Eastwards beyond Jordan nothing remained of the Greek cities of classical times save one or two groups of deserted ruins. Southwards in Beersheba, once the site of several prosperous towns, all trace of urban life had long lain buried under the encroaching sand.'

Visitors wrote of the poverty and desolation they found there: in the nineteenth century, Mark Twain, in his book *Innocents Abroad*,* and in the first decade of the present century Sir Frederick Treves recorded their impressions of the country, the latter signalling the gist of his account in the title he gave it: *The Land that is Desolate*. Another writer who paid his first visit to Palestine about the same time as Treves was 21-year-old T.E. Lawrence. In a letter from Beyrout, dated 2 August 1909, he wrote:

'. . . it is such a comfort to *know* that the country was not a bit like this in the time of Our Lord . . . The country was well-peopled, and well-watered artificially: There were not 20 miles of thistles behind Capernaum! and on the way round the lake they did not come upon dirty, dilapidated Bedouin tents . . . Palestine was a decent country then, and could so easily be made so again. The sooner the Jews farm it the better: their colonies are bright spots in a desert . . .'

---

* 'Palestine sits in sackcloth and ashes. Over it broods the spell of a curse that has withered its fields and fettered its energies . . . Nazareth is forlorn; about the ford of Jordan where the hosts of Israel entered the Promised Land with songs of rejoicing one finds only a squalid camp of fantastic Bedouins . . . Palestine is desolate and unlovely. And why should it be otherwise? Can the curse of the Deity beautify a land? Palestine is no more of this work-day world. It is sacred to poetry and tradition − it is dream-land.' (Mark Twain, *Innocents Abroad*, 1869)

More than 20 years later Lawrence's comments were reflected in a report, in 1932, by Lewis French of the Indian Civil Service on the conditions in the Beisan area, which the British found

'inhabited by fellahin who lived in mud hovels, suffered severely from the prevalent malaria and were of too low intelligence to be receptive of any suggestions for improvement of their housing, water supply or education. Large areas of their lands were uncultivated and covered with weeds. There were no trees, no vegetables. The fellahin, if not themselves cattle thieves, were always ready to harbour these and other criminals. The individual plots of cultivation, such as it was, changed hands annually. There was little public security, and the fellahin's lot was an alternation of pillage and blackmail by their neighbours the Beduin ... The Beduin, wild and lawless by nature, were constantly at feud with their neighbours on both sides of the Jordan, and raids and highway robberies formed their staple industry: while such cultivation as the Beduin were capable of filled in the intervals of more exciting occupation.'

Nevertheless, as the Palestine Royal Commission pointed out: 'poor and neglected though it was, to the Arabs who lived in it Palestine − or, more strictly, Syria, of which Palestine had been a part since the days of Nebuchadnezzar − was still their country, their home, the land in which their people for centuries had lived and left their graves.' Sympathetic recognition of these facts emerged in a motion in the House of Lords on 21 June 1922, introduced by a Liberal Peer, Lord Islington, in which he declared that the Palestine Mandate was 'inacceptable to this House' because 'it was opposed to the sentiments and wishes of the great majority of the people of Palestine ... Zionism runs counter to the whole human psychology of the age.' It involved bringing into Palestine 'extraneous and alien Jews from other parts of the world.' Jewish immigration would be a burden on the British taxpayer, and a grave threat to Arab rights and development.

Islington found support in the debate in Lord Sydenham, who claimed that

> 'we have dumped down 25,000 promiscuous people on the shores of Palestine, many of them quite unsuited for colonising purposes, and some of them Bolsheviks, who have already shown the most sinister activity. The Arabs would have kept the Holy Land clear from Bolshevism . . . The Mandate as it stands will undoubtedly, in time, transfer the control of the Holy Land to New York, Berlin, London, Frankfurt and other places.'

The Peers present in the House made their views on the matter quite clear: in the division which followed the debate 60 voted against the Balfour Declaration, and only 29 for it. In Palestine itself the campaign against the Declaration had been strengthened by the recruitment of the 28-year-old Haj Amin el-Husseini, who, it will be remembered, had been convicted for his part in the Jerusalem pogrom, but on 8 May 1921, after receiving a special pardon, had been appointed Mufti of Jerusalem. Later he became President of the newly-created Supreme Moslem Council, giving him full authority over considerable religious funds. Half of his salary was paid by the Government of Palestine. How rapid was his rise from convicted criminal to effective head of the Muslim community in Palestine!

A week before Haj Amin's appointment, on the first day of the month, there had been a severe outbreak of Arab violence, first in Jaffa, where 13 Jews were murdered in the Immigration Centre, and on the following days in some neighbouring colonies. Horace Samuel has left an account of the disorders, writing that the British Commandant of Police in Jaffa, though aware that demonstrations were being held there that day, 'judged that this was the appropriate moment to go to Gaza for a day's shooting. Equally unfortunate the fatal measure was adopted of issuing rifles and ammunition to the predominantly Arab police.'

In neighbouring Tel Aviv both the authorised and unauthorised demonstrations passed off without any major incident and then dispersed.

'Shortly after this the Arabs of Jaffa, who had apparently begun to arm themselves, started to murder, wound, and loot the Jews under the official protection and assistance of a considerable number of the Jaffa police. In many cases the observance of a benevolent neutrality was insufficient, and the police gave full vent to their patriotism by shooting at Jews, or personally participating in the breaking open of Jewish shops. On the first day of the riots alone in Jaffa twenty-five Jews were killed, while many Jewish shops were looted to the tune of about £50,000.

'The most tragic and dramatic feature of the whole business was the attack on the Zionist Commission Immigration Depot, situated well in the heart of the Arab quarter. A mob of Arabs, including a certain number of Arab prostitutes and their bullies, began to attack this building with stones and sticks, but were at first successfully kept at bay by the immigrants. Finally, reinforcements for the attackers were supplied by certain Arab policemen, well equipped with rifles, bombs, and ammunition. The door was forced by the police, and under their leadership and escort the mob burst into the building. Thirteen of the immigrants were murdered, including one woman. Women who were attending to the wounded were fired at to discourage them from so undesirable a practice. Policeman No. 500, Adib Kayal, a member of a distinguished Jaffa family, attempted to persuade a Jewish girl to succumb to his gallant overtures by pointing his rifle at her. Fortunately, Eros was interrupted by Mammon, and while the representative of law and order was engaged in robbing her of a chain, the girl escaped.

'The riots of the 1st of May and the massacre of the Jews in the Immigration Hostel were a pretty broad hint that the Jaffa Arabs resented any further immigration into the country. Under these circumstances the High Commissioner, preferring a policy of tact to one of drastic repression, within forty-eight hours of the massacre telephoned to Mr. Miller, the Assistant Governor of Jaffa, instructing him to announce to the Arabs that in accordance with their request, immigration had been suspended.'

Despite this surrender the colony of Petach Tikvah was attacked on 5 May by thousands of armed Arabs from the adjacent villages who were beaten off by a detachment of Indian cavalry after looting about 600 head of cattle and shooting four of the colonists. On the same day Rehovot and K'far Saba were attacked, the latter being destroyed. On 6 May Hedera was attacked, with damage estimated at £25,000.

It should not be assumed that the Government failed to take punitive action against the offenders. A collective fine was imposed on the villages which had attacked Hedera, but the Arabs informed the Government that they preferred not to pay, and the matter was apparently allowed to rest there. Likewise, though warrants were issued against specific persons resident in Tulkarem on a charge of being concerned in the attack on Hedera, no effort was made to execute the warrants, on the grounds that 'Their arrest would provoke excitement and resentment and friction. All this was easily avoidable by refraining from executing the warrants. Why, therefore, be provocative?'

Samuel's close knowledge of these events derives from his professional involvement in the preparation of the prosecution of those responsible for the perpetration of the various atrocities. The task was a considerable one, involving the proofs of about 500 witnesses, and accordingly a private enquiry agent of British nationality was engaged to assist the prosecution, but 'who, immediately he got on the track, was promptly ordered by the military authorities to leave the Jaffa district.'

However, the Administration did not remain entirely inactive in the matter. Policeman No. 500 (Adib Khayal) was convicted and sentenced to five years for his exploits in the Immigration Hostel. Two Jews from Petach Tikva were charged with firing a revolver during the attack on the colony, and a third, Blum, for many years a resident in that colony, was charged with lancing one of the attackers from the Arab villages of Yehoudiyeh. From the evidence at the hearing it was established that Blum had in fact accompanied the Indian Lancers who had dispersed the mob.

> 'Under these circumstances, peasant after peasant swore "blind" that he had been lanced personally and physically by Blum. The train of logic was simple and easy to recon-struct. He must have been struck by the enemy. Blum was the enemy – therefore he had been struck by Blum.'
> (Samuel, op. cit., pp. 70–76)

In both these cases the evidence was deemed to be insufficient, and all three Jews were acquitted. So the outbreak petered out in a series of criminal prosecutions, and a Committee of Enquiry, who reported *inter alia*, that Zionism was unpopular with the Arabs, that the police were inefficient, and that it was 'not improbable that there are persons among the sheikhs and money-lenders who do what they can to promote discontent.'

Of this 'Commission of Enquiry' John Marlowe writes more fully that it was 'appointed by the High Commissioner and presided over by the Chief Justice, Sir Thomas Haycraft, (and) found that "the fundamental cause of the Jaffa riots and the subsequent acts of violence was a feeling among the Arabs of discontent with and hostility to the Jews due to political and economic causes and connected with Jewish immigration and with their conception of Zionist policy as derived from Jewish exponents".' In other words, it was the socialist ideas of the Zionists and general Zionist policy that were mainly responsible. It was regrettable that the encouragement given to the Zionists should inevitably result in an Arab frenzy of murder, rape, robbery, pillage and destruction.

12

The Haycraft Commission of Enquiry, after finding that 'the racial strife was begun by Arabs' and that 'the police were, with few exceptions, half-trained and inefficient, in many cases indifferent and in some cases leaders of or conspirators in the violence', finally recommended that the Zionist leaders should implicitly accept the Government's policy on the Jewish National Home and 'should abandon and repudiate all pretensions that go beyond it'.

It seemed therefore incumbent on the Government to issue a Statement of Policy, and in 1922 it accordingly published a White Paper (Cmd 1700). This denied that the Balfour Declaration meant to turn Palestine into a Jewish State, and promised to limit Jewish immigration to the economic absorptive capacity of the country.

These two documents, the Haycraft Report and the 1922 White Paper, were the forerunners of a series of Commission and Committee Reports, together with other White Papers on Palestine, which appeared during the following twenty-five years of the period of the Mandate. As we shall note, they formed a progressive pattern of retreat from the initial concept of the Balfour Declaration. When Balfour first presented the formula contained in the Declaration to the British Cabinet he said:

'As to the meaning of the words "National Home", to which the Zionists attach so much importance, he understood it to mean some form of British, American, or other protectorate, under which full facilities would be given to the Jews to work out their own salvation and to build up, by means of education, agriculture and industry, a real centre of national culture and focus of national life. It did not necessarily involve the *early* establishment of an independent Jewish State, *which was a matter of gradual development* in accordance with the ordinary laws of political evolution.'

The British Cabinet, accepting this explanation, accordingly voted for the issuance of the Balfour Declaration. Lloyd George subsequently wrote (*The Truth About the Peace Treaties*, 1938, pp. 1138–39):

'There has been a good deal of discussion as to the meaning of the words "Jewish National Home" and whether it involved the setting up of a Jewish National State in Palestine. I have already quoted the words actually used by Mr. Balfour when he submitted the Declaration to the Cabinet for its approval. They were not challenged at the time by any member present, and there could be no doubt as to what the Cabinet then had in their minds. It was not their idea that a Jewish State should be set up immediately by the Peace Treaty without reference to the wishes of its inhabitants. On the other hand, it was contemplated that when the time arrived for according representative institutions to Palestine, if the Jews had meanwhile responded to the opportunity offered them by the idea of a National Home and had become a definite majority of the inhabitants, then Palestine would thus become a Jewish Commonwealth.'

President Wilson, too, speaking not only with the authority of the President of the United States but also as a statesman involved in the history of the Balfour Declaration and its meaning, declared on 22 March 1919:

'I am persuaded that the Allied nations, with the fullest concurrence of our own Government and people, are agreed that in Palestine shall be laid the foundations of a Jewish

Commonwealth' (as reported the following day in the *New York Times*).

At the time that these statements were made it was manifestly clear that any such development in Palestine would have to be dependent on Jewish immigration into that country. As Lloyd George remarked:

'The notion that the Jewish immigration would have to be artificially restricted in order to ensure that the Jews should be a permanent minority never entered into the heads of anyone engaged in framing policy. That would have been regarded as unjust and as a fraud on the people to whom we were appealing.'

Of course the authors of the various reports which repeatedly stressed the need to limit Jewish immigration on the grounds of 'economic absorptive capacity' would have rejected out of hand any suggestion that this formula was a device to ensure that the Jewish community in Palestine would remain a minority, but they now make very curious reading. The Hope-Simpson Report, which was issued on 21 October 1930, stated that:

'If all the cultivable land in Palestine were divided up among the Arab agricultural population, there would not be enough to provide every family with a decent livelihood; until further development took place and the Arabs adopted better methods of cultivation, there is no room for a single additional settler, if the standard of life of the fellaheen is to remain at its present level . . .'

The Palestine Royal Commission Report of July 1937 referred to that statement, commenting that 'Sir John Hope-Simpson visited Palestine and made a thorough investigation into all questions connected with land and its possible development', and then went on to quote the 1932 reports submitted by Mr. Lewis

French. These are summarised as follows:

(1) Unless there is a marked change in the methods of cultivation, the land in Palestine is unable to support a large increase in the population.
(2) Any such change must necessarily be a very slow process spread over many years, and depends largely on the extension of education in the Arab villages.
(3) The general indebtedness of the fellaheen is a serious hindrance to the desired progress.

Some light on these comments emerges from an account included in the Palestine Royal Commission Report

'by a Jewish eyewitness of the condition of the Maritime Plain in 1913. It was, we believe, at the time it was written, a truthful and disinterested description:'

'The road leading from Gaza to the north was only a summer track suitable for transport by camels and carts. The track was dry and open for travel in the summer months only. In the rainy season it was impassable. In the villages on both sides of the tracks and as far as the hills to the east no orange groves, orchards or vineyards were to be seen until one reached Yabna Village. Trees generally were a rare sight in these villages . . . Nor were there any vegetable gardens to be seen in any of these villages except at Jora on the sea (Asqalan). In the Hawakir around the villages – small plots fenced around by cactus hedge – one could find in the winter green onions and in the summer cucumbers and water melons. In all the villages dotting the plain between Gaza and Jaffa there was only one well in a village and in the smaller villages there were not wells at all . . . Not in a single village in all this area was water used for irrigation. Water was scantily used for drinking purposes by man and beast.

'Houses were all of mud. No windows were anywhere to be seen. The roofs were of caked mud. Every house was divided in two parts – one part slightly elevated above the other. The family lived in the elevated part while in the lower part the cattle were housed. The cattle were small and poor. So were the chickens.

'The fields were sown with wheat, barley, kursena and lentils in the winter – and with dura and sesame in the summer. Fields used for summer crops one year were sown with winter crops the next year, and so on in rotation. The ploughs used were of wood. European ploughs were not known in the whole area. Not a village could boast of a cart. Sowing was done by hand: harvesting by the scythe and threshing by animals. Fields were never manured . . . The sanitary conditions in the villages were horrible. Schools did not exist and the younger generation rolled about in the mud of the streets. The rate of infant mortality was very high. There was no medical service in any of the villages distant from a Jewish settlement. In passing a village one noticed a large number of blind or half-blind persons. Malaria was rampant . . .

The Royal Commission Report makes reference to these conditions in its para. 66, on page 242, writing that:

'The Arab charge that the Jews have obtained too large a proportion of good land cannot be maintained. Much of the land now carrying orange groves was sand dunes or swamp and uncultivated when it was purchased. Though today, in the light of experience gained by Jewish energy and enterprise, the Arabs may denounce the vendors and regret the alienation of the land, there was at the time at least of the earlier sales little evidence that the owners possessed either the resources or training needed to develop the land . . .'

The evidence given before the United Nations Special Committee on Palestine in 1947 revealed that

> 'of the one million dunams of land acquired by the Jews during the last 25 years, more than half was thought to be uncultivable and unhealthy waste land. The total area reclaimed is more than 600,000 dunams. More than half of northern Palestine – about eight million dunams – consists of hill country, of which only about two million dunams, according to Government statistics, are cultivated. This very low ratio of cultivation is the result of centuries of neglect. By deforestation, over-grazing and improper cultivation, large areas have been reduced to rocks and boulders. The soil itself is of the highest fertility . . .'

A Jewish witness claimed:

> 'Our Arab neighbours have improved and intensified their land use during the past 15 years of rapid Jewish growth. This improvement has taken place often as a direct consequence of resources made available by Jewish land purchases. Other stimuli have been Jewish urban markets, the example of Jewish farm methods, and the aids made available through Jewish paid taxes. It is a notable fact that in Transjordan, under the same Mandatory rule, but from which Jewish immigration was excluded by the partition of 1922, the Arab farmer shows no corresponding progress, despite the availability of large land reserves.'

Official figures revealed that the average income of the Arab farmer increased from the year 1931 to 1939 by approximately 30 per cent (disregarding the gain in citrus). By 1945, again utilising official figures (and disregarding wartime price advantages), the income of the average Arab farm family was approximately 50 per cent higher than in 1931. This gain revealed great progress in land use and in farm management. 'The Arab fellah has diversified his farm and has greatly increased his production of vegetables, olives, fruits, eggs and fodder. He has been able to raise his standard of living notably and at the same time pay off the greater part of his debts.'

In the light of these facts, which were accepted at face value by the 1947 UN Special Committee, the comment in the July 1937 Royal Commission Report that Sir John Hope Simpson's estimate of the total cultivable land was not a sufficiently scientific and final calculation to justify a reversal of immigration policy may well be regarded as an egregious understatement. If it was used by the British Government to justify a limitation of Jewish immigration based on Simpson's assessment of the 'economic capacity' of the country, it can only be regarded, at best, as a grievous error which contributed to the monstrous tragedy to which Ben-Gurion referred in his evidence before UNSCOP:

'When the White Paper was introduced in 1939, Mr Churchill said that this was a mortal blow to the Jewish people. I am sorry to say, he did not exaggerate. The White Paper, in closing the gates of Palestine to Jews in the hour of the greatest peril, is responsible for the death of tens of thousands, perhaps hundreds of thousands of Jews who could have been saved from the gas chambers had Palestine been open to them. Just before the war we applied to the Colonial Secretary for permission to bring over 20,000 Jewish children from Poland and 10,000 youths from the Balkan countries. Permission was refused, and those 20,000 children and the 10,000 youths were put to death. There were times when Jews could still escape from Nazi-occupied territories, but the gates of their National Home were closed by the Mandatory Power and they were sent to their death in Dachau and Treblinka . . . Palestine is now the only place in the civilised world where racial discrimination still exists in law.'

13

Article 4 of the League of Nations Mandate for Palestine provided that:

'An appropriate Jewish agency shall be recognised as a public body for the purpose of advising and co-operating with the Administration of Palestine in such economic, social and other matters as may affect the establishment of the Jewish national home and the interests of the Jewish population in Palestine, and, subject always to the control of the Administration, to assist and take part in the development of the country.'

The first constituent meeting of the Jewish Agency was held at Zurich on 11 August 1929. To this event the Arab response came with tragic swiftness. Of what followed in the next few weeks there may have been some forewarning in the withdrawal by the authorities of the three rifles issued as a sealed emergency reserve from a Jewish settlement near Tiberias, leaving the inhabitants at the mercy of armed attackers. There had never been a time in the history of the return when some measure of protection had been more urgently needed. Isolated settlements were always subject to armed attacks: it was for this reason that sealed armouries, however modest, had been permitted to them. There has never been any explanation of this action. The High Commissioner, Sir John Chancellor, was at that time in England, on leave.

On 16 August a vast crowd of Moslems swarmed across the narrow pavement fronting the Western Wall which had for centuries been permitted to the Jews for their prayers. The

Shammas (Beadle) was beaten, the prayer books were torn to pieces and burnt. On the following day 17-year-old Abraham Mizrachi was fatally stabbed in a Jerusalem street. At his funeral on 21 August the police were reported to have used considerable violence against the crowd of Jewish mourners when the latter sought to depart from the prescribed route.

On 22 August the Arab newspaper, *Falastin*, wrote: 'The atmosphere is tense and it is apprehended that tomorrow, when many fellaheen assemble for prayers in Jerusalem, a substantial answer will be given to these incidents.' The newspaper proved to be remarkably well-informed. Soon after midday on Friday 23 August Arab mobs emerged from the Old City armed with knives and clubs and proceeded, as anticipated, to murder Jews. The slaughter continued without interruption for two hours before the police were allowed to fire upon the murderers. On the same afternoon a student in the Jewish theological seminary in Hebron was murdered, and on the following morning the Jewish community in that town was decimated in a massacre perpetrated by a mob estimated by the (Arab) Acting District Officer of Police to number 'about four thousand': there were only some fifty or sixty police available.

At the time of this outbreak Col. F.H. Kisch, the Chairman of Palestine Zionist Executive, was in London, on leave. He decided to return at once to Palestine, which he reached on 1 September, on the same day that the High Commissioner, Sir John Chancellor, issued a Proclamation which commenced:

'I have just returned from the United Kingdom to find to my distress the country in a state of disorder and a prey to unlawful violence. I have learnt with horror of the atrocious acts committed by bodies of ruthless and bloodthirsty evil-doers, of savage murders perpetrated upon defenceless members of the Jewish population, regardless of age and sex, accompanied, as at Hebron, by acts of unspeakable savagery, of the burning of farms and houses in town and country and of the looting and destruction of property. These crimes have brought upon their authors the execration of all civilized peoples throughout the world. My first duties are to restore order in the country, and to inflict stern punishment upon those found guilty of acts of violence. All necessary measures will be taken to achieve those ends.'

The wording of this Proclamation offended the susceptibilities of the Arab leaders, and the High Commissioner had to issue a subsequent Proclamation 'which largely counteracted the effects of the first, being regarded as a kind of apology for the strong words of condemnation which the High Commissioner had used . . .' On 2 September Col. Kisch saw the High Commissioner and then spent the rest of the day conferring with the military and police authorities, with a view to improving conditions of security for the Jewish population. He left for Safad on 3 September. 'The Diary which follows tell its own story from that date. In these riots 129 Jews were killed and 318 injured.'

These last sentences are from Kisch's *Palestine Diary*, published in 1938 by Victor Gollancz, seven years after the author's retirement from the Zionist Executive. He could not have known at that time that Britain would be needing his services in the World War which broke out in the following year, when he returned to active service in the British Army and was sent to Egypt, where by 1941 he was Chief Engineer, Eighth Army, with rank of Brigadier. He was responsible throughout all North Africa for maintaining the water supply lines for military construction during the advances and demolition during the retreats, and for designing mine fields and anti-mine measures. Almost at the end of the fighting he was killed while inspecting a German minefield and was buried in Tunisia. He was decorated by the British and French governments. Kefar Kisch and the Kisch Memorial Forest in Lower Galilee are named after him.

Frederick Hermann Kisch was born in 1888 in Darjeeling, India, where his father was in the Indian Civil Service. Kisch finished in second place at the Royal Military Academy, Woolwich, and joined the Indian Army. In the First World War he was wounded in France and again in Mesopotamia. After the war he headed the Military Intelligence section of the British Delegation at the Paris Peace Conference of 1919–21. He was by this time a Lieut-Colonel, but nevertheless failed to obtain a nomination to the Staff College and resigned from the Army.

In his *Foreword* to Kisch's *Palestine Diary*, Lloyd George discusses the failure of the British Government to honour the pledges given to World Jewry in the Balfour Declaration, and asks:

'What has been the course of events which led up to this collapse of British administrative capacity? Was it inevitable, and our policy misjudged from the start; or could the aims set out in the Balfour Declaration have been in fact achieved, if those appointed to carry them out had been wiser in their methods, and been more loyally supported and encouraged by the home Government in the honouring of our pledged word to the Jewish People?

'A very valuable light is thrown on this issue by the diary of Colonel Kisch. It is a first-hand account, written from day to day by one who had the fullest possible knowledge and experience of what was taking place, that tells us just how the difficulties developed which have led to the present impasse, and how they were handled by the authorities we had appointed. For the historian it is a record of the greatest possible importance. The reliability of Colonel Kisch as a witness is beyond question.'

On 4 September Kisch visited Rosh Pinah, where he was told that 'the Arabs are still taking every opportunity to loot and pillage following the example of Safad, a tendency which they attribute largely to the fact that none of the Safad offenders has yet been punished. Nor has any action yet been taken against the villages which are known to have looted Yesod Hamalah.' He then went on to Safad.

'The Jewish quarter at Safad is a terrible sight, Sephardim Street, where the attack began, being entirely gutted and pillaged. It appears that the attackers, not content with shooting and stabbing their victims, brought with them tins of petrol in order to set the place alight. In this zone, the houses having been reduced to a mass of ruins, there is no hope of reconstruction. I was informed – and this is important – by an old Jew who was one of the first to be attacked and whose life was spared, that he had recognized his attackers as neighbours who had traded with him, and with whom he had been on friendly terms for years. He remonstrated with them, but they savagely continued their blows. I saw one family of five orphans – girls – whose father, mother and grandfather had been murdered in their presence.'

At Deganya B., on the following day, he was informed of the 'anxiety in regard to some of the Arab police', which led to the District Officer being asked

'that no police should enter the colonies without special orders. The representative of the PICA colonies expressed lack of confidence in the Government with reference to the fact that just a month earlier the authorities had taken away the arms which had been with them for eight years. This point was raised in a number of settlements, and it is not unnatural that the removal of the Government armouries within a period of one to three months before the riots, has given rise to strong feelings against certain officers of the Administration and the police.'

At Beit Alfa he was told that

'it will not be possible for Jews to return to Beisan until after the instigators have been punished. About 45 families are involved. Strong views were expressed on the tendentious character of the Official Bulletin No. I, which stated that *"yesterday morning a clash occurred between Arab and Jewish residents of Beisan."* (I subsequently drew the High Commissioner's attention to this Bulletin, as also the Bulletin No. 5, which, referring to the atrocious attack at Safad on August 29 when 45 Jews were killed and wounded, said: *"Disorders broke out at Safad on the 29th"*.)'

At Nahalal he 'was informed that robberies in the neighbourhood were increasing and that no punishments were being inflicted: it was submitted that village *mukhtars* should be made financially responsible for security.' On 11 September he visited Hebron. His Diary of that date gives too full an account to be afforded space here, but contains some details which need to be recorded. The morning after the murder of the theological student

'found most of the Yeshiva students taking refuge at the house of Mr. Slonim, the bank manager, who was both respected and liked by the Arab inhabitants. At about 10.30, after agitators had been crying out through the town that Jews were massacring Moslems in the streets of Jerusalem, riots broke out simultaneously in several parts of the city.

'After the first blood had been drawn the rioters behaved like madmen, and Slonim's house became a real scene of slaughter; some nineteen persons were murdered there. It is said that one local Moslem tried to keep the rioters from this house, and that he was thrown over the stone staircase. The house, which I inspected, has been closed by the police but is kept in the state in which it was left by the rioters, the floors and furniture covered with bloodstains, pillows and mattresses ripped to pieces, the prayer-books burnt.

The Scrolls of the Law were retrieved by the police and are held at our disposal.

'I also visited the Hadassah Hospital which was broken into, one room being set on fire. This is a real indication of the madness which took possession of the crowd, since the Hadassah is everywhere recognised as an institution which is also of constant service to the Arabs . . . After seeing the town and gathering such information as I could, I visited the cemetery where exhumation was in progress: a ghastly sight of which I will give no description. Fifteen bodies had been disinterred by the time of my visit. In the evening we learnt of the distribution in the streets of Jerusalem of a terrible anti-racial proclamation issued by the Arab Youth Association and printed at the Moslem Orphanage Press, which is the press of the Moslem Supreme Council.'

Too long to reproduce here in full, it exhorted 'The Sons of the Fatherland' to

'keep away from the Jew who has killed your innocent Arab brethren with weapons purchased with the money you paid in buying his goods and which he intends to utilize for the acquisition of the land remaining in your hands in order to drive you away from your Fatherland . . . O Arab! Remember that the Jew is your strongest enemy and the enemy of your ancestors since olden times. Do not be misled by his tricks for it is he who tortured Christ, peace be upon him, and poisoned Mohammed, peace and worship be with him. It is he who now endeavours to slaughter you as he did yesterday . . .

'In Tel Aviv there are 1,365 refugees from the mixed districts of Jaffa for whose safety, if they return to their homes, the Government do not feel able to give a guarantee.

At Rehovot there are 120 refugees from Hulda, Kefar-Uriah and Beer-Tuviah, where our settlements have been completely destroyed.' (op. cit., p. 265)

14

Following the pattern commencing in 1921, when the Jaffa riots gave rise to the Haycraft Commission of enquiry and the 1922 White Paper, the 1929 riots were followed by the Shaw Commission of Enquiry in that same year, and a White Paper in 1930. The Shaw Commission's terms of reference were 'to enquire into the immediate causes which led to the recent outbreak in Palestine and to make recommendations as to the steps necessary to avoid a recurrence.' It consisted of Sir Walter Shaw, former Chief Justice of the Straits Settlements, as chairman, and three Members of Parliament, Sir H. Betterton (Conservative), R.H. Morris (Liberal) and H. Snell (Labour).

As to the causes of the trouble the Commission stated: 'There can be no doubt that racial animosity on the part of the Arabs, consequent upon the disappointment of their political and national aspirations and fear for their economic future, were the fundamental cause of the outbreak of August last.' The Commission accepted most of the Arab claims, and recommended that a new statement of policy should be issued, containing 'a definition in clear and positive terms' of the meaning of the passages of the Mandate providing for 'the safeguarding of the rights of the non-Jewish communities.' It recommended that immigration policy be reviewed to prevent a repetition of what the Commission described as the excessive immigration of 1925 and 1926; and that a special inquiry should be undertaken into the prospects of introducing improved methods of cultivation and that a new land policy be introduced to cater for the natural increase in the rural population.

The Commission's Report, which was published in 1930, made it clear that British opinion was swinging slowly but definitely against the Zionists, and concluded that:

'the claims and demands which from the Zionist side have been advanced in regard to the future of Jewish immigration into Palestine will have been such as to arouse among Arabs the apprehension that they will in time be deprived of their livelihood and pass under the political domination of the Jews . . . There is incontestable evidence that in the matter of immigration there has been a serious departure by the Jewish authorities from the doctrine accepted by the Zionist Organization in 1922 that immigration should be regulated by the economic capacity of Palestine to absorb new arrivals.'

The Shaw Report recommended an early declaration of the British Government as to the policy which was to be pursued 'in regard to the regulation and control of future Jewish immigration into Palestine.' The Government's response came with its appointment of Sir John Hope Simpson to report on questions of immigration and land settlement, and a preliminary statement accepting the substance of the Shaw Report. These views proved to be unacceptable to the Permanent Mandates Commission of the League of Nations at an extraordinary session following the 1929 riots. It criticised severely the British Government for failing to suppress immediately the anti-Jewish riots, thus proving itself powerless to protect Jewish life – the essential condition for the development of the Jewish National Home. In the opinion of the Mandates Commission, the adoption of 'a more active policy . . . a firmer and more constant and unanimous determination – would have diminished the antagonism from which the country suffers.' The establishment of the Jewish National Home and the foundation of self-governing institutions were defined as the two objects of the Palestine Mandate. The Mandatory authorities were called upon to show a firm hand 'to all sections of the population which are rebelling against the Mandate . . .'

The British Government made no attempt to conceal its anger with this censure or to exhibit any immediate compliance with its injunctions. Indeed, the action it took on 12 May, when it withdrew 2350 Immigration Certificates which had been issued two days before by the Palestine Government for the half-yearly Schedule April to September 1930, thus suspending all further labour immigration until the conclusion of Sir John Hope-Simpson's investigations, could well be regarded as an act of defiance. On the subject of the growing rift between the British Government and the Permanent Mandates Commission of the League of Nations John Marlowe wrote, in a chapter on the Shaw Report:

'Two things are apparent from this Report. First, the British Government, whose predecessors had in fact drafted the Mandate in co-operation with the Zionist Organization, had now begun to use, and were to continue to use, language which implied that the Mandate was an onerous obligation imposed on Great Britain by the League of Nations which they were attempting to fulfil out of loyalty to the League of Nations. Secondly, in view of the fact that the Permanent Mandates Commission, more interested in legal interpretation than in political realities, had always been inclined to criticize restrictions on the development of the National Home, the Report was concerned to minimize those aspects of the Shaw Report which appeared to recommend such restrictions. In this way, via the 1930 White Paper and the subsequent Macdonald "Black Letter", the British Government became involved in a process of "double talk" which was to make their intentions less instead of more explicit.' (op. cit., pp. 119–20)

One example of this 'double talk' is to be found in the extraordinary statement in the Shaw Report that:

'It is our belief that a feeling of resentment among the Arabs of Palestine consequent on their disappointment at their continual failure to obtain any measure of self-government is greatly aggravating the difficulties of the local Administration.'

It seems incredible that the Commission could have been so ill-informed, or ill-advised, as to have been unaware of the British Government's attempt in 1923 to proceed with an arrangement for the formation of a Legislative Council on lines already discussed with the Arab Delegation appointed by the Fourth Arab Congress and the Zionist Organization in 1921.

An Order-in-Council dated August 10 set out arrangements for a Legislative Council consisting of eleven official and twelve elected non-official members, of whom eight were to be Moslem, two Christian and two Jewish. Elections were to be held in the following February, but when the Arab Delegation returned from London in September a Fifth Arab Congress held at Nablus resolved to boycott the proposed elections on the grounds that the powers reserved to the High Commissioner included the control of immigration, and that official members of the Council plus the two Jewish members could together outvote the Arab members. These limitations meant that the Arab members would have been unable to use the Legislative Council for blocking legislation providing for the implementation of the Balfour Declaration policy, as written into the Mandate. In the face of this boycott the Administration postponed *sine die* the promulgation of the Legislative Council and substituted for it a nominated Advisory Council consisting of the same number of members of each race, as had been provided for in the plan for a Legislative Council. But the Arabs boycotted the Advisory Council as well, with the result that this too was abandoned. The High Commissioner later expressed the view to a Cabinet Committee that the rejection of the Legislative Council proposals was due to the advice given to the Arab Delegation by its English friends. (Colonial Office C.P. 106, 1923)

These 'English friends' might be identified with a group of some eighty Conservative M.P.s who had presented a memorandum to the Cabinet Committee which was appointed, during the summer of 1923, to review British policy in Palestine. The Colonial Office presented a Memorandum which, in company with memoranda from its Middle East Department and from the three services on the strategic importance of Palestine, pointed out that abandonment of the Balfour Declaration policy would also involve abandonment of the Mandate and the consequent abandonment of Palestine, which would be inadvisable for strategic reasons and for reasons of prestige. The Middle East Department, the Naval Staff, and the Air Staff together expressed the view that a British regime in Palestine was vital for the defence of the Canal, particularly in view of the possibility of a withdrawal from Egypt.

With these papers before them, the Cabinet Committee decided that it was 'well nigh impossible for any Government to extricate itself' from the Balfour Declaration, but it would attempt to meet Arab complaints of discrimination against them with the offer of an Arab Agency. Accordingly a proposal was prepared and sent to the High Commissioner. It stated that

'H.M.G. are prepared to favour the establishment of an Arab Agency in Palestine which will occupy a position exactly analogous to that of the Jewish Agency under Article 4 of the Mandate, i.e. it will be recognized as a public body for the purpose of advising and co-operating with the Administration in such economic, social, and other matters as may affect the non-Jewish population and, subject to the control of the Administration, of assisting and taking part in the development of the country. As regards immigration the Arab Agency will have the right to be consulted as to the means of ensuring that the rights and position of other sections are not prejudiced.'

In October the High Commissioner reported that Arab leaders

had been consulted about this proposal and that they had 'expressed themselves unable to accept the proposal as falling short of the demands of the Arab population'. That, for the time being, represented the British Government's last attempt to secure Arab consent to a policy of equality of obligation. And yet, as we have seen, the Shaw Report could permit itself to ventilate the belief that Arab resentment arose from 'their disappointment at continual failure to obtain any measure of self-government'!

The Passfield White Paper, which was issued at the same time as the Hope-Simpson Report again proposed the establishment of a Legislative Council: . . . 'H.M.G. trust that on this occasion they will secure the co-operation of all sections of the population.' It was highly critical of many aspects of the Zionist policy and programme, and castigated Histadruth, the Jewish Federation of Labour, for adopting 'a policy which implies the introduction of a new social order based on communal settlement and the principle of self-labour'.

The publication of the Passfield White Paper provoked universal condemnation. General Smuts sent a telegram to the Prime Minister, Ramsay Macdonald, urging its repudiation. Lord Melchett, announcing his resignation from the Council of the Jewish Agency, wrote that 'the grotesque travesty of the purpose of the Mandate given in the Government Paper can only be described as an insult to the intelligence of Jewry and a deliberate affront to the Mandates Commission'.

Weizmann wrote an open letter to the Colonial Secretary announcing his resignation as Chairman of the Zionist Organisation and Jewish Agency. Writing of the Passfield White Paper in *Trial and Error*, he said that 'it was considered by all Jewish friends of the National Home, Zionist and non-Zionist alike, and by a host of non-Jewish well-wishers, as rendering, and intending to render, our work in Palestine impossible'. He had for some time been aware of the hostile attitude of the Passfields. 'I had a conversation,' he wrote, 'with Lady Passfield (the former Beatrice Webb), in the presence of Josiah Wedgwood who, in those days, as always, stood staunchly with us. What I heard from Lady Passfield was: ''I can't understand why the Jews make such a fuss over a few dozen of their people killed in Palestine. As many are killed every week in London in traffic accidents, and no one pays any attention''.'

The Passfield White Paper was never, in fact, implemented, and the years that followed gave the lie to most of the smears included in that Paper and the accompanying Shaw and Hope-Simpson Reports. During those years a tremendous increase in Jewish immigration accompanied increased employment, increasing wages, and increasing agricultural and industrial production. The resultant prosperity was shared by both Arabs and Jews to an extent, which, while it lasted, created an illusion of the continued possibility of political peace, if not of political progress. Land sales continued apace, and such Arab tenants as were evicted for the most part found employment in enterprises started by Arab landlords from the proceeds of their land sales. The emollient effects of economic prosperity even resulted in some measure of economic co-operation between Arabs and Jews.

15

'There are in this part of the world six million people doomed to be pent up in places where they are not wanted, and for whom the world is divided into places where they cannot live, and places into which they cannot enter.' Chaim Weizmann to the 1936 Royal Commission on Palestine.

On 15 September 1935, the National Socialist National Convention in Nuremberg decreed that: 'A citizen of the Reich is only that subject who is of German cognate blood and who, through his conduct, shows that he is both desirous and fit to serve faithfully the German people and Reich.' A further statute, the Law for the Protection of the German Blood and of the German Honor, prohibited marriage and extramarital relations between Jews and Germans. The effect of these two statutes was to render stateless the Jews of Germany.

For the helpless victims of these enactments, the ideal of the Jewish National Home was transformed into a dire necessity for their survival. When, some three years later, an international conference was convened at the town of Evian, on Lake Geneva, to arrive at some common policy on the refugee problem, nation after nation declined to relax its immigration regulations to accommodate these stateless and homeless people.

The Australian delegate told the Conference: 'Since we have no racial problem, we are not desirous of importing one.' The British Government declared that there was no territory available for the settlement of Jewish refugees anywhere in the British Colonial Empire, while in Palestine only very limited immigration could be considered. Golda Meyerson (Golda Meir) was present at the Conference on its final day, 15 July, when a resolution was passed stating that 'the countries of asylum are not willing to undertake any obligation toward financing involuntary obligation'. When invited by a journalist to comment on the resolutions of 'sympathy' towards the plight of the refugees, she replied: 'There is one ideal I have in mind; one thing I want to see before I die – that my people should not need expressions of sympathy.'

It is worth noting that in 1933 the British Government had been given an undertaking by leaders of the Anglo-Jewish community that all expense of maintenance or accommodation of refugees would be borne by the Jewish community without cost to the State. Despite this assurance there was widespread antagonism towards refugees, fuelled in part by traditional xenophobia and in part by the fear that immigration would aggravate unemployment. The British Medical Association opposed the admission of more than a small number of refugee doctors, while Lord Dawson of Penn, the President of the Royal College of Physicians, told the Home Secretary in 1933 that 'the number that could usefully be absorbed or teach us anything could be counted on the fingers of one hand'. The *Daily Mail* warned: 'Once it was well known that Britain offered sanctuary to all who cared to come, the flood gates would be opened, and we should be inundated by thousands seeking a home.' Six trade unionists complained to the *Daily Herald* about its support for refugees, declaring that 'charity begins at home'. The *Observer* warned that a mass influx might lead to outbreaks of anti-Semitism. In a discussion in the Cabinet in July 1938 the Home Secretary stated that 'while he was doing his best, there was a good deal of feeling growing up in this country – a feeling which was reflected in Parliament – against the admission of Jews to British territory.'

In Palestine itself the campaign against the immigration of Jews to that country came to a head in April 1936, in the form of a full-scale rebellion under the open leadership of Haj Amin el Husseini, the Mufti of Jerusalem. Politically, the rebellion was well timed. Italy had, after open preparation, invaded Abyssinia. Britain had condemned this aggression and had concentrated warships at Haifa and Alexandria. Large numbers of British and Italian troops faced each across Libya's border with Egypt. At a League of Nations meeting sanctions were applied against Italy. Italy responded by broadcasting in Arabic, from the Bari station, attacks on Britain in general and British rule in Palestine in particular. Arab newspapers in Palestine were subsidised with Italian money, and after the rebellion had broken out the rebels were kept supplied with arms and ammunition.

The close relations which the Mufti established with the Italians at this time marked a step in his progress towards open co-operation with the Axis Powers. On 15 July he called on the German Consul-General in Jerusalem to assure him of the Palestinian Arabs' 'sympathy for the New Germany' (Documents on German Foreign Policy, Series D, Vol. VI, No. 566). In his capacity as leader of the Palestinian Arabs he might be seen as acting at this time in concert with other Middle East groups against the British and French roles in the region, when the Egyptians deemed it opportune to press Britain for an Anglo-Egyptian treaty to establish the independence of Egypt. This was concluded and signed on 26 August 1936, and was accompanied by a two-year defence pact which permitted Britain to station forces on the Suez Canal.

In Syria also the nationalists were successful in raising riots against the French in January 1936. These were followed by a general strike, and on 1 March the French conceded defeat and agreed to negotiate a treaty which would give Syria the status of an Independent Power in alliance with France. Thus the Palestine Arab Rebellion of 1936 followed the pattern of the Syrian Arab rising: the Palestinian's general strike succeeding the formation of the Arab Higher Committee from the ranks of the Arab leaders. This Committee was headed by the Mufti, who had by then promoted himself to the dignity of 'Grand Mufti', a designation which became widely accepted by his supporters. A snapshot of him in conversation with Heinrich Himmler identifies him as 'Seiner Eminenz dem Grossmufti'.

The career of this character makes astonishing reading. Before 1917 he was an officer in the Turkish army. Returning to Palestine before the end of the war, he reported to his cousin, Musa Kazem (who later became Mayor of Jerusalem, and was elected President of the Arab Executive in 1920, the year of the Jerusalem pogrom). The reader will recall Haj Amin's prudent withdrawal across the Jordan at that time to avoid serving the prison sentence imposed on him for his part in the organisation and direction of the disturbances. He was pardoned and allowed to return to Jerusalem, and then, in extraordinary fashion, 'appointed' to the position of Mufti of Jerusalem.

The normal procedure for this appointment involved a contest between candidates at an electoral college convened by the Moslem religious authorities. From these a shortlist of three would be submitted to the High Commissioner, who would then select one for the appointment. While it is not clear how it was that Haj Amin was originally entered for the contest, there is no mystery about his failure in the poll, where he received the lowest number of votes and was thus disqualified from inclusion in the shortlist of three.

The successful candidate chosen by the High Commissioner was one Sheikh Jurallah. The campaign to reject Jurallah is believed to have been launched by E.T. Richmond, chief Adviser to the High Commissioner on Moslem affairs. It is known that the High Commissioner did not send Haj Amin a letter of appointment, and in fact the appointment was never gazetted, but nevertheless Haj Amin became Mufti of Jerusalem. It was from that exalted position that he was freely able to organize the 1936 riots and build up two well-defined rebel armies operating from Galilee and Samaria. These comprised regular full-time troops augmented by 'territorials' who would on occasion return to their normal occupations, thus acting as a reserve. In addition to these two armies various armed bands operated around Hebron and in other parts of the country. All these groups were directed from the Mufti's two headquarters, Jerusalem and Damascus.

It was the action of one of these guerrilla groups on 27 September which roused the Administration from its hitherto perfunctory attitude towards the rebellion. The District Commissioner of Galilee, Mr. L.Y. Andrews, and his police escort were murdered at Nazareth. This time the rebels had gone too far. The Arab Higher Committee was declared to be illegal, and the Mufti was deprived of his position as President of the Supreme Moslem Council. Four members of the Higher Committee were arrested and deported, while the Mufti repeated his 1920 disappearing act and escaped capture (if, indeed, this had been intended) and travelled to his Damascus headquarters.

'There is no doubt,' wrote John Marlowe, 'that his escape was deliberately connived at by the Administration' (*Rebellion in Palestine*, Cresset Press, 1946, p. 186), while Nicholas Bethell, in *The Palestine Triangle* (Deutsch, 1979), wrote: 'The Mufti took sanctuary in the *haram esh-Sarif*, the most holy shrine in Jerusalem, where no British soldier or policeman would enter, then escaped overland and by boat to Lebanon, probably with British connivance' (p. 35).

'After the dismissal of the Mufti from his official posts, the Supreme Moslem Council and the Wakf funds were put under the direct control of the Administration. Investigation proved what had long been apparent, namely, that the Mufti had for sometime been diverting a substantial part of the funds at his disposal from their legitimate objects to the purpose of the rebellion. The maintenance of mosques and the general interests of the Moslem religion in Palestine had been grossly neglected. It was strange that the Administration did not see fit to give more publicity than it did to this aspect of the Mufti's activities. No organised attempt was made in this or in any other direction to try to discredit the Mufti and his actions among the people of Palestine.' (Marlowe, op. cit., p. 187)

The French permitted him to work from his headquarters in Damascus, from where he was able to direct the rebellion unhindered, the French insisting that 'the Mufti had shown no signs of an incorrect attitude'. Nevertheless, they were probably relieved when in October 1939 the Mufti (disguised, it is said, as a woman) left Damascus to reappear a few days later in Baghdad. (CAB, 24 282). From there, on 20 January 1941, he sent his secretary, Osman Haddad, to Berlin with a letter to Hitler, in which he repeated his sympathy with Nazi Germany and prophesied 'the well deserved defeat of the Anglo-Jewish coalition'. He proposed a German-Arab alliance to achieve Arab independence, end the Jewish National Home, and solve 'the Jewish question' on a joint basis. Few could now possibly question the form that proposed joint solution would have taken.

'I conclude,' he wrote, 'by wishing your Excellency a long and happy life and brilliant victory and prosperity for the great German people and for the Axis in the very near future. I beg your Excellency to believe in my sentiments of great friendship, of gratitude, and of admiration.' The letter was signed by him as 'Grand Mufti of Palestine'. (*Documents on German Foreign Policy 1918–45*, HMSO, Series D, Vol. XI, pp. 1151–55)

Prior to this communication the Foreign Ministry in Berlin had received a letter from the Chargé d'Affaires in Italy (dated 15 November 1940), reporting the visit to Rome of the Grand Mufti's Secretary, and also the arrival in Rome of Tewfik al-

Shakir, who asked for continued collaboration between Italy and the Arab countries, with 'particular emphasis on the request that the Nationalists in Palestine be supported with money, arms, and ammunition'. (ibid, pp. 586–7)

At the Mufti's house in Zahawi Street, Baghdad, Rashid Ali, who had formerly been Prime Minister of Iraq and the Minister of the Interior, met the four colonels ('The Golden Square') to plan the coup of April 1941 which restored Rashid Ali to the premiership. In the following month the conspirators were routed by a British force which, strangely, included an Irgun group under the command of David Raziel. Raziel lost his life when his car was bombed by German aircraft at Habbaniya, the British base.

Before the end of May Baghdad was in British hands, and the Mufti was on his way to Iran, making his third escape from capture. Trapped in the Japanese embassy in Teheran, where he had taken refuge, it now seemed certain that he could not now avoid falling into British hands. But while the British were discussing the pros and cons of having him in their custody, he travelled to Rome with members of the Italian community, in Italian disguise. There he was officially welcomed by Mussolini. On 6 November he arrived in Berlin: three weeks later he was received by Hitler.

16

The sequence of riot, followed first by Commission of Enquiry and then by White Paper, which had emerged during the period of the Palestine Mandate, was again repeated with the 1936 Arab Rebellion. A Royal Commission of Enquiry in 1936 to investigate the causes of unrest in Palestine was succeeded by the White Paper (Cmd. 5513) of July 1937, and the Woodhead Commission of 1938. In 1939 there came further White Paper (Cmd. 6019), which remained official British policy until the end of the Mandate.

The 1936 Commission held its first public session on 18 November. On 24 November its members questioned Andrews, the acting Director of Development for the Galilee District, on the Arab charge that Arab farmers had been displaced by Jews. He was already on the Arab blacklist for having given hospitality to the members of the Commission, to which he happened to be officially attached, and his reply to the effect that there was little evidence to support the Arab charges contributed to the sealing of his fate.

'Yelland Andrews, District Commissioner for Galilee, was high on the assassination list because he had organised the Peel Commission's programme and was thought to have influenced it in favour of partition. He realized his danger and took all the proper precautions. Then on 26 September he telephoned Foot with the good news that the rebel command in Damascus had removed his name from the list and that he was going to church in Nazareth to celebrate. He and his bodyguard Peter McEwan were not on the alert as they entered a narrow lane near the Anglican church. Arab gunmen shot them both dead.' Bethell, p. 34.

Condemnation of his murder was not universal. Thomas Hodgkin, a British academic, wrote to the New Statesman and Nation two weeks after his death, deploring the 'jingo resentment at the murder of a British official by members of a subject race . . . Terrorist movements under British Imperialism . . . can be understood only as the expression of strongly held political beliefs which are denied an adequate constitutional outlet . . . It is surely misleading to describe an action like the assassination of Mr. Andrews as a ''dastardly murder''.'

This view received some support from at least two members of the Foreign Office. Sir George Rendel, the head of its Eastern Department, wrote on 28 October: 'I think this letter has a great deal of good sense in it.' (Foreign Office Papers, 371/20819), while another member of his department, Terence Brenan, noted on the same day that there was 'unfortunately a lot of truth in this letter . . . The whole history of the last 20 years in Palestine have (sic) made it abundantly clear that by no other means than terrorism could the Arabs hope to get what they consider a square deal.' (ibid, 371/20818)

Both officials had previously made known their personal views on the subject of Jewish immigration into Palestine and its effect on Muslim relations. On 15 October they recorded their responses to a protest which had been signed by all the Muslim members of the Central Legislatures in India and presented to the Viceroy on 10 October. It protested that Britain had 'surrendered itself to the world Jewry intrigue and is involved in financial transactions with them', and continued: 'We beg his Excellency to inform the responsible Ministers in England of our feelings and sentiments, who should not lose us for the sake of foreign Jews, who at a crisis would not be able to give any help.' Brenan noted 'we cannot afford to ignore this warning', while Rendel wrote that it was 'a reaction which, I think, is likely to grow stronger and more dangerous the longer the policy is continued.'

On October 15 Ronald Campbell, of the Egyptian Department of the Foreign Office, warned of the hostility of the Egyptians to any future Jewish Palestinian State, and of the dangers of adopting a policy 'which would be hateful to the Arabs'. On the same day Rendel minuted (Foreign Office Papers, 371/20816)

'the culture of the leading Jews in Palestine, as I know by personal experience, is predominantly German. The Jewish immigrants of the better class are mostly of German origin or tradition, and have not only kept a culture of a strongly Germanic character, but have even retained a curious loyalty to Germany and to German ideals. A Jewish state is therefore likely to acquire a very Teutonic complexion, and it is by no means inconceivable that if there was some turn of the wheel in Europe, a no longer actively Jew-baiting Germany might find a ready-made spiritual colony awaiting her in a key position in the Middle East.'

On the day following Andrew's attendance Dr. Weizmann was called before the Commission to give evidence and submit to cross-examination. He appeared again on 26 November: this was not a public session and so was not reported in the published evidence, but Vera Weizmann's diary of that date notes: 'They were all kind and understanding, with the exception of Rumbold.'

Sir Horace Rumbold, a former British Ambassador in Berlin, Deputy Chairman of the Royal Commission, clashed frequently with Jewish witnesses during the course of the hearings. On 30 November he asked Moshe Shertok, the head of the Political Department of the Jewish Agency, whether Tel Aviv was being built up deliberately as 'a sort of artificial creation with a view to getting more and more immigrants in and creating a sort of snowball process.' The Commissioners appeared to regard the growth of Tel Aviv unfavourably, closely examining the Mayor, Israel Rokach, during the 5 January 1937 hearing on the plans for the growth of the city. To Lord Peel's comment that Tel Aviv's growth reminded him of a large American town, and Rokach's response that he indeed hope that it would grow as large as Los Angeles, Rumbold asked sarcastically: 'With the cinema business and all?'

With Shertok in the witness box for three days Rumbold was able in his interrogation to display all the skills of a prosecuting barrister, asking whether the Jewish Agency took into account 'the economic absorptive capacity' of Palestine when granting labour certificates to European Jews, and then countering immediately Shertok's affirmative reply with the riposte that the granting of certificates to German Jews since 1933 'really had nothing to do with the absorptive capacity of the country'.

When Eliahu Epstein gave evidence, on 3 December, of the illegal immigration into Palestine of Syrian Arabs from the Hauran, amounting, he maintained, to as many as 8,000 over the previous five years, and the employment by the Government of 10,000 illegal Arab immigrants, some from the Hauran, some from Transjordan, in the port of Haifa, Rumbold demanded: 'If you debar various people from Transjordan and Hauranis from coming in to work in the port, your contention is that the Government would be able to employ Jews, it would give more opportunity to Jewish labour? Is that your contention?' Winston Churchill rebuked him when he referred to the Arabs of Palestine as 'the indigenous population' subjected in 1918 'to the invasion of a foreign race' and pointed out that the Arabs came to Palestine after the Jews: he objected to them being described as 'a foreign race'. (Churchill evidence to the Peel Commission, 8 March 1937: Churchill papers, 2/317)

The evidence given before the Commission was not by any means the only element in the shaping of its conclusions and in influencing the terms of its report. The views of the Arab rulers and leaders were sympathetically received and recorded by members of the Eastern Department of the Foreign Office. On 4 January 1937, the British Ambassador in Baghdad, Sir Archibald Clark Kerr, reported to the Foreign Office that in the view of the Prime Minister of Iraq 'the solution of the problem of Arabs in Palestine' was more important 'than any other question of the day'. (F.O. 371/20804)

This Foreign Office file also recorded a minute by Lacy Baggallay of its Eastern Department, dated 13 February 1937, saying that in his opinion King Ibn Saud of Saudi Arabia 'would probably cease to exert any moderating influence' if a solution emerged which did not satisfy Arab opinion outside Palestine. When the British High Commissioner in Palestine, Sir Arthur Wauchope, suggested that Jews should be allowed to form armed units to protect their settlements against the frequent attacks of Arab bands, Baggallay minuted: 'I can conceive nothing more likely to convince Arab opinion that His Majesty's Government was definitely and finally committed on the side of the Jews . . .'

The same Foreign Office file records a note by Sir Robert Vansittart, the Permanent Under-Secretary of State, dated 18 February and stating: 'We shd set our faces most resolutely against the recruitment of Jews for use against Arabs. This wd be a vast mistake.' The slant of Foreign Office policy in the discussion of the proposed partition of Palestine into Jewish and Arab States emerges from a note by Baggallay on 22 April stating that the decision to proceed with partition is viewed inside the Foreign Office primarily 'from the point of view of our relations with the surrounding Arab countries'. (F.O., 371/20806)

The Peel Commission Report was presented to the Cabinet on 25 June and released for publication (Cmd. 5479) in July. It is described by Bethell: 'An elegantly written work of some 400 pages, the report remains one of the standard historical works on Mandatory Palestine.' (op. cit., p. 30). After examining the claims of both Jews and Arabs, it concludes that the only solution to 'the existing deadlock' is a further partition of Palestine. 'Partition seems to offer at least a chance of ultimate peace. We can see none in any other plan.'

'There is little moral value in maintaining the political unity of Palestine at the cost of perpetual hatred, strife and bloodshed, and there is little moral injury in drawing a political line through Palestine if peace and goodwill between the peoples on either side of it can thereby in the long run be attained.' (Palestine Royal Commission Report, p. 375)

17

If all parties had agreed to accept the Peel recommendation of Partition, Britain would have with that measure been released from many of the problems attending her rule over a state claimed as their homeland by two conflicting peoples while at the same time maintaining her presence in the Land under the new Mandate proposed by the Commissioners. She would then have presided over an enclave which would have included both Jerusalem and Bethlehem and, extending to Jaffa, would also have incorporated the towns of Ramle and Lydda. Britain would thus have maintained her foothold in Palestine.

The Palestine Royal Commission Report omits to make this point in its 'Plan of Partition' (covered in Chapter XXII of the Report), but instead explains the 'new Mandate' as a measure to execute 'a sacred trust of civilization'. Paragraph (10) of this chapter states:

> 'The Partition of Palestine is subject to the overriding necessity of keeping the sanctity of Jerusalem and Bethlehem inviolate and of ensuring free and safe access to them for all the world. That, in the fullest sense of the mandatory phrase, "is a sacred trust of civilization" – a trust on behalf not merely of the peoples of Palestine but of multitudes in other lands to whom those places, one or both, are Holy Places.'

The Arabs, however, greeted the proposal of partition with a renewal of violence. It failed to satisfy their demands for the termination of the Mandate and Arab sovereign rule over the whole country. The 1937 Arab Conference at Bludan, in Syria, presided over by the Prime Minister of Iraq, expressed its support for the Palestine Higher Committee in its rejection of partition and resolved that 'we must make Great Britain understand that it must choose between our friendship and the Jews. Britain must change her policy in Palestine or we shall be at liberty to side with other European Powers whose policies are inimical to Great Britain.'

There could be no question about the identity of the other European Powers with whom the Arabs threatened to side. In the previous year Mussolini had conquered Ethiopia and Hitler had marched into the Rhineland. The intervention of both Axis powers in the Spanish Civil War then being fought posed a challenge to both Britain and France. With the prospect of a European war between the democracies and the dictatorships becoming closer, the friendship of the Arab States could be of vital importance to Britain, with her problems of bases and communications as well as oil supplies. The message from Bludan was loud and clear: 'Do as we say, or count us among your enemies.'

There is reasonable ground for surprise at the Arab rejection of the Peel proposals, which would appear to have been designed to win the approval of the Arabs, who would have received under its terms nearly 90 per cent of the entire country west of the Jordan, while of the remaining area some 400 square miles would remain under British rule. The Jewish State, covering in its entirety a few hundred square miles, would be split near its southern end by the Jerusalem-Jaffa 'corridor', resulting in a 100-square-mile enclave below Jaffa. From Tel-Aviv northwards there would be a narrow strip 40 miles in length with an average width of little more than 10 miles. Indeed, to the west of Tulkarm (facing the centre of the strip) the width of the proposed Jewish State would have measured approximately seven miles. Arab forces successfully attacking the sector at this point would reach the sea in minutes, splitting the coastal strip into two 200-

square-mile sectors, while the enclave below Jaffa would be completely encircled.

The remaining area of the proposed Jewish State covered the greater part of Galilee; the frontiers of the State totalled some 300 miles. With knowledge of the unrelenting hostility of the Arabs, a cynic might suggest that it was designed for easy annihilation. Ironically this prospect was graphically illustrated in a Beirut cartoon which appeared on 31 May 1967, depicting a repulsive stereotype, bearded, with an enormous hooked nose and displaying a Star of David, his ill-favoured features convulsed with fright as he topples backwards over the cliffs at the edge of the sea, retreating from a ring of huge guns pointing at him from north, east, and south-west; the Arabic inscriptions on their barrels no doubt indicating their countries of origin.

The Arabs could well have regarded this tiny, vulnerable state as an acceptable compromise but, instead, they rejected it outright. Their witnesses at the Royal Commission session on 12 January 1937, the Mufti and Awni Bey, expressed their views with brutal clarity. The Mufti demanded the annulment of the Balfour Declaration and the creation of an Arab State over the whole area of Palestine. When Rumbold asked him whether such a state could 'assimilate and digest' the 400,000 Jews already there, the Mufti replied briefly and without equivocation – an emphatic 'No!' Awni Bey informed the Commissioners that: 'Every Arab in Palestine will do everything possible in his power to crush down Zionism, because Zionism and Arabism can never be united together . . . What we say is that we want a National Palestine Government – we object to the existence of 400,000 Jews in this country.'

The Zionist leaders (though not all of their followers) were prepared to consider the partition of the country for the creation of independent Arab and Jewish States, but found it impossible to accept the Peel prescription for a mini-state which had no prospect of survival. They could hardly have been unaware of the pattern of partition which, commencing in 1921, eroded the declaration included in the terms of the Mandate, which provided that the Mandatory should be responsible for administering the Mandate 'in favour of a national home for the Jewish people'. Article 2 of the Mandate specified: 'The Mandatory shall be responsible for placing the country under such political, administrative an economic conditions as will secure the establishment of the Jewish national home, as laid down in the preamble' The Mandate, however, did not attempt to specify precise dimensions for the site of a Jewish National Home, so that there was possibly no legal constraint on a programme of erosion of the original area available for the resettlement of Jews in Palestine, and for 'reconstituting their national home in that country' (to quote the Preamble to the Mandate).

The first division of the area of the Mandate took place in 1921, when out of the total of 44,000 square miles covered by the Mandate 34,000 square miles were handed over to Arab rule. While the exclusion of Jews from this appropriated area was not specified in the Royal Commission Report, it had this to say:

> 'We understand that the Government of Trans-Jordan would emphatically refuse to encourage Jewish immigration in the teeth of popular resistance; and it must be remembered that not only is Trans-Jordan free from those Articles of the Mandate which apply to the establishment of the National Home, but its Government is recognized as an independent Government, and the High Commissioner, though he is entitled to advise the Government of Trans-Jordan, would scarcely regard the question of Jewish immigration as one on which he could press his advice.' (p. 309)

The interpretation of this must be left to the reader. Although this partition was confirmed after the issue of the Mandate, it was not the first time that the British had handed over portions of the

Land to other parties. Shortly after the Armistice, Lord Curzon had presented a Foreign Office memorandum to the Eastern Committee of the War Cabinet, emphasising that Britain would never tolerate the presence of another power in Palestine.

'The old phrase, Dan to Beersheba, still prevails. Whatever the administrative subdivisions, we must recover for Palestine, be it Hebrew or Arab, or both , the boundaries up to the Litani on the coast, and across to Banias, the old Dan.'

After this meeting the British Cabinet decided to retain control of the Mosul-Kirkuk oil fields in Upper Mesopotamia, at that time under British military occupation. But under the Sykes-Picot Agreement of 1916 the Mosul area had been included in the French protectorate, and she was not willing to surrender it to the British without due compensation. To the resourceful British this was not an insurmountable problem. They drew some new lines on the maps: Upper Galilee from Ras en-Naqura up to the Litani was thus 'transferred' to the French and added to the Lebanon as a contribution to the 'Greater Lebanon' which the French were in the process of creating, and the Golani was presented in like fashion to Syria. The frontiers shown on the maps were swiftly altered, and Britain got Mosul. Palestine lost Upper Galilee and the Golan Heights: the Zionist leaders described the new O.E.T.A. frontiers as 'depriving Palestine in the north of its head, in the east of its right arm, and in the south of its legs.' (*Palestine*, 8.2.1919)

In the Six-Day War of June 1967 Golan was restored to its former place in the Land. South Lebanon (Upper Galilee) remained in Arab occupation. From October 1968 onwards guerrilla groups entered south-eastern Lebanon, and then proceeded to expand across the country, reaching the large refugee camps along the coastline, and establishing the 'state within a state' which ultimately created a political crisis in Lebanon, plunging the country into civil war and posing a constant threat to Israel.

18

'It seems clear that the Peel partition proposals were adopted because the British Government thought (and probably had good reason for thinking) that these proposals would be acceptable to moderate Arab opinion outside Palestine: it seems clear that they were abandoned as and when it became apparent that the principle of partition was not so acceptable.' (Marlowe, op. cit., p. 147)

George Rendel of the Foreign Office had no illusions about the attitude to the partition proposals of the Arab world, with which he was closely and constantly in touch. In a Foreign Office memorandum dated 27 October 1937, and entitled 'Palestine. Immediate Problem', he pointed out that:

> 'We have many enemies in Europe, and there are clear signs that the Arabs are already turning to them for help against us. Our Palestine policy will thus not only earn us the hostility of all the Arabs, both inside and outside Palestine, but is calculated to bring about an increasingly close association between those Arabs and our European rivals, the consequences of which may be far-reaching and extremely serious to ourselves.' (F.O.371/20818)

He went on to explain that: 'The trouble in Palestine is political and not criminal, though naturally our political opponents are using criminal measures, since no others are at present open to them', and in a note dated 5 November he argued that many of the Arabs who had been described as 'thugs' were, in fact, 'sincere Arab patriots'.

He had attended a meeting on 29 October to discuss the Palestine question with representatives of the War Office, the Colonial Office and the Air Ministry. Rendel represented the Foreign Office. In his report he wrote: 'I suggested that the hostility of the Palestinian Arabs to the transfer of territory which they regarded as their own to Jewish immigrants from Central Europe, whom they regarded as aliens, was a deep-seated and natural sentiment which was likely to grow stronger as our policy developed.' (Foreign Office papers, 371/20818)

It was clear that Rendel was now devoting a good part of his time to campaigning on behalf of the Arabs. On 11 November he wrote in a 13-page memorandum that the Arabs of Palestine must be assured 'that they will no longer be in danger of becoming a minority in their own country, or of finding practically its only fertile portions taken from them and handed over in full sovereignty to alien immigrants.' The Jews should never be allowed to reach 'more than 40 per cent of the total population of the country'. He received full support for these views from the Foreign Office Assistant Adviser for League of Nations Affairs, Roger Makins, who wrote in a memorandum dated 12 November: 'I would view with dismay the possibility that Egypt, Iraq, Turkey and Persia would work against us at Geneva . . . The alienation of the Moslem countries might be total.' (Foreign Office papers, 371/20810)

The Foreign Secretary, Anthony Eden, recorded his approval of the Makins memorandum, writing: 'This is important. I have great confidence in Mr. Makins' judgement, and little doubt that he is right.' Eden added that Makins' argument 'should find its place in our memorandum for the Cabinet.' (ibid) That memorandum, signed by Eden, declared that Palestine was 'an Arab country, the best area of which is being handed over to an alien and particularly dangerous invader ... It has been suggested to me that there is only one way in which we can now make our peace with the Arabs, and avoid the dangers I have indicated above, that is, by giving the Arabs some assurance that the Jews will neither become a majority in Palestine, nor be given any territory in full sovereignty.' (ibid)

Eden personally advised the British Ambassador in Washington of this new policy on 26 November, writing that the alternative they were now seeking to the Peel Commission recommendations must be one 'which would not give Jews any territory exclusively for their own use'. (Foreign Office papers, 371/20821) By the end of the year Weizmann, the Zionist leader, had become fully aware of the direction of the new policy now being adopted by the British, writing to Sir John Shuckburgh, the head of the Middle East Department, that the British were yielding to pressure from Moslem and Arab states to ensure, in Palestine, a single Arab State and 'the reduction of the Jews to permanent minority status.'

'Jews are not going to Palestine', he went on, 'to become in their ancient home "Arabs of the Mosaic Faith", or to exchange their German or Polish ghetti for an Arab one. Whoever knows what Arab government looks like, what "minority status" signified nowadays, and what a Jewish ghetto in an Arab State means — there are quite a number of precendents — will be able to form his own conclusions as to what would be in store for us if we accepted the position allotted to us in these "solutions" ... Could there be a more appalling fraud of the hopes of a martyred people than to reduce it to ghetto status in the land where it was promised national freedom?' (Churchill papers, 2/315)

In *Trial and Error* Weizmann describes those measures, taken towards the end of 1937, as 'the first steps towards the nullification of the Balfour Declaration; actual nullification came with the White Paper of 1939. It was the classic technique of the step by step sell-out of small nations which the great democracies practised in the appeasement period.' The Peel Report he describes as

'an extraordinary document. On the one hand it testified to the achievements of the Jews in Palestine, on the other hand it recommended measures which seemed to us to be in complete contradiction with that testimony. The report put an end to the persistent falsehood that Jewish land purchases and land development had led to the displacement of the Arabs; then it recommended severe restrictions on Jewish purchases of land. It asserted that Jewish immigration had brought benefits to the Arab people; then it recommended the severe curtailment of Jewish immigration. And it did this last in a form which was all the more shocking because it practically conceded the point made by the Arab terrorists, and undermined the very foundations of the Mandate.'

Against this background it is difficult to understand the motives of the British Government in appointing, in January 1938, a Palestine Partition Commission 'to recommend boundaries for the proposed Arab and Jewish areas and the British enclaves that would (a) afford a reasonable prospect of the eventual establishment of self-supporting Arab and Jewish States: (b) necessitate the inclusion of the fewest possible Arabs and Arab enterprises in the Jewish area and vice versa; and (c) enable the British Government to carry out its "Mandatory responsibilities".'

This commission, headed by a senior Indian civil servant, Sir John Woodhead, left for Palestine in April, stayed for four months, and published its report (Cmd. 5854) in October. While it recommended three alternative plans of partition, it reported that 'we have been unable to recommend boundaries which will afford a reasonable prospect of the eventual establishment of self-supporting Arab and Jewish States'. This conclusion fitted admirably the policy which the Government had been pursuing for almost a year, giving credence to Weizmann's sour comment that the instructions which had been given to the Commission 'were such as to foredoom any sort of plan . . . Plans would be offered for the planned purpose of being rejected.' (op. cit., p. 486) The Jews could only reject the offer of the 500-square-mile mini-state which the Woodhead 'Plan C' had to offer: the Arabs would not concede even this tiny plot, which surely must have been inspired by Low's famous cartoon (see p. 33), and the British were able to agree that partition was not practicable.

The members of the Commission had not been unanimous in arriving at their conclusions. While some had stressed Arab fears that the Jews had acquired the most fertile land, Sir Alison Russell, a former Chief Justice in Tanganyika, commented:

'It has been alleged that the Jews have acquired the best land in Palestine. It does not appear to me a fair statement. That much of the land now in possession of Jews has become the best land is a truer statement . . . It was impossible not to be impressed when inspecting some of the bare rocky places where Jewish settlements have been or are in the course of being made. Such remarkable efforts may well disturb statistics.'

The new Colonial Secretary, Malcolm MacDonald, demonstrated his awareness of the new doctrine when on 24 October he told his colleagues on the Cabinet Committee that if Britain were to insist upon the partition of Palestine into an Arab and a Jewish State 'we should forfeit the friendship of the Arab world'. It was at this meeting that the Cabinet's Palestine Committee decided to make a public announcement to the effect that 'the setting up of independent Arab and Jewish States is impracticable'. (Cabinet papers, 27/651) There can be little doubt that this decision may have been influenced by the note from the Egyptian Prime Minister to Neville Chamberlain some five days earlier, urging him to adopt a solution in Palestine that would 'win for your country the goodwill and deep gratitude of Arabs and Moslems throughout the world.'' (ibid)

On 4 July Malcolm MacDonald pointed out to Weizmann that 'the final adoption of the policy of partition would be followed at once by a considerable rebellion in Palestine which would receive material and moral support from the Arabs and Moslems elsewhere'. Moreover, Britain would 'lose much of the friendship of the authorities and peoples of a number of surrounding countries like Egypt, Saudi Arabia, Iraq and Syria ... serious trouble for us in Palestine would be an additional inducement to our enemies in Europe to start some active aggression, the outcome of which would be war.' (Cabinet papers, 24/278) The question again arises: if the Government had so firmly decided that the adoption of partition was dangerously inimical to British interests, why the farce of appointing the Woodhead Commission to draw up plans for partition and 'to recommend boundaries for the proposed Arab and Jewish areas and the British enclaves'?

There was support for this rapidly burgeoning Government policy in some organs of the British press. The *Sunday Express* told its readers on 19 June: 'There is a big influx of foreign Jews into Britain. They are over-running the country. They are trying to enter the medical profession in great numbers ... Worst of all, many of them are holding themselves out to the public as psycho-analysts', thus compounding the awesome threat to the British way of life by an overwhelming deluge of invaders who are not only Jews but also, if the dreadful word may be used, psychoana-lysts! The psychoanalyst, the newspaper proceeded to explain, 'often obtains an ascendancy over the patient of which he makes base use if he is a bad man'.

A month later the Home Secretary, Sir Samual Hoare, warned his colleagues at a meeting of the Cabinet Committee on Refugees that 'there was a good deal of feeling growing up in this country – a feeling which was reflected in Parliament – against the admission of Jews to British territory'. The Committee had been discussing the possibility of Jewish refugees finding a haven in some of the British colonies. (Cabinet papers, 23/94) This was only five days after the close of the Evian Conference, where, as we have seen, the delegates one by one refused to relax the immigration regulations of their countries to accommodate the desperate victims of the Nazis.

With virtually every door closed to them – with the world, as Weizmann had described it – divided into places where they could not live, and places which they could not enter – more and more of these hapless refugees, fleeing from Poland and Germany and central Europe, were desperately seeking routes to Palestine. Some travelled down the Danube to the Black Sea ports of Constanza (Romania) or Varna in Bulgaria, then through the Aegean to the Mediterranean. The British responded immediately, pressing the Governments of all the countries on this route to close all land and sea escape routes to the refugees. The Greeks were the first to respond, and the British Minister in Athens telegraphed the Foreign Office in London to say that the Greek Government 'have now instructed their Missions abroad, including Vienna and Warsaw, not to issue transit visas through Greece to Jews whatever the destination stated'. (Foreign Office papers, 371/21888)

19

'There was a man of genius who might well have become also a man of destiny.' (Winston Churchill on the death of Major-General Orde Wingate)

The desperate need for the organisation of local defence groups to counter Arab attacks on isolated farms and settlements gave rise to the Haganah. By 1936 this organisation embraced most of the able-bodied men and youths in the settlements as well as large numbers from the towns and cities. During the 1936–39 Arab rebellion the British Security Forces, although not affording the Haganah official recognition, nevertheless co-operated with it and supervised the training of thousands of its members. From its ranks the Jewish Settlement Police (JSP) were sworn in as Supernumerary Police, receiving arms and uniforms from the Administration and training by British Army and Police officers. As the Arab revolt increased in intensity, members of Haganah were incorporated into British Army units fighting the rebels, and the JSP was formed into a militia of twelve battalions.

In the summer of 1938 special Night Squads were established under the command of Orde Wingate, who had been given the rank of Captain when he was posted to Palestine in 1936 to take part in the British attempts to contain the Arab terror campaign, and later promoted to Major. Major-General R.J. Collins, in his biography of Field-Marshal Lord Wavell, refers to:

> 'Wavell's selection of one of his Intelligence officers, a certain Major Wingate, to raise and command an irregular corps, which later became known as the ''S.N.S.'' (Special

Night Squads). This body of men – half-British and half-Jew – operated almost entirely by night. Lightly equipped and with little or no transport, they soon became the bugbear of the Arab gangs who, hunted by the regular columns by day, were then harried by the S.N.S., who took up the pursuit by night. These squads, which used tracking dogs, highly trained and capable of following a cold scent, were dreaded by the Arabs. It was for successful operations with his S.N.S., who established a reign of terror, killed many Arabs and prevented the sabotage of the oil pipe-line from Iraq, that Wingate received his first D.S.O., and was registered in Wavell's retentive brain for further use if occasion arose.' (*Lord Wavell*, Hodder and Stoughton, 1947, p. 173)

On 12 January 1937, just four months after his arrival in Palestine, he wrote to his cousin Sir Reginald Wingate, a Governor-General of the Sudan, to report his impressions of conditions in Palestine. This letter is too lengthy to repeat here in full, but some of his observations may be worth recording.

'The military strength, past, present and future, of the whole Arab group is quite negligible, as I need not tell you. The potential military strength of the Jews, especially if we adopt my recommendations, is equivalent to at least two British Army Corps when trained and organised. The administration of Palestine and Transjordan is, to a man, anti-Jew and pro-Arab. This is largely due to the fact that we seem to send only the worst type of British official to Palestine. They hate the Jew and like the Arabs who, although he shoots at them, toadies to them and takes care to flatter their sense of importance. The history of the last six months is a sad one indeed. The troubles started in such a way that we could have stopped them with half the force we had. Owing purely to the vacillation of H.E. and the pro-rebel sympathies of the entire civil service, what might have proved a mere riot developed into armed rebellion. The

121

Jews, who never broke the law and remained loyal throughout, had to witness their work destroyed, their families threatened, their blood spilt, and the blame for all laid on their shoulders. The Jews are loyal to the Empire. You have no idea of what they have already done here. You would be amazed to see the desert blossom like a rose; intensive horticulture everywhere – such energy, faith, ability and inventiveness as the world has not seen. We have only to train it . . . We are in for a war sooner or later – for pity's sake let us do something just and honourable before it comes. Let us redeem our promises to Jewry, and shame the devil of Nazism, Fascism and our own prejudices.' (*Orde Wingate*, 1959, p. 179)

Holding these views, and uninhibited in expressing them, it was inevitable that he would ultimately clash with higher authority. At army headquarters there had been long-standing objections to the arming or military training of Jews, on the grounds that this would encourage them to engage in armed conflict with the Arabs. The Jews, it was argued, were under the protection of the regular forces, and so did not need to bear arms for the defence of their lives or their property.

The crunch came after a massacre of Jews at Tiberias, on 2 October 1938. Christopher Sykes has described what happened.

'Under well-preserved secrecy, and following a careful plan, a large gang of rebels had infiltrated to selected points in the town . . . Nineteen Jews, of whom ten were small children, were murdered. Many of them were killed by being burned alive after having been stabbed. The massacre might have been on a larger scale if the assassinating party had not given themselves up early to looting and carousal. What made the incident doubly disgraceful to British rule was the fact that on the very night of the attack a British battalion had arrived at Tiberias and taken up quarters in a Turkish fort serving as barracks. They had so little notion of conditions of guerrilla warfare as to settle therein without establishing a picket line, and as a result of their carelessness they were effectively surrounded by a few brigands with automatic weapons. Police and men of the Transjordan Frontier Force from Samakh on the south shore came to the rescue too late. The battalion had been kept within the walls till the massacre was over and the gangsters out of the town.' (*Orde Wingate*, 1959, p. 179)

At the time that the British regulars were penned up in their barracks Wingate, with less than twenty men, happened to be at Kafr Meshka, a few miles to the west of Tiberias. He was unable to reach the town in time to prevent the massacre, but led his men to its western exit and there laid an ambush for the murderers. Some were drunk with looted wine; all were intoxicated with their triumph over an entire British battalion. Fifty of them paid with their lives for their night's work. If Wingate had not been in the area they would have got away scot-free. General Sir Edmund Ironside, Governor of Gibraltar and Commander-in-Chief Designate of the Middle Eastern Theatre, drove from Haifa, where he had stayed the previous night, to Tiberias on the day following the massacre. 'When he reached Tiberias he was confronted with the spectacle of the charred corpses being carried away from the wrecks of buildings, and he heard with indignation the dismal tale of how the British battalion had failed in its task. He dismissed the commanding officer on the spot.' (Sykes, p. 180)

On that same day Wingate led the Special Night Squads into action for the last time. After taking an overdue leave, which he spent in London, he returned to Jerusalem on 12 December to find that his S.N.S. headquarters at Ein Harod had been closed down and the camp dispersed. Sykes wrote of this measure:

'The decision to remove him from the little force he had

raised meant what it appeared to mean. The authorities were "apprehensive of the lines on which the S.N.S. organisation was developing", by which they meant that Wingate was chiefly concerned with the political object of associating Jews to the greatest possible extent with offensive operations against the rebels, although he was well aware that this was contrary to policy.' (Sykes, p. 194)

The final step towards the abolition of Wingate's Special Night Squads was taken on 23 January. On that day a Divisional Conference of Intelligence Officers proposed a recommendation to Force Headquarters that: 'The conference is generally opposed to the dressing up of Jews as British soldiers; in particular it is considered undesirable to have a proportion of Jews in S.N.S. detachments: these should be entirely British . . . In short, if it is desired to conciliate the Arab, we should not provoke him by using Jews in offensive action against him.'

Wingate protested that . . . 'men of whatever race or creed who fought bravely under British officers against rebels should not be described by any officer holding His Majesty's Commission as "dressing up as British soldiers".' Although General Montgomery, after seeing this memorandum, sent a message to Wingate saying that he disapproved of the language used by the Conference, and would make amends to the Jews by recommending certain squadsmen for decorations, the policy of 'dejudification' was continued. Inexperienced young men were put in charge of squads and were said to have discriminated against Jews, selecting them for menial tasks. Wingate was condemned to the routine of Staff duty.

There he lingered and languished until 10 May, when he was informed that he was to return to England to serve as Brigade Major in an Anti-Aircraft Brigade. General Haining, G.O.C. Palestine, had finally succeeded in his efforts to transfer him. His military service record followed him to England. It read: 'Orde

Charles Wingate, D.S.O. is a good soldier, but, so far as Palestine is concerned, he is a security risk. He cannot be trusted. He puts the interest of the Jews before those of his own country. He should not be allowed in Palestine again.'

20

Wingate was punished in 1938 for his Zionist sympathies as was Meinertzhagen in 1920 – both were removed from the Palestinian arena. When Wingate left England on 19 September 1940, to join Wavell in Cairo, where the latter had been appointed Commander-in-Chief of the British Forces in the Middle East, he carried with him a letter signed by a high officer in the Army which read 'You are going on a mission to the Middle East. Under no circumstances, while you are in this area, will you visit Palestine. In case you should do so as a civilian, you will note that your passport has been endorsed: ''The bearer of this passport should not be allowed to enter Palestine''.'

It should not be thought that every critic of British policy in Palestine received the same stern treatment. E.T. Richmond, after retiring from the Palestine Secretariat, where he had been in charge of Arab affairs, had, in the *Nineteenth Century* of July 1925, attacked the Mandate as an 'iniquitous document', but nevertheless returned to Palestine as Director of Antiquities, in 1938. In the February 1938 issue of the same journal he launched another attack, dealing with 'the aggression which for twenty years we have been committing against the Arab people.' He seemed to be confident that these views would not earn him any condemnation from his employers.

It would appear that they were now vigorously engaged in measures of atonement for the 'aggression'. On March 10 the new High Commissioner in Palestine, Sir Harold MacMichael, was informed by the Colonial Office that no more than 2,000 immigrants of independent means, i.e. with a personal capital of £1,000, should be allowed to enter Palestine in the six months from April to September 1938. This instruction was perfectly timed. Five days after it had been issued Hitler marched into Vienna, sealing the fate of a further 180,000 Jews (in addition to some 40,000 people of Jewish decent, including many baptised Christians).

By 31 May their condition had become desperate. On that day the British Consul-General in Vienna informed the British Ambassador in Berlin that: 'the distress and despair amongst the Jews are appalling. This consulate-general is literally besieged every day by hundreds of Jews who have been told to leave the country and who come vainly searching for a visa to go anywhere.' (Foreign Office papers, 371/21635)

But where? Palestine, as we have just noted, was virtually closed against them. Almost every other country declined to help them. On 17 April Czech villagers heard cries of distress coming from a breakwater in the Danube. There they found 51 Austrian Jews, including an 82-year-old Rabbi and many women and children, who had been dumped there by stormtroopers and left without food or adequate clothing. Although the villagers were willing to offer them shelter, the Czech authorities refused to allow them to stay, and on the night of April 18 they were driven back across the Hungarian frontier. The Hungarians likewise refused to have them, and on the following night they were driven back into Austria.

The communication from Consul-General Garner to Sir Neville Henderson, quoted above, was by no means the only advice on the plight of the refugees to be received in Whitehall. On August 30 the British Minister in Egypt, Charles Bateman, wrote to Malcolm MacDonald, warning him that 'the balloon in Europe may go up this autumn' and it was necessary to guard against Arab hostility, which might close the Mediterranean and Red Sea to Britain. The only way out, he wrote, was by 'placating the Arabs . . . The Jews? Let us be practical. They are anybody's game these days. There were six million of them homeless in Europe. In no way would Palestine ever be able to take them all. There would have to be a halt to immigration sometime. So why not now? They had waited two thousand years for their home and they would just have to wait a little longer before getting "their last pound of flesh". And as for Parliament, the government would have to bring the pro-Jew element into line by pleading what is practicable as opposed to what is desirable.'

'Please don't think from all this that I am pro-Arab or anti-Jew,' he proceeded. 'I think them each as loathsome as the other.' He wanted Britain to invite the Mufti to London and to promise him a complete stoppage of Jewish immigration in return for him calling off the revolt. While the Foreign Office were in agreement with him on the question of immigration, some of its members hoped that they would be able to deal with Arab moderates rather than with the Mufti. Lacy Baggallay noted that, with this exception, 'Tell Mr. Bateman that we sympathize with all that he says.'

In the meantime the authorities in Palestine were sending out their own signals to all concerned. For nearly three years they had had to endure incessant terrorism, and they were now determined to show that they were no longer willing to tolerate it. So, on 5 June two young Jews were sentenced to death for firing at an Arab bus on the Acre-Safad high road. A third young Jew, tried for the same offence, was found to be insane and ordered to be detained. The bus had not been hit, and nobody had been injured. The three youths were all of good character and absolute novices in the use of firearms. John Marlowe commented:

'The attempted crime was bungled in a pathetic fashion. The motive for this amateurish attempt was clear. For the last several weeks the Jewish community of Safad had been continually subjected to Arab attacks. Many Jews had been killed, including a young girl who had been stabbed in a ditch while fleeing from a car which had been fired upon by Arab bandits. The effect of such incidents on youths of impressionable age and living in the midst of them may be imagined. It may be asserted absolutely definitely that if the youths had been Arabs they would, in similar circumstances (if they had been sentenced to death at all), have been reprieved. There had been a similar case before a Military Court not long previously, when some Gaza fishermen had been sentenced to death and subsequently reprieved in view of their clean record and the fact that no death or injury had resulted from their action. Hardened ruffians convicted of murder during the 1936 disturbances had been reprieved. But the Administration was out for Jewish blood. It wanted to hang a Jew in order to give the Arabs a demonstration of its impartiality. Major-General Haining, the G.O.C. (who had just taken over from General Wavell), acting on the urgently expressed wishes of the Administration, which made great play of the effect a reprieve would have on Arab opinion, confirmed the sentences. Subsequently, on its being proved that one of the prisoners was under eighteen, his sentence was commuted. The remaining youth of the three, Shlomo Ben Yussuf, was to die. Great efforts were made by Jews all over the world to obtain a reprieve. Representations were also made by the Polish Government, whose subject Ben Yussuf was. Although the G.O.C. had confirmed the sentence, the final word remained with the High Commissioner, in whom was vested His Majesty's Prerogative of Pardon. But the Palestine Administration, whose past weaknesses had brought about the conditions which provided the provocation for the crime, decided to make this the occasion for a show of firmness. Ben Yussuf was executed on the morning of 29 June ... As a demonstration of firmness it was ludicrous: all it demonstrated was the Administration's extraordinary and discreditable desire to curry favour with the Arabs. The effect of the execution was to increase the Arab's contempt, the Jew's dislike, and many other people's disgust for the Administration. Members of the Administration were immoderately pleased about it, and seemed to think that they had scored a notable triumph.' (*Rebellion in Palestine*, pp. 198–99)

The Arabs responded to this incident in characteristic fashion. Two or three weeks after the death sentence was passed (but six days before it was carried out), they kidnapped three youths from the Emek settlements: their dead bodies were found some weeks later. In Jerusalem the Haram esh Sherif became a rebel fortress. By 17 October the rebels were in almost complete control of the Old City, and on the following day it was announced that the Military Authorities had taken over control of the Jerusalem District from the Civil Power. Their troops succeeded in penetrating the walls of the Old City, forcing the rebels to retreat into the Haram esh Sherif, from which at night they escaped into open country after climbing over the walls. The troops were able to search most of the city for arms but, in deference to Moslem susceptibilities, refrained from violating the sanctity of the Haram itself. ('Haram esh Sherif' means 'Noble Sanctuary'.)

Meanwhile, in London the Cabinet continued to deliberate on the possibility of reaching an agreement with the Arabs. MacDonald believed that once the Arabs could be satisfied that there would be no Jewish majority in Palestine they might then agree to Jewish immigration 'on a reasonable scale'. (CAB. 24 279) There was now general agreement in the Cabinet that partition was no longer possible, and on 2 November MacDonald told his colleagues that: 'There was much to be said for allowing the Mufti to represent the Palestine Arabs – he was the only man who could deliver the goods.' (CAB. 23 96) On 9 November the Report of the Woodhead Commission was published. It was accompanied by a Statement of Policy from the British Government. The Government announced that it had decided to reject the policy of partition.

21

'British policy in Palestine between 1919 and 1939
represented an attempt on the part of successive British
Governments to impose the policy of the Balfour
Declaration on a reluctant Arab majority. The 1939
White Paper was an expression of the British
Government's intention to terminate this policy and to
substitute for it a policy of imposing the will of the Arab
majority on a reluctant Jewish minority.' (John Marlowe,
Rebellion in Palestine)

The news that the British Government had decided against a policy of partition received an immediate welcome from the Arabs. Six days after the Government's announcement Fakhri Bey Nashashibi wrote to the High Commissioner expressing the 'unlimited satisfaction' of the Arabs with the Government's decision, and the hope that at the forthcoming Conference the further Arab demands would be conceded. The Government's response came without delay. On 23 November the Colonial Secretary informed the House of Commons that the Arab leaders of the rebellion who had been deported to the Seychelles would now be granted facilities to attend the Conference; and a few days later announced that they would in fact be unconditionally released to enable them to represent the Arab case at the Conference. They left the Seychelles on 19 December 1938.

The Conference opened on 7 February 1939. On 9 February the Arabs demanded recognition of the Arab right to independence in Palestine; the abandoning of the Jewish National Home; the abrogation of the Mandate and its replacement by a Treaty of Alliance with an independent Arab Palestine; and immediate prohibition of land sales to Jews together with immediate cessation of immigration. The Government response amounted to a prompt acceptance of these demands. It proposed to the Jewish delegates a termination of the Mandate and their attendance at a Round Table Conference, to be held in the autumn, which would lay down the constitution of an independent Arab State in Palestine under the protection of Great Britain, in which the Jews would be a minority safeguarded by British guarantees.

The concept of a Jewish minority in an Arab State with its safety dependent on British 'guarantees' could only be rejected by the Jewish delegates, with their recollection of the fate of the Assyrian Christians whose safety was similarly guaranteed by the British when they were left to the mercy of the Arabs of Iraq, by whom they were rounded up and promptly massacred. However acceptable the Government's proposals may have been to the Arab delegates, it became abundantly clear that the Jews were not willing to acquiesce in any arrangement which exposed the Palestinian Jews to annihilation, and many left the Conference before its termination.

The Government attempted to reach a compromise with the Arab demands by making a number of recommendations. The economic absorptive basis of immigration would be abandoned. 75,000 Jews were to be admitted to Palestine over a five-year period, after which there would be no further immigration without the consent of the Arabs. Land sales to Jews would be restricted as follows: 63.4 per cent of the land of Palestine would be barred to Jewish purchase, and a further 31.6 per cent would be subject to restrictions of Jewish purchase, leaving about 5 per cent in which Jewish purchase would be permitted.

This final revelation of the Government's new policy on Palestine filled Jews everywhere with despair. On March 16 Rabbi Stephen

Wise, after praising Britain's past record in the defence of democracy, spoke emotionally about the prospect of Britain abandoning a solemn pledge in order to appease Hitler, Mussolini and the Mufti:

> 'Do you know what a permanent minority status means? It means that for 1900 years we have prayed and dreamed, and for 60 years we have worked and toiled and our best have put their most into the upbuilding of Eretz Israel, and after all that, and the promise of the Mandate and the Balfour Declaration, Palestine would become nothing more than another Jewish ghetto.'

A week later, speaking in a debate in the House of Commons, MacDonald attempted to defend the White Paper by reminding the House: 'We have some interests of our own in Palestine. We have, for instance, certain vital strategic requirements.' Leopold Amery's response was to announce that he would vote against the Government's call for approval of the White Paper:

> 'I could never hold my head up again to either Jew or Arab if I voted tomorrow for what, in good faith, I repeatedly told both Jews and Arabs was inconceivable, namely, that any British Government would ever go back upon the pledge given, not only to Jews, but to the whole civilized world when it assumed the Mandate.'

The new Palestine White Paper was published by the Government on 17 May and debated in the House of Commons on 22 May. Amery spoke out against it as he had promised he would.

> 'The White Paper is a direct invitation to the Arabs to make trouble. As for the Jews, they are now told that all the hopes that they have been encouraged to hold for 20 years are to be dashed to the ground, all their amazing

effort wasted – in so far as it was an effort to create a National Home – all the pledges and promises that have been given to them, broken. That is to be their reward for loyalty, for patience, for almost unbelievable self-restraint – these people will be content to be relegated to the position of a statutory minority, to be denied all hope of giving refuge and relief to their tortured kinsfolk in other countries, that they will wait passively until, in due course, they and the land they created are to be handed over to the Mufti?'

On the following day Winston Churchill made his contribution to the continued debate. During the course of his speech Churchill touched upon the vexed question of immigration into Palestine. He pointed to the large Arab immigration into Palestine which had been taking place since the beginning of the Mandate. The Arab immigrants had been attracted by its new-found prosperity; they had made their way into the Land from many countries, some very distant.

'So far from being persecuted, the Arabs have crowded into the country and multiplied till their population has increased more than even all Jewry could lift up the Jewish population. Now we are asked to decree that all this is to stop and all this to come to an end. We are now asked to submit, and this is what rankles most with me, to an agitation which is fed with foreign money and ceaselessly inflamed by Nazi and by Fascist propaganda. ... Now, there is the breach; there is the violation of the pledge; there is the abandonment of the Balfour Declaration; there is the end of the vision, of the hope, of the dream.'

At the close of the debate the final vote was 268 to 179 in favour of the Government. In the United States President Roosevelt commented: 'Frankly, I do not see how the British Government reads into the original Mandate or into the White Paper of 1922 any policy that would limit immigration.' The Permanent Mandates Commission of the League of Nations unanimously declared that: 'the policy set out in the White Paper was not in accordance with the interpretation which, in agreement with the mandatory Power and the Council, the Commission had placed upon the Palestine Mandate.' The matter would have to be referred to the Council of the League, which would consider the Commission's report at a meeting on 8 September.

In the meantime the British continued without restraint to implement the policies adumbrated in the White Paper, particularly those referring to the restrictions placed on Jewish immigration. On 26 May the Foreign and Colonial Office representatives attended an Inter-Departmental Conference on the subject of 'illegal' immigration into Palestine. The official minutes reveal that the discussion centred on the question of how to prevent further Jewish refugees from Central and South-eastern European countries from embarking on ships en route for Palestine, and that agreement was reached that strong pressure should be brought at once upon the Governments of Greece, Hungary, Poland, Rumania and Yugoslavia, to take effective measures to put a stop to the traffic.

One conclusion arrived at was that the Rumanian Government 'should be asked to take them back' and then set them *en route* to the eastern European towns from which they had fled. To encourage Rumanian agreement to this suggestion, the British Government would be prepared 'to supply free of charge, food, water and any necessary medical supplies at the Roumanian port of embarkation in each case sufficient for a short period, say 15 days, while the negotiations were proceeding with the Roumanian Government.' (Foreign Office papers, 371/24090) On the following day Sir Ronald Campbell, the British Ambassador in Belgrade, requested the Yugoslav Government 'to co-operate with His Majesty's Government in putting a stop to attempts to land at ports in Palestine Jewish refugees embarked in ships flying the Greek or some other flag at ports in various European countries, including Yugoslav ports in the Adriatic.' (Foreign Office papers, 371/24091)

22

The meeting of the Council of the League of Nations, planned for 8 September 1939, did not take place. On 1 September the Germans had invaded Poland, initiating the most devastating and destructive war in our history.

The first hostile shots fired by British forces in that war were aimed, on 2 September, at an unarmed illegal immigrant ship, the *Tiger Hill*, as it landed 1,400 Jewish refugees on Tel-Aviv beach. Fleeing from the threat of death in their European homeland, two of these unfortunates met with it immediately on their arrival at the Promised Land. Although Britain was at war with Germany (the British ultimatum delivered to the Germans at 9 a.m. on 3 September expired at 11 a.m. on the same day), her efforts directed towards the bottling-up in Europe of the Germans' most vulnerable victims continued undiminished.

On the first day of the war, while Warsaw was being heavily bombed by the German invaders, the Foreign Secretary, Lord Halifax, was telegraphing the British Ambassador in Ankara to put pressure on Turkey 'to do what they can to delay ships carrying illegal immigrants' (Foreign Office papers, 371/24094). One week later, on 8 September, the Foreign Office received a request from the American Ambassador in Berlin, who had been put in charge of all British interests there, asking whether 'German nationals of the Jewish race who hold immigration permits issued by British authorities in Germany will be allowed to enter Britain'. The British reply, dated 18 September, stated: 'On the outbreak of war all visas previously authorized or granted became void, and it is left to the individual to make an entirely fresh application which will be dealt with in accordance with the war time regulations which do not contemplate the grant of visas to refugees of this nature'. (Foreign Office papers, 371/24100) In short – 'No!'

On this same day Dr. Weizmann pleaded with Malcolm Mac-Donald for permission to allow 20,000 Polish Jewish children to enter Palestine. This number would have fallen within the total of the special quota envisaged in the White Paper published before the outbreak of the war. The economic burden of supporting them would be accepted by the Jewish people. 'We pledge ourselves to provide for them' continued Weizmann. 'It therefore depends on your decision alone whether the lives of Jewish children shall be saved or not.'

This appeal was discussed in the Colonial Office on the same day. The minutes recorded:

'Mr. MacDonald said that his own view had at first been that we should make some effort to meet this request, on humanitarian and other grounds. On reflection, however, he had felt that it must be turned down. Technically it might be possible for us to admit 20,000 Polish children to Palestine straight away without going back on our pledge to the Arabs not to exceed the immigration figures laid down in the White Paper and our decision to hold up the current immigration quota owing to illegal immigration.

'The position about the 25,000 refugees is that it has always been intended that they should be introduced gradually over the five-year period, and in fact the first quota period made provision for a certain number of these refugees, although it subsequently had to be cancelled for the reason already mentioned. In any case, it has always been contemplated that these refugees should include persecuted Jews of all countries, and not only Poland.

'It might be possible to get round the technical difficulty of our promise with regard to illegal immigration by keeping the children in Cyprus or some such British territory until the new quota period began, and then introducing them into Palestine. But he thought that, even though this might not actually be breaking our promise, it would certainly be so regarded by the Arabs.

'Furthermore, there were technical difficulties about getting the children there and making arrangements for the reception of so large a body at once, whatever Dr. Weizmann might say about accepting responsibility for their maintenance. The position in all the Middle Eastern countries was delicate, and he thought that to accept Dr. Weizmann's proposal might have serious consequences.

'There was, furthermore, the consideration that H.M.G. were at war and everything must be subordinated to the winning of the war. However brutal it might sound, to remove 20,000 children from Poland at this moment would *pro tanto* simplify the German economic problem.

'As against this must be set the possibility of hostile comment in America and other countries should this chance of relieving distress in Poland be missed. But here against the stress weighed equally on Christians and Jews alike, and the Christians were far the more numerous. On the whole, therefore, he felt that, without saying anything about Arab sentiments, he should reply to Dr. Weizmann that the acceptance of his request might prejudice the successful prosecution of the war, and, for that reason, must be turned down.' (Foreign Office papers, 371/23251)

Grief at the probable fate of the 20,000 Jewish children must surely be mollified by the thought that their sacrifice may ultimately have contributed to 'the successful prosecution of the war', while at the same time avoiding offence to 'Arab sentiments'. There was a further bonus in this Colonial Office ruling: they would not have to go back on their 'decision to hold up the current immigration quota owing to illegal immigration'. Let the blame fall on those immigrants who illegally salvaged their own lives without regard to the retribution the innocents would have to suffer. Dr. Weizmann had overlooked these when he pleaded with MacDonald: 'It therefore depends on your decision alone whether the lives of Jewish children shall be saved or not.'

It was a terrible responsibility to place on any man. He was, perhaps, fortunate, that the decision could be shared with Lacy Baggallay, who took the official minutes, and those others at the meeting. In due course, when 'the successful prosecution of the war' had been achieved, the victors would be greeted by the monuments to that decision in the form of the mountains of children's footwear outside the crematoria across Nazi Europe.

Devotion to 'the successful prosecution of the war' did not detract from the intensity of the attempts to halt the flow of 'illegal' refugees: it would seem that at that time the Royal Navy was largely engaged in the business of intercepting immigrant ships, while the Colonial Office continued to apply pressure on foreign Governments with a view to preventing 'the little death-ships', as they came to be called, from leaving European ports. On 15 September the Colonial Office official responsible for Jewish immigration, J.S. Bennett, was able to report:

'Rumania has prohibited the departure of Jews to any destination. Turkey has been asked to obstruct (on sanitary and safety grounds) the passage of ships carrying Jewish immigrants through the Bosphorous. Greece has introduced legislation with heavy penalties for any of their nationals engaging in the trade. Panama has promised to put a stop to the irregular use of her flag. All other countries concerned have been strongly pressured to co-operate and have undertaken to do so. We can only wait and see.'

When the Italian Ministry of Foreign Affairs offered to facilitate the passage of German Jewish refugees seeking to reach Palestine through Italian ports, the Foreign Office, on 25 September, rejected the suggestion on the grounds that the Cabinet Committee on Refugees had decided to suspend the emigration of German nationals in war-time. (Foreign Office papers, 371/24078) The 'illegal' immigration was discussed at the Foreign Office on 29 December. A minute from this meeting by G.M. Warr read: 'The only hope is that all the German Jews will be stuck at the mouths of the Danube for lack of ships to take them . . .' (F.O. 371/24097)

In Palestine itself the British displayed a determination to crack down on the illegal possession of arms. An opportunity to pursue this came on 5 October, when the future Israeli General Moshe Dayan, who had been a member of Orde Wingate's Special Night Squads, in company with 42 other Haganah men, armed and in uniform, marching in military formation, were seen by a British patrol. They were immediately arrested and taken to a police station.

They were brought to trial on 27 October. Their defence was that they were a group of young men training to prepare for the fight against Nazi Germany: they had no doubt that they might be called upon to assist British troops when the time came, and wanted to be ready for that task. If one can accept the account in *Trial and Error* of the atmosphere in Palestine, and the Middle East generally, at the time of Rommel's swift advances towards Tobruk and Egypt in the critical months of 1942, their preparations might then seem to have been both praiseworthy and justified. Weizmann was in America at that time, working on a synthetic rubber programme for the American Government, when a correspondent from Cairo and Palestine flew in to see him, with 'a shattering story. The Egyptians were preparing to receive the ''conquerors'' in great style. Mussolini was ready to fly over at a moment's notice, and a beautiful white charger was to carry him into Cairo, where, like Napoleon, he would address his armies at the foot of the Pyramids. I saw in my mind's eye the mountebank posturing in imitation of his great hero, and the picture was a little revolting.

'Equally serious, if without the touch of the grotesque, was the news the correspondent brought from Palestine. There, he said, the Arabs were already preparing for the division of the spoils. Some of them were going about the streets of Tel Aviv and the colonies, marking up the houses they expected to take over: one Arab, it was reported, had been killed in a quarrel over the loot assigned to him. The correspondent further reported that General Wavell had called in some of the Jewish leaders and told them confidentially how deeply sorry he was that the British Army could not do any more for the *Yishuv*: the troops were to be withdrawn towards India, the Jews would have to be left behind, and would be delivered up to the fury of the Germans, the Arabs and the Italians. The correspondent had also heard that the Jewish leaders had held a meeting and made decisions of despair: they were to be divided into two age groups: the members of the older group would commit suicide: the younger ones would take to the hills to fight their last battle there and sell their lives as dearly as possible: thus the National Home would be liquidated.'

'What could be the fate of the Jews of Palestine if Rommel broke through,' Weizmann goes on to ask, 'after what was happening to the Jewish communities of conquered Europe?' He went to see the American Chief of Staff, General Marshall, explaining:

'what faced us if the needed munitions did not reach the

British in time . . . The story of how the supplies were rushed across the Atlantic and Africa, of how they arrived in the nick of time, of how the tide was turned at the last moment, has been told many times. But perhaps no one remembers those agonizing days more vividly than the Jews of Palestine, for whom that near-miraculous rescue of the Homeland from complete annihilation still has in it a Biblical echo . . .'

But in October 1939 the British were not yet fighting Rommel: it was the period of 'the phoney war', and they were fighting the Jews. Sir Harold MacMichael, the High Commissioner for Palestine, his Army commander Lieutenant-General Michael Barker and Malcolm MacDonald together agreed that the Haganah could not be regarded as Britain's ally. Its aims, they thought, were to establish a Jewish army and to secure 'eventual Jewish military supremacy in Palestine'. (CAB 67 4) It could be used against the British. The Haganah had to be suppressed with 'the firmest possible measures'. They were sentenced on 30 October to long terms of imprisonment. Weizmann complained to Halifax that 'Men who have done distinguished service with the British forces in Palestine are now lying in prison on rags, half-starved, and treated as criminals.' General Barker had no illusions about the offenders. 'This was a most serious thing. Their aim was clear. They were preparing for rebellion against Great Britain . . . In Great Britain the build up of a private army would be considered high treason.' (Z4/14847)

In February 1941, Lord Moyne was appointed Colonial Secretary, and before the end of the month Dayan and his 42 Haganah colleagues were released from Acre fortress. The British were now prepared to use the services of these ex-convicts. In the June 1941 invasion of Syria, Dayan lost an eye while acting as a guide to the Allied forces. Yigal Allon, later to become famous as a Major-General in Israel's army, crossed the Lebanese border with a small Jewish force, captured a bridge over the Litani river, and brought four Vichy French prisoners back to Palestine. Twenty-three young Jewish volunteers lost their lives when their boat, the *Sea Lion*, with Major Anthony Palmer in charge, was lost after they set out to destroy the oil refineries at Tripoli, on the Lebanese coast. Later it was disclosed that these and other participants in the war were being secretly trained through M14, a branch of military intelligence, and SOE, the Special Operations Executive. The SOE received considerable help from the Haganah's intelligence centre in Haifa.

But at the end of 1939 the British relationship with the Jews was of a different order. Sir Reginald Hoare, the British Minister in Bucharest, complained on 27 December that: 'In spite of repeated representations, illicit traffic in Jews continues.' It appears that on the Danube there were at that time the steamship *Sakaria*, with 700 refugees on board: the *Ahms*, with 3,000, and another party of 1,000 iced up at Klavada. The *Sakaria* had no lighting or heating: there were cases of pneumonia among the passengers. The *Rudnichar* had left Varna the previous day, carrying 400 passengers, inciting an angry telegram to Sir George Rendel in Sofia from Halifax: 'HMG and Government of Palestine are making every effort to check this traffic. . . . Strongest efforts have in fact been made over the past six months to persuade Romanian government to prevent entry and transit of Jews in this manner . . .' (CO 733 429)

In January 1940, the British Government issued and distributed a memorandum on Jewish illegal immigration to Palestine. Its theme appeared to be that the motives for illegal immigration were

'largely political . . . Illegal immigration is not primarily a refugee movement . . . The problem is . . . an organized invasion of Palestine for political motives, which exploits the facts of the refugee problem and unscrupulously uses the humanitarian appeal of the latter to justify itself The

Gestapo are known to assist the Jews in organising and despatching these parties. It is clearly to the interests of the German Government to promote this traffic, since it serves the double purpose of ridding them of Jews and causing embarrassment to His Majesty's Government.'

This memorandum (PRO FO 371/25238/274) was dated 17 January 1940. It was followed on 5 February by another, which suggested 'the possibility of there being agents of the German Government amongst them and the consequent danger to the internal security of Palestine'. (J.E.M. Carvell, PRO FO 371.25239/150) A further slant on the sinister motives behind immigration was offered by Sir John Shuckburgh, the Deputy Under-Secretary of the Colonial Office, on 27 April 1940 in a minute which declared:

'I am convinced that in their hearts they hate us; they hate all Gentiles. . . . So little do they care for Great Britain as compared with Zionism that they cannot even keep their hands off illegal immigration, which they must realise is a very serious embarrassment to us when we are fighting for our very existence.'

23

Within a few weeks of the German invasion, the boundaries of Poland were sealed against the Jews trying to escape from the murderous excesses of the soldiers and the police. Hundreds of thousands fled eastward to the Soviet-occupied areas: many were refused entry by the Russians, who sent them back to the German zone. Frantic and helpless in this grim game of battle-dore and shuttlecock, they turned desperately in every possible direction: northwards to Lithuania, south to Hungary and Rumania in their efforts to escape the tightening noose. The measure of their success was revealed in an intelligence report (MI PRO FO 371/42840), which stated that by the end of 1943 90 per cent of the 3,300,000 Jews of Poland had been killed.

By the end of 1939 between 14,000 and 15,000 Polish Jews had managed to cross the borders into Lithuania. On 15 June 1940, Soviet troops entered the country, and on 3 August Lithuania became the 16th Soviet Republic. It was invaded by the Germans in the following June, and within a few weeks was subjected to the 'provisional regulations' which preceded the application of the 'final solution'. All Jewish property was confiscated and an allowance limited to 20 pfennig (about 5 cents) per day per person was permitted to the Jews.

Their ultimate fate is no secret. The meticulous German attention to detail has left a grim legacy in the shape of the 195 reports submitted by the *Einsatzgruppen* to Berlin from the end of June 1941 to 24 April 1942. Report No. 88, 19 September 1941, contains the following: '. . . a detachment of *Einsatzkommando* 3, assisted by a Lithuanian *Kommando*, has carried out actions in the following towns: Raseintai, Rokiskis, Zarasai, Birzai, and Prienat.

147

These executions bring the total number to date of persons liqui-dated by *Einsatzkommando* 3 (with the assistance of Lithuanian partisans), to 46,692.'

Einsatzgruppe A was commanded by *SS-Brigadefuehrer* Stahlecker, whose detailed report on the activities of his unit makes grim reading. It discloses how 'local anti-Semitic forces were organized . . . to carry out pogroms against the Jews'. One 'auxiliary unit of 300 men was formed under the command of Klimaitis, a Lithua-nian journalist . . . the group very meticulously fulfilled its tasks, especially in the preparation and carrying out of large-scale liqui-dations.' An Appendix to this report gives the number of Jews killed by Stahlecker's units up to the end of October 1941 in Kaunas, Siauliai, Vilna and their vicinities as 80,311. By the end of December 1941 the report indicates that 136,421 Jews had been murdered in Lithuania (excluding Vilna). After the libera-tion of Lithuania by the Soviet army in the summer of 1944, most of the Lithuanians who had taken part in the murders fled to Germany, where, after the war, they were classified as Displaced Persons and were aided as Nazi victims.

Hungary, too, proved to be no more than a temporary halt on the road to annihilation. Under the rule of its Regent, Admiral Horthy, its Jews were deported in their thousands to Auschwitz. Raoul Wallenberg, a special Swedish diplomatic emissary, was able by his efforts to save some 5,000: most of the others perished. When Rumania became a satellite of Nazi Germany in 1940, the Jews of that country were immediately subjected to a reign of terror at the hands of the Iron Guard. On 21 January 1941, this organisation carried out a pogrom in Bucharest. Aided by local hooligans, they slaughtered and looted without restraint. Some wealthy Bucharest Jews were arrested by the Iron Guard, murdered and their bodies hung on meat hooks in the municipal slaughterhouse, bearing the legend 'kosher meat'.

Flight from this incredible martyrdom seemed to commentators like John Shuckburgh to be an irresponsibly selfish 'illegal immigration which they must realise is a very serious embarrassment to us when we are fighting for our very existence.' It is of course possible that those that had survived or escaped from these determined attempts of total annihilation may have been selfishly more conscious of the imminent threat to their own continued existence than they were of Britain's battle for its national existence, but nevertheless they blindly sought every avenue of escape. The countries represented at the Evian Conference had made it quite clear that they were not prepared to open their doors to Jewish refugees: Palestine remained as their only hope. But their determination to reach that haven was surpassed by Britain's resolve to prevent them from achieving that aim.

H.F. Downie was the Colonial Office official principally concerned with Palestine. Criticised for commenting in March 1941 that some aspect of Zionism 'makes one regret that the Jews are not on the other side in this war' (PRO CO 733/445), he found some support in a minute of 27 April written by a Foreign Office official, R.T.E. Latham, stating:

'One has, in matter emanating from the Middle Eastern Department of the Colonial Office, to take into account Mr. Downie's inward and spiritual conviction that illegal immigration is only the outward and visible sign of a world-wide scheme to overthrow the British Empire. It is only if one realises that he regards the Jews as no less our enemies than the Germans that certain features of this draft become explicable . . . If one has a personal conviction that the Jews are our enemies just as the Germans are, but in a more insidious way, it becomes essential to find reasons for believing that our two sets of enemies are linked together by secret and evil bonds, and it becomes our duty to say that they are so linked, irrespective of the evidence we can produce . . .'
(PRO FO 371/27132)

In May the British Ambassador in Belgrade had requested the Yugoslav Government to co-operate with Britain in her efforts to stop 'illegal' immigration. A group of more than 1,000 Jews, using the Danube as a route of escape from the Nazis, found themselves blocked by ice on the river and forced to remain at the river port of Kladovo in Yugoslavia. In desperate straits, without food or money, they had appealed for aid to the American Jewish Joint Distribution Committee. Downie, at the Colonial Office, called for measures to prevent such assistance reaching the party on the grounds that 'such assistance of this kind amounts to not only conniving at, but also actively helping, the passage of illegal immigrants towards Palestine.' (PRO FO 371/25238/322) The Kladovo group never reached the Promised Land: they were interned by the Yugoslav authorities in a camp near Belgrade. They were all murdered after the German occupation of Yugoslavia in April 1941.

No power on earth could persuade these unfortunate people to wait passively in their countries of origin for the murder squads to dispose of them. In their thousands they sailed down the Danube to the ports where they hoped to find vessels of any kind to take them on to Palestine. On 3 September 1940, over 3,000 refugees hailing from Prague, Vienna and Danzig set off in four steamers which conveyed them down the Danube to the Rumanian port of Tulcea. There they boarded three Greek cargo boats, renamed the *Atlantic*, *Pacific*, and *Milos*, in which, under the Panamanian flag, they continued the voyage to Palestine.

Conditions on these boats were appalling. A group of survivors have left a description of the ordeal of the *Atlantic*:

'The *Lebensraum* was restricted to a space of 45 cm. per person. In this way children, babies, women, old people, cripples, were pressed together ... the boat was supplied with a little fuel and food which may be stretched to last us a fortnight with utmost thrift. The crew were apparently "pirates". In front of the lavatories, the number of which was by no means sufficient, there were long queues of people waiting. These conditions became almost unbearable when due to the bad food and the spoiled water, the majority of the passengers suffered from diarrhoea ... When the wind blew up people got sea-sick. So we sailed and lived almost for three months.' (Deposition by Drs. Erwin Bloch and R. Hirsch)

By the time the *Atlantic* reached Crete on October 16 there was no fuel, water or food left, and typhoid had broken out. The Greek captain and crew attempted to desert in the only usable lifeboat, but the harbour police, supplying the ship with some inferior-quality coal, ordered them to move on. After a few miles, the captain with some members of the crew abandoned the ship after throwing most of the coal overboard. The remaining crew members, together with the passengers, took over the ship and continued through the Dodecanese, but after three days the boat was again without fuel. By demolishing the superstructure the passengers contrived to provide wood to keep the boat moving, and finally they reached Cyprus. On 12 November the *Atlantic* was towed into Limassol by tugs. Six days later the Governor of Cyprus reported to the Foreign Office that an inspection of the vessel had revealed:

'Gross overcrowding; standing room on deck only; below, lack of ventilating light; no ablution or laundry facilities at all; no proper cooking facilities for such numbers. Director of Medical Services considers that every day's delay in taking passengers off increases risk already high of epidemic death toll which would probably be very high as passengers are suffering from exposure and hardship and are emaciated.' (PRO FO 371/25242/117)

Despite the 'risk of epidemic death toll', the Governor refused to allow the passengers to land in Cyprus 'as political reaction to their landing here will be most undesirable', and the *Atlantic* arrived in Haifa under British escort on 24 November, to join the *Milos* and the *Pacific* which had been intercepted off the coast of Palestine by patrol vessels and were being held while preparations were made to transfer their passengers to a liner, the *Patria*, pending their transport to Mauritius. On 15 October the Colonial Office had telegraphed the Governor of Mauritius, inquiring: 'Could you as a matter of urgency provide accommodation for a considerable number of Jews who are endeavouring to enter Palestine illegally? They would have to be kept under restraint and this involves the construction of a camp surrounded by barbed wire and the provision of guards.' (ibid)

The Government explained its action in an official communiqué:

'There can be no doubt that these persons must be classed as illegal immigrants, that is to say persons seeking to enter Palestine against what is well known to be the law of the country. H.M.G. are not lacking in sympathy for refugees from territories under German control. But they are responsible for the administration of Palestine and are bound to see to it that the laws of the country are not openly flouted. Moreover they can only regard the revival of illegal Jewish immigration at this present juncture as likely to affect the local situation most adversely and prove a serious menace to British interests in the Middle East. They have accordingly decided that the passengers of the S.S. *Pacific* and S.S. *Milo* shall not be permitted to land in Palestine but shall be deported to a British colony . . . and shall be detained there for the duration of the war. Their ultimate disposal will be a matter for consideration at the end of the war but it is not proposed that they shall remain in the Colony to which they are sent or that they should go to Palestine. Similar action will be taken in the case of any further parties who may succeed in reaching Palestine with a view to illegal entry.' (PRO FO, ibid)

The Government's firm intention to proceed with these measures brought protests from within Palestine and from the U.S.A., and on 20 November a general strike was observed by the Jews in Palestine. In London Winston Churchill attempted to counter the deportation order (PRO PREM 4/51/1/87), but the Colonial Secretary (Lord Lloyd) replied that since the order had already been announced it should be carried out, arguing that the illegal immigrants 'generally include a proportion of militant young Jews who are likely to cause trouble . . . revocation would be interpreted only in one sense, viz., as a surrender to Jewish agitation. If such an impression were created, not only would more and more shiploads be encouraged to descend upon us, but the political effect in the Middle East would be altogether deplorable.' (ibid)

As the remaining passengers from the *Atlantic* were being transferred to the *Patria* on the morning of 25 November the ship was blown up by explosives in its hull, and 267 of the refugees were drowned. When the *Zionist Review* of 29 November denounced the deportation policy as an 'act of inhumanity', Shuckburgh retorted: 'The Jews have no sense of humour and no sense of proportion.' (PRO CO 733/430/76021)

The survivors from the *Patria* and the remaining passengers on the *Atlantic* were transferred to internment camps on the mainland. To the suggestion that they should be permitted to remain in Palestine, Lloyd responded that 'if this were allowed, he feared that it was only too likely to encourage further acts of sabotage by other illegal immigrants, in order to obtain a similar concession', but after discussion the Cabinet decided that the survivors of this disaster should be allowed to remain in Palestine 'as a special act of clemency, having regard to the sufferings which these immigrants had undergone in the S.S. *Patria*.'

When General Wavell, the British Commander-in-Chief in the Middle East, learned of this decision he dispatched a 'most

153

immediate' cable to Anthony Eden, the Secretary of State for War:

> 'Have just heard of decision re *Patria* immigrants. Most sincerely trust you will use all possible influence to have decision reversed. From military point of view it is disastrous. It will be spread all over Arab world that Jews have again successfully challenged decision of British Government and that policy of White Paper is being reversed. This will gravely increase prospect of widespread disorders in Palestine, necessitating increased military commitments, will greatly enhance influence of Mufti, will arouse mistrust of us in Syria and increase anti-British propaganda and fifth column activities in Egypt. It will again be spread abroad that only violence pays in dealing with British ... Please exert all your influence. This is serious.' (PRO PREM 4/51/2/116)

This plea was dealt with by Churchill in a personal telegram in which he set out the Cabinet's views and at the same time expressed his personal opinion that 'it would be an act of inhumanity unworthy of the British name to force them to re-embark.' Nevertheless, the British would proceed with the deportment of the 1,580 passengers who had been left on the *Atlantic* after the explosion in the *Patria*, and on 10 December the High Commissioner was able to report to the Colonial Office that this 'carefully planned joint operation (was) successfully carried out by the naval, military, and police personnel concerned', although 'Certain initial resistance was dealt with by uniformed policemen calling the military forces held in reserve'. (PRO FO, ibid)

'The military forces held in reserve' were deployed on 9 December encircling the camp where the refugees were being held with military vehicles and troops, while within the camp policemen made, in the words of the Inspector-General of Police,

154

'a show of strength'. An account of the manner in which the 'initial resistance was dealt with' tells that:

> 'The refugees had decided to resist by refusing to pack their few belongings and by refusing to dress: both males and females lay down naked on their beds . . . Policemen, armed with sticks, belaboured some of the men with blows, and carried them naked on blankets to the waiting lorries. They brought out over a hundred of the first batch, all of them wounded, completely naked. Many of the old men fell on the ground and kissed it. They pleaded with tears before the police officer that they had already passed through Dachau and Buchenwald.'

24

*'As the escape routes were sealed so too was the fate of the
majority of the Jews imprisoned in Nazi Europe.'
(Bernard Wasserstein:* Britain and the Jews of Europe
1939–1945, *Clarendon Press, Oxford, p. 80)*

While the *Atlantic* survivors were awaiting deportation in the
camp at Athlit, another immigrant ship set out for Palestine from
the Bulgarian Black Sea port of Varna. The *Salvador*, flying the
Panamanian flag, carried between 350 and 380 passengers. The
British attempts to prevent her departure had failed, but the
Foreign Office instructed the British ambassadors in Athens and
Ankara to impede, by every means, the passage of the ship
through the Straits into the Aegean. On 12 December the
Salvador was wrecked in the Sea of Marmara, and over 200 of the
passengers were drowned.

The head of the Foreign Office protested to the Bulgarian
Minister in London at his country's 'connivance in the ship's
departure' (PRO FO 371/25242), and the head of its Refugee
Section, T.M. Snow, wrote on 17 December: 'There could have
been no more opportune disaster from the point of view of
stopping the traffic'. (PRO FO 371/25241) On the following day
the British Ambassador in Ankara received the following message
from the Foreign Office: 'In interests of Middle East stability
please press Turkish Government to do everything possible to
prevent survivors from attempting to reach Palestine by overland
or other route.' The ambassador's replied two days later: 'I am
informed by Turkish Government that survivors are in pitiable
state at Istanbul. Turkish government are going to inform

156

Bulgaria.' In the margin of this note (CO 733 430) is scribbled the single word: 'good!'

As the German grip on Europe tightened the flow of illegal immigrants from the area virtually dried up, and the Foreign Office was able to concentrate on the dangers nearer home. An anti-alien campaign began to emerge in some organs of the press, and the question arose of the necessity for distinguishing between 'friendly enemy aliens' and those with Nazi or Fascist sympathies. It was disclosed that in some of the internment camps set up by January 1940 there had been fighting between Jews and Nazi sympathisers. A Mass Observation survey at the end of April reported pronounced anti-alien sentiment among 'the middle and upper classes': on 23 April the Conservative M.P. for Salisbury asked in the House of Commons: 'Would it not be far better to intern all the lot and then pick out the good ones?'

A memorandum on the 'Fifth Column Menace' written by the British Minister at the Hague was circulated in Whitehall. The British Consul-General in Zurich reported that he had been warned by a German contact 'that we must not trust too much the German Jewish refugees in England'. (PRO FO 371/24388) The British Embassy in Madrid informed the Foreign Office: 'It was evident that the new weapon was the fifth column and that the basis of the fifth column everywhere except in the Iberian peninsula was Jewish refugees from Germany and Austria ... England would not be safe until the whole 80,000 had been placed in concentration camps.' That memorandum (PRO FO 371/25189) was dated 6 February 1940: by the end of May the Government had interned all category 'B' enemy aliens.

Women were included. *The Times* reported: 'At one of the London receiving centres, there were young nuns, babies only a few weeks old, and boys and girls ... Several of the older women were in tears. All carried gas masks.' Galician Jews long resident in Britain were interned on the ground that Galicia had formed part of the Austrian Empire before 1918. In Tyneside a man who had lived in Britain since the age of three was interned. The great majority of the detainees were Jewish refugees. In January the Jewish Secretary of State for War had been made to resign. Sir Alexander Cadogan, the Permanent Under-Secretary at the Foreign Office, noted in his diary on Monday 1 January: 'H. told me Hore-Belisha must be got our of W.O. and will be offered Ministry of Information. This blinding – and exquisitely funny. I hadn't time to get my breath, but on thinking it over, came to the conclusion that Jew control of our propaganda would be major disaster.'

On Wednesday, 3 January, his diary entry again refers to this matter. 'H.J.W. (Sir Horace Wilson?) came about Hore-Belisha's appointment. Told him what I knew and that I understood it was settled so hadn't criticised it to H (Lord Halifax?). But if question was still open, and since he asked my opinion, I thought it catastrophic.' On the next day: 'Told H.P.M. had much better make one bite of the cherry and get rid of H-B altogether. He will get the worst of both worlds if he merely shifts him. H. said he saw this, and would put it to P.M. . . . H. tells me that P.M. has sacked H(ore)-B(elisha) from W.O. but offered him B(oard) of T(rade). This just misses the point. P.M. had an awful interview and had much better just gone the little bit further and said he had no post to offer him . . . One can only spend the night in prayer imploring the Almighty the H-B may refuse B(oard) of T(rade). But H-B will take no account of Jehovah in this.' (*The Diaries of Sir Alexander Cadogan 1938–1945*, Cassell, 1971, pp. 241–42)

Later in the year the Government decided to enforce large-scale deportations of aliens, and some 8,000 were sent overseas, mainly to Canada and Australia. A War Office communication to the Foreign Office, dated 31 July 1941, revealed that the 2,400 aliens who were transported to Australia on the troopship *Dunera* had been maltreated and robbed by soldiers on board. The commanding officer and two N.C.O.s were court-martialled for these offences and severely disciplined: compensation was paid by the British Government to the victims. (PRO FO 916/90/19) In the same month a Home Office report by H.M. Commissioner of Prisons revealed that when 1,714 aliens arrived in Quebec aboard the *Ettrick* a great part of their baggage was stolen when they were searched by British and Canadian soldiers. He found that the internees, most of whom were Jewish refugees, had been subjected to anti-Semitic insults and petty persecutions by their guards. (Home Office papers 45/23515 [GEN 200/117/163])

On 30 June 1940, the Blue Star Liner *Andorra Star* sailed for Canada with 1,190 deportees: it was torpedoed off the coast of Ireland by a German submarine at 6 a.m. on 2 July and 599 of the passengers were drowned. Some of the passengers were refugees. On 8 July the Secretary of the Parliamentary Committee on Refugees, H.W. Butcher, M.P., received a letter from a woman refugee, Mrs. Theresa Steur. She wrote:

'Out of the chaos of Nazi Austria, my husband and I saved only each other. Country, home, family, friends, career, books, income, everything was lost, but my husband and I clung to each other resolutely, through grave dangers, and finally reached this country and refuge ... We refugee wives were proud and satisfied when our men volunteered for admission into the army. These applications were rejected ... On 25 June, my husband, an Austrian of Polish birth and parentage, was arrested. I have heard nothing of him since, have still, after two long weeks, no idea where he is. All I definitely know is that German and Austrian internees of category ''C'' were drowned in the Atlantic.'

Butcher forwarded this letter to the Foreign Office: it is filed under (PRO) FO 371/25248/331.

The *Andorra Star* incident marked the end of the policy of the deportation of internees from Britain. It was not, however, the last of the tragedies at sea leading to the death of these helpless victims fleeing from the certainty of death at the hands of the Nazis and their collaborators. On 12 December 1941, the S.S. *Struma*, a 240-ton converted yacht, left Constanza under the command of a Bulgarian captain, carrying 769 Jewish refugees. In the previous month the American Minister in Bucharest had written to the State Department in Washington that in view of the reign of terror then prevailing in Rumania, the only solution facing the Rumanian Jews seemed to be 'a refuge abroad to which these unfortunate people would be able to emigrate, probably with no worldly possessions whatsoever.' (FRUS 1941 vol. II, pp. 871–74)

The authorities in Jerusalem had learned about the voyage even before the ship set sail, and on 9 October the High Commissioner had been in touch with the Foreign Office, who in turn, two days later, brought pressure on the Turkish Government to bar passage through the Straits to the *Struma*. The Turks pleaded that they were prevented by the terms of the Montreaux Convention from taking such action. The *Struma*'s engine broke down when the ship had reached Istanbul after three days sailing: and the Turkish authorities would not allow the passengers to go ashore while repairs were being effected. A British naval intelligence report to the Admiralty described the conditions on board as 'appalling'. This was confirmed by a Jewish Agency communication to the Chief Secretary of Government, Palestine, dated 13 February 1942, which stated that there was only one lavatory and one small kitchen on the ship, and no fresh water for drinking or washing. Air in the hold was foul, but there was no room on deck for all the passengers. There was no sick bay, despite the numerous cases of dysentery and of mental illness.

Such were the conditions which the unfortunate refugees were called upon to endure for over two months while efforts were made to repair the engine. Discussions on 20 December between

Sir Hughe Knatchbull-Hugessen, the British Ambassador in Ankara, and the Assistant Secretary-General of the Turkish Ministry of Foreign Affairs, on the problems attending the ultimate disposal of the refugees were reported to the Foreign Office (PRO CO 733/449), where they were received with the utmost displeasure.

The Turks had informed Sir Hughe that they were unwilling to agree to any measure which might result in the survivors being left in Turkish territory, but would allow the ship to proceed if His Majesty's Government would promise to admit the refugees to Palestine. Sir Hughe had replied that His Majesty's Government 'did not want these people in Palestine' and that they 'had no permission to go there', but at the same time he could not readily agree, from a humanitarian point of view, to the Turkish proposal to send the ship back into the Black Sea.

'If the Turkish Government must interfere with the ship on the ground that they could not keep the distressed Jews in Turkey, let her rather go towards the Dardanelles. It might be that if they reached Palestine, they might despite their illegality receive humane treatment.'

Officials of the Colonial Office were not slow in expressing their anger at this suggestion. On 23 December S.E.V. Luke minuted 'This is the first occasion on which . . . the Turkish Government has shown any signs of being ready to help in frustrating these illegal immigrant ships, and the Ambassador then goes and spoils the whole effect on absurdly misjudged humanitarian grounds.' On the same day E.B. Boyd added: 'Sir H. Knatchbull-Hugessen had a heaven-sent opportunity of getting these people stopped at Istanbul and sent back to Constanza, and has failed to avail himself of it.' (ibid)

The Colonial Secretary, Lord Moyne, sent, on the next day, an even stronger protest to Richard Law, Parliamentary Under-Secretary at the Foreign Office, declaring:

'The landing (in Palestine) of seven hundred more immigrants will not only be a formidable addition to the difficulties of the High Commissioner . . . but it will have a deplorable effect throughout the Balkans in encouraging further Jews to embark on a traffic which has now been condoned by His Majesty's Ambassador . . . I find it difficult to write with moderation about this occurrence which is in flat contradiction of established Government policy, and I should be very glad if you could perhaps even now do something to retrieve the position and to urge that (the) Turkish authorities should be asked to send the ship back to the Black Sea, as they originally proposed.' (ibid)

Support for this view came from the High Commissioner in Palestine, Sir Harold MacMichael, who insisted in a cable to the Colonial Office (with a copy to Ankara) that it was 'most important both from policy and security points of view that these illegal immigrants should be prevented from coming to Palestine.' These pronouncements resulted in an instruction to the British Embassy in Ankara to correct the false impression of British policy which may have been conveyed to them by the British Ambassador in the discussions with the Turkish Foreign Affairs Ministry seven days previously, and the Turks were informed that 'His Majesty's Government saw no reason why the Turkish Government should not send *Struma* back into the Black Sea if they wished.' (PRO PREM 4/15/1/40)

The Turkish Government, however, were now faced with a number of reasons for not acceding to the British request. The Turkish engineers had been unable to mend the ship's engine: it appeared to be damaged beyond repair. The Rumanian Minister in Ankara had informed the Turkish Government that the passengers on board the *Struma* had left Rumania illegally and would not be allowed to return. Finally, the captain of the *Struma* reminded the Istanbul Port Captain on 10 January 1942, that his ship was registered under the Panamanian flag, that Panama had declared war on Germany on the day that the *Struma* had left Constanza, and that it was therefore dangerous for the ship to proceed without being escorted by a Turkish warship. Furthermore, the condition of the ship was such that he could take no further responsibility for the voyage.

Faced with this situation, the Turkish Government informed the British Ambassador on 9 February that, in the absence of any other solution, they would send the ship and its passengers back in about a week's time in the direction from which they had come. One member of the Foreign Office, Oliver Harvey, was so shocked by this decision that he asked, in a minute dated 11 February: 'Can nothing be done for these unfortunate refugees? Must H.M.G. take such an inhuman decision? If they go back they will all be killed.' (PRO FO 371/32661) C.W. Baxter, a less sympathetic colleague, minuted on the following day that 'if we were to accept these people, there would, of course, be more and more shiploads of unwanted Jews later! . . . Personally, I feel strongly that it would be unwise for us to intervene, and that our intervention would only mean more shiploads later and more suffering.'

Harvey was allowed to put his views to Moyne's private secretary and also to write to Eden, pleading in his note: 'After all, these unfortunate people are on our side. The exodus could hardly assume very great proportions, and it should be able to sort out the enemy agents.' (ibid) Three days later the High Commissioner cabled the Colonial Office: 'It has been decided to admit to Palestine Children from the *Struma* between the ages of eleven and sixteen years. . . . No repeat no adults can be accepted.' In a long cable on 17 February he stressed the objection that the passengers were in the main professional people and if admitted to Palestine would add to 'the unproductive element in the population.' But the Turks insisted that if the children travelled to Palestine it would have to be by sea, on a British boat: they would not permit the children to travel overland across Turkey. The Foreign Office could find no way of ending this deadlock, and on 23 February the British Passport Control Officer at Istanbul reported that the Turks were preparing to tow the *Struma* 'towards the Black Sea where she would doubtless be cast adrift outside Turkish territorial waters.' Two days later, a Foreign Office minute recorded: 'The ship is today reported as having sunk with all on board.'

25

The Foreign office report that 'all on board' had sunk with the *Struma* was not strictly accurate. David Stoliar, who had jumped overboard when the ship started to sink, was picked up 24 hours later by a Turkish motor launch. After two weeks in hospital he was consigned to prison. In March 1942 he was included in a group of 20 refugees whose application for admission to Palestine was rejected by the High Commissioner on the ground that the 'basic principle that enemy nationals from enemy or enemy-controlled territory should not be admitted to this country during the war applies to all immigrants'. The admission of these immigrants would be likely to 'open the flood-gates and completely undermine our whole policy regarding illegal immigration.' (19 March 1942. PRO CO 733/446)

In sheer numbers, when compared with the hundreds of thousands of Jews being slaughtered in Central and Eastern Europe, the *Struma* total may have appeared insignificant. Only a few weeks previously 34,000 Jews had been murdered by *Einsatzgruppen* at Babi Yar, near Kiev. Heydrich revealed at the Wannsee Conference of 20 January 1942, that at that date only half of the 250,000 German Jews had been killed: there were still eleven million left in Europe who must be subjected to the Final Solution. Why then did the *Struma* tragedy, with less than 800 victims, prompt so much grief and horror throughout the Yishuv – the Jews of Palestine?

The Germans, with their collaborators, had never made any secret of their intentions – complete annihilation. But the governments of the various countries whose actions and decisions had contributed to the outcome of the *Struma* disaster had professed to be either neutral in the conflict or at war with Germany. Their actions could only have achieved German approval, in the same measure as they resulted in universal Jewish protest.

The 769 *Struma* passengers – half of whom were women or children – had paid more than 1,000 U.S. dollars each for their places in this derelict converted 240-ton yacht. Before the vessel left port Rumanian officials came on board and confiscated most of the provisions and all of the passengers' valuables. After she had foundered the Turks placed every obstacle to the passengers' going ashore while the repairs were being attempted, but offered, as they informed His Majesty's Government, to give every possible assistance to the ship if it was allowed to proceed to Palestine. The Rumanians would not allow the passengers, who were Rumanian citizens, to return to their country, on the grounds that the ship had left illegally. The British declared (PRO FO 371/32661/25) that it was impossible to send the boat to Cyprus (as an alternative to Palestine) because, owing to the war, there would be no accommodation for the passengers.

Within Palestine the High Commissioner, Sir Harold MacMichael, bore the brunt of the despair and anger which swept the Jewish population. The underground movements posted 'WANTED' notices on the walls in towns and villages bearing his portrait and blaming him for the 'MURDER OF 800 REFUGEES DROWNED IN THE BLACK SEA ON THE BOAT "STRUMA".' When the news of the disaster was officially confirmed in the country's newspapers, a 12-hour strike was called in protest. There can be little doubt that the ranks of the two dissident organisations were at this time augmented by many of the younger generation of Palestinian Jews.

Nevertheless, this hostility of the radical groups towards the Administration and the British Government for what they regarded as their blatant anti-Zionist attitudes existed side by side with the urgent desire of the Yishuv to make some tangible contribution to the war effort through enlistment in the fighting services. In August 1940 Weizmann had written to Churchill that 'Palestinian Jewry can furnish a force of 50,000 fighting men, all of them in the prime of their strength', and in the following month was summoned to attend a meeting which considered a five-point programme for the formation of Jewish battalions and a Jewish desert unit.

Although Churchill gave his approval to this programme the military authorities raised difficulties for its implementation, and it was not until some time later that a Jewish Brigade was officially formed. Despite this delay, by the middle of 1941 Palestinian Jews were fighting side by side with the Allies in Syria and in Iraq. Most of the 1,700 Palestinians who joined the R.A.F. in 1940 when its personnel were being transferred to England to take part in the Battle of Britain were Jews. Altogether 33,000 Palestinian Jews enlisted in the British Army, and fought not only in the Middle East but also in Crete, North Africa and Europe. The Palestinian Pioneer Corps sent to France in the early days of the War was 75 per cent Jewish. 90 per cent of the Palestinian A.T.S. were Jewish.

Some of these Jewish volunteers elected to fight behind the German lines. Twenty-three-year-old Hannah Senesh, Hungarian-born and a writer of poetry, was captured by the Nazis after being parachuted by the British behind their lines. She was executed in Budapest on 4 November 1944, after being cruelly tortured. Enzo Sereni, another Jewish parachutist, was murdered in Dachau two weeks later. The 9,000 Arabs who enlisted in Palestine included groups from Syria, Lebanon and Transjordan: it was not long before their numbers were reduced through discharges and desertion by more than half.

Wavell, Commander-in-Chief in the Middle East, was throughout strongly opposed to the creation of any Jewish fighting units.

When the discussions with Weizmann on the creation of Jewish fighting units were in progress he had cabled the War Office: 'I am strongly opposed to raising this force at the present time. It is vitally important that for the next six months at least I should be as free as possible from commitments and anxieties in Palestine.' (PRO FO 371/27126)

Churchill had no illusions about Wavell's prejudices and sympathies, writing, on 1 May 1941: 'General Wavell, like most British army officers, is strongly pro-Arab. At the time of the licences to the ship-wrecked illegal immigrants being permitted, he sent a telegram, not less strong than this, predicting widespread disaster in the Arab world, together with the loss of the Busra-Baghdad-Haifa route. The telegram should be looked up, and also my answer in which I overruled the General and explained to him the reasons for the Cabinet decision. All went well and not a dog barked . . .' (ibid)

The Wavell telegram to which Churchill here refers was sent to Eden on 30 November 1940. Four days earlier Wavell had recommended action to open the Basra-Baghdad road, at that time under the control of Rashid Ali and the pro-Axis 'Four Colonels': now he was threatening to 'withdraw recommendation of 26 Nov. to open Basra-Baghdad road, as certain result will be great increase of anti-British feeling and action in Iraq. Please exert your influence. This is serious'. (PRO PREM 4/51/2/116) While Wavell won the support of both the Foreign Office and the Colonial Office for these views, Churchill replied:

'I wonder whether the effect on the Arab world will be as bad as you suggest. If their attachment to our cause is so slender as to be determined by a mere act of charity of this kind, it is clear that our policy of conciliating them has not borne much fruit so far. What I think would influence them more would be any kind of British military success. I therefore suggest that you should reconsider your statement about the Basra-Baghdad-Haifa road' . . . (1 Dec. 1940)

The force mustered in Palestine to accomplish the near-500-mile desert march to Habbaniya, the British air base to the west of Baghdad, amounted to no more than 2,000 men. The swift defeat of the Iraqi forces, which enjoyed the support of some sixty German aircraft, invites comment on Wavell's petulant willingness to abandon the attack in order to avoid 'great increase of anti-British feeling'. The scratch force from Palestine had included Glubb's Arab Legion and members of the Irgun. Nicholas Hammond, an SOE instructor, reported that 'The Jews had a very good network in Iraq. We prepared explosive devices for them to plant in Rashid Ali's supply dumps.' Irgun's role ended when its commander Yaacov Meridor was killed in action.

Meridor was by no means the only Jewish casualty of that campaign. On 30 May, after the British forces had crossed the Washash Canal two or three miles to the west of Baghdad, a deputation, headed by the Mayor of Baghdad and an army officer, called at the British Embassy in the city, to announce that the ex-Mufti, together with Rashid Ali and some German and Italian officials, had fled to Persia. On the next morning an Iraqi deputation bearing a flag of truce appeared at the Iron Bridge on the Canal, and a cessation of hostilities was agreed. For the next two days British troops were stationed outside the city while savage mobs massacred Jews and looted their property. Women were raped and abducted. Neither the British nor the Regent, who had returned to his capital on the morning of 1 June, made any effort to intervene. Iraqi army and police officers also were passive witnesses of the pogrom. Various figures have been given for the casualties: Christopher Buckley wrote, in an official account for H.M. Government, that 'Serious riots broke out in Baghdad that night, directed by the worst elements of the population, against the Jews, and about 700 persons lost their lives.' (*Five Ventures*, His Majesty's Stationery Office, 1954, p. 35)

26

The discussions on the question of the most suitable style of propaganda to be employed by the Allies in the closing stages of the war were relieved by touches of humour. The problem of whether to emphasise or suppress reports of the persecution of Jews in broadcasts or the distribution of leaflets encouraged one Foreign Office humorist to suggest that 'the air for the Jew string' would not be an effective propaganda. (PRO FO 371/42724/3)

Mr. A. Walker's amusing minute was dated 4 April 1944. That he was by no means the only comic in the Foreign Office was revealed by the lyrical response of Dwight Chaplin (of the Foreign Office's Enemy Branch), addressed to Mr. Churchill, to the offer of one Mr. S. Sass of Colombia to reorganise the German steel industry after the war:

> From Africa's shore, from Colomb's sunscorched strand,
> Urgent there streams an eager Hebrew band,
> Imbued with our desire to serve the aims
> Of Allied justice, see them stake their claims
> To jobs in Germany. *They* know the ropes,
> And *their* control will answer all our hopes.
> 'Let us but serve, and we will prove our worth.
> 'Till Hitler came and rudely thrust us forth
> 'We helped the men who laid the powder train.
> 'So you can trust us not to help again.
> 'Good Germans we? Perhaps, but all the same
> 'Profit or loss we'll play the Allies game.'
> Such altruistic offers shall we spurn,
> Nor rather trusting to these helpers turn.

Loose them like vultures on the German scene
And hope they will not pick the carcase clean
Or, worse, revert to type and aid the Hun
To germanize the world with tank and gun?
Prudence invites we leave them where they are
And hitch our wagon not to David's star.
Paris we know, well worth a mass,
Berlin not less by Bellow-Fellow Sass.
(FO 371 40816/U5266. 9.6.44)

When the board of Deputies of British Jews submitted measures to bring aid to the Jews of Rumania and Hungary, the head of the Southern Department of the Foreign Office, A.R. Dew, complained: 'In my opinion a disproportionate amount of the time in this office is wasted in dealing with these wailing Jews.' (PRO FO 371/42817/16) This minute was dated 1 September 1944, at the time that the German armies were in retreat in Europe, and the gas chambers were being dismantled, with the survivors transferred to other camps. In the United States a War Refugee Board was charged with: 'taking all measures within its power to rescue the victims of enemy oppression who are in imminent danger of death, and otherwise to afford such victims all possible relief and assistance consistent with the successful prosecution of the war.'

This statement was circulated to U.S. embassies in London and other capitals. When Eden saw it he commented that in addition to its stated war aims the W.R.B. was formed with the intention of 'placating the large Jewish vote'. (PRO CAB 95/15/31) Friction arose between the British and American Governments over the dispatch of relief funds for Jews in occupied Europe, to which Britain was opposed on the grounds that the blockade of Nazi Europe needed to be strictly maintained, and for that reason she had consistently rejected applications to send relief supplies to Jews in Europe.

While the last part of that statement was known to be the truth, it should be remembered that during the entire period of the occupation of Greece by the Axis Powers, from 1942 to the end of the war, the Allies supplied the entire food needs of the population. The Report of the International Committee of the Red Cross on its activities during the Second World War, published in Geneva in 1948, reveals that between autumn 1943 and 1945 40 million dollars' worth of foodstuffs (up to 35,000 tons per month) were permitted to go through the blockade to Greece. While there can be no question that the Greeks were fully entitled, in view of their resistance to the Axis, to every possible help, the difference between the treatment they received in the matter of food supplies and that meted out to the Jews was manifest.

When the W.R.B. approved a proposal by the Joint Distribution Committee to give $100,000 to the International Red Cross for the relief of Jews in Hungary and Rumania, Eden commented:

'If we object, we run the risk of being held up by the War Refugee Board (which is engaged on a publicity campaign) as obstacles to a humanitarian measure which would probably save many Jewish lives. If we merely acquiesce, we allow the United States Government to get the credit for a piece of rescue work which critics will say should have been attempted long ago, while if we, too, agree to remit money to the International Red Cross, we may be committed to a relaxation of our financial blockade which may prove of real advantage to the enemy ... we should emphasize that we wish to help the refugee cause as much as the United State Government and desire to co-operate with them fully. But we cannot overlook the fact that providing the enemy with foreign currency may increase his powers of resistance, and so ultimately cause more suffering than will be relieved.' (PRO CAB 95/15/138)

These differences between the British and the United States Governments on the approach to the European refugee problem were to become more pronounced after the English general elections in July 1945, following the end of the war in May, resulted in the election of a Labour Government. In April 1944 the Labour Party National Executive Committee had published a statement of support for a Zionist programme in terms which had troubled the Zionist leaders. It read:

'There is surely neither hope nor meaning in a Jewish National Home unless we are prepared to let the Jews, if they wish, enter this tiny land in such numbers as to become a majority. There was a strong case for this before the war, and there is an irresistible case for it now, after the unspeakable atrocities of the cold-blooded German-Nazi plans to kill all the Jews of Europe . . . Let the Arabs be encouraged to move out as the Jews move in. Let them be compensated handsomely for their land, and their settlement elsewhere be carefully organized and generously financed.'

Weizmann commented: 'I remember that my Labour Zionist friends were, like myself, greatly concerned about this proposal. We had never contemplated the removal of the Arabs, and the British Labourites, in their pro-Zionist enthusiasm, went far beyond our intention.' (*Trial and Error*, p. 535) However, within three months of taking office Britain's Labour Government repudiated that pledge. Instead of proceeding with the abrogation of the White Paper which had pronounced a death sentence on fulfilment of the Jewish National Home, and taking steps towards the relief of the thousands of Jews still being held in detention camps, the Labour Government decided to appoint a new Commission of Enquiry.

The 1946 Commission of Enquiry differed from its predecessors in that it was Anglo-American, thus involving for the first time the American Government in the problems with which the

British had wrestled alone throughout the war. Its terms were 'to examine political, economic, and social conditions in Palestine as they bear upon the problem of Jewish immigration' and 'to examine the position of the Jews in the countries of Europe where they have been the victims of Nazi and Fascist persecution.'

The Report of the Anglo-American Commission of Enquiry was published on 20 April 1946. Its principal recommendations were that 100,000 Jewish refugees from Europe should be admitted into Palestine over a period of two years, and that land sales to Jews should no longer be restricted. Neither of these recommendations accorded with British policy, and the British lost little time in conveying their own views to the Americans. A letter written to the British Prime Minister, Mr. Attlee, by President Truman on May 8 urging immediate action on the Commission's recommendations, received a frosty reply on 27 May in which Attlee refrained from giving British assent to the American request. Instead he sent Truman a list of 43 matters which, he claimed, would have to be taken into account before any consideration could be given to the admission into Palestine of the Jews from the camps. One of the 43 items concerned the disbanding of the Haganah, the Jewish defence organisation.

In less than a week from the date of this letter, the 'Report of the Anglo-American Committee of Enquiry regarding the problems of European Jewry and Palestine' (Cmd. 6808) was discussed at a conference of Arab rulers at Inchass, a country palace of King Farouk of Egypt, and its proposals were rejected. Those present called for an immediate end to all Jewish immigration into Palestine and the prevention of all further sales of land to Jews. Attlee was thus enabled, in presenting his views to Parliament on the limitation of immigration, to reinforce his argument with President Truman by citing the unanimous views of the representatives of seven Arab countries on this question. His other demand, the disbanding of Haganah,

175

appeared to be approaching fulfilment on 30 June, when the Jewish leaders in Palestine were arrested and the Jewish Agency was occupied.

27

On the day following the mass arrests and detentions in Palestine a Member of Parliament, Richard Crossman, addressed the House of Commons on the subject of that action. In the course of his speech he submitted that the Anglo-American Committee's condemnation of terrorism was linked with its statement that

'Palestine is now a semi-military or police state . . . When, therefore, the Prime Minister speaks of the necessity of restoring law and order it is important to remember that what he really means is the restoration of the authority of the police, the restoration of the authority of a state hated by both Jew and Arab. Granted that the form of restoration which he has chosen in arresting 2,000 Jews may gain somewhat greater consent from the Arab population, it remains true that, so far as the Jewish population is concerned, no consent to such methods can be achieved. I hesitate to believe that when we talk of the restoration of law and order we on this side of the House are meaning that kind of restoration of law and order which has occurred in past history. We cannot be referring to what has happened in several countries – pushing down by brute force people who are genuinely struggling for their liberation.

'It is right that this House should be deeply concerned about the cost of British lives – and I would add that this has been very much smaller in the Jewish revolt than in the Arab revolt – but it is always as well to remember that while we are indignant that British soldiers should be killed we should be even more indignant if we discover that they are being killed in an unjust war . . . I must say frankly to the House that what we are trying to impose on the Jewish community is a reimposition of the White Paper, something which no Jew in Palestine accepts as either law or order.'

The Report of the Anglo-American Commission of Enquiry pointed out that the Jews

'were with Britain in the fight against Fascism but they were against Britain in the struggle against the White Paper, which they felt was not only unjust but totally inhuman as preventing the escape to Palestine of men, women and children in imminent danger of death in Nazi Germany and Nazi-controlled Europe. When the war ended and the Labour Government came into power the White Paper still remained in force. The Jews, who had expected an immediate fulfilment by a Labour Government of the programme with regard to Zionism, felt a sense of outrage when no change of policy occurred ... To use the words of one Jewish leader: "Our present crisis in Europe and in Palestine is felt by us to be our Dunkirk."'

'I have risen to second the Motion for the Adjournment because I feel desperately that the Government's present line of action will not work ... Whom have they arrested? Practically every trade-union leader and Socialist leader in Palestine, practically every leader of the Palestine Labour Party, of trade unions, co-operatives and co-operative retail organisations. They have arrested the whole of what we might call the political Left. These have been chucked into gaol in the belief that they are the leaders of the resistance movement. ... It would be grossly improper for a Member of the House who was not a Jew to regard this as solely a question between the British Government and the Jews ... The Mufti has made it quite clear that once the British Government has liquidated the Jews in Palestine, he will demand and achieve by violence the removal of the British

178

from Palestine. I have one more point to make. The Government says that it would, of course, deal with the Arab violence too. Let me remind the House that Arab violence is organized from outside Palestine. There are no fewer than six Arab states which could organize arms and hire guerrillas and send them into Palestine. Although the Government have cracked down on the Haganah, it cannot crack down on these allies who have said that they will use violence to get their way. It is a somewhat one-side destruction of private armies which is being done by the disarming of the Jews in Palestine, while the Iraqi army, the Transjordan army, are all there, and the Arab League, with a British Brigadier to consult, denounces the Anglo-American report, and breathes fire and slaughter.'

When, on a Thursday evening in October 1945, Mr. R.H.S. Crossman was informed by the Chief Labour Whip that the Foreign Secretary, Ernest Bevin, had assigned him for a special job ('something about Palestine'), he immediately sought out Bevin's Parliamentary Secretary, Hector McNeil, and protested that he 'knew nothing about Palestine and was quite unsuitable for the job'. He was not aware, at that time, that those deficiencies were, in Bevin's view, excellent qualifications for this assignment.

Crossman was the youngest man in the British team. In Washington he met Bartley Crum, the youngest man in the American team. Crum, a Catholic lawyer, later wrote:

'The night before I left Washington I had spent an evening with several of Richard Crossman's wartime associates in New York. They told me of his brilliance and of the extraordinary work he had done during the war as Deputy Director, Psychological Warfare Division, SHAEF. A former Oxford Don, assistant editor of the liberal *New Statesman and Nation*, at 39 Crossman was a Labour M.P., considered by many of the party's left-wing spokesman on foreign affairs, and a Socialist theoretician of recognised influence. He came of an old, Conservative family; his father was a High Court judge in England . . . I found him most refreshing, with an agile mind, a quick sympathy, and a gift for striking swiftly at the nub of complicated questions.'

On the morning on which his boat drew into New York, Crossman wrote in his diary:

'We start with a blankness towards the philosophy of Zionism which is virtually anti-Zionist. We have a feeling that the whole idea of a Jewish national home is a *dead end* out of which Britain must be extracted; that, whereas it is obvious that Arab independence in the end *must* be granted, we have not a similar obligation to permit the Jews in Palestine the fulfilment of Zionism . . .'

The Committee sat in London from 25 January to 1 February, and then went on to the Continent, where they met survivors of the extermination camps. They heard the Arab case in Cairo, which they left on 6 March for Palestine. On the very next day Crossman met Ben-Gurion, with whom he was discussing Crossman's book, *Plato Today*, 'when one of the High Commissioner's aides tapped me on the shoulder and said it might be a little undiplomatic if I remained in conversation with Ben-Gurion for too long.'

There were no similar inhibitions suggested at his next meeting.

'I went out to a party in the Mufti's villa, given by Mrs. Antonius, the widow of George Antonius (his book, *The Arab Awakening*, has been standard reading for the British members of the Committee). Mrs. Antonius seems to have a political salon in true French style. It was a magnificent party – evening dress, Syrian food and drink, and dancing on the marble floor. As far as I could see, the party was fifty-fifty Arab and British.

'It is easy to see why the British prefer the Arab upper class to the Jews. The Arab intelligentsia has a French culture, amusing, civilised, tragic and gay. Compared with them the Jews seem tense, *bourgeois*, central European. As we motored back, a British official said to me: "There are two societies in Jerusalem, not three. One is Anglo-Arab and the other is Jewish. The two just can't mix".'

On 8 March Crossman visited Weizmann at the Zionist leader's home in Rehovot. The two talked alone from 5 p.m. until after midnight. Weizmann asked him whether he was anti-Semitic. 'When I said, "Of course", I felt that our friendship had begun. For, if a Gentile denied his latent anti-Semitism, Weizmann concluded that he must either be lying, or, even worse, deceiving himself.' In his book, *A Nation Reborn* (Hamish Hamilton, 1960), Crossman wrote:

'By what right do I, an English Gentile, claim to talk about Weizmann's Zionist faith? My answer is that, in the course of this century, the histories of Great Britain and the Jewish people have been tragically yet providentially intertwined – and the man chiefly responsible for this was Chaim Weizmann. As for myself, I can claim expert knowledge neither of Zionism nor of the Middle East. My mind was empty, if not open, when I was pitched into the Palestine problem by Ernest Bevin's decision to appoint me, in the autumn of 1945, one of the two British M.P.s on the Anglo-American Commission of Enquiry. Since Mr. Bevin was a careful man, and was hopeful that this commission's report would help his own plans for Palestine, it is not difficult to conclude that I started our 120-day investigation without any bias in favour of Zionism. Looking back now, I can see that Mr. Bevin was playing for time: the main function of our Commission was to postpone for 120 days the very awkward decision that faced him.' (op. cit., p. 13)

Those '120 days of intense concentration' (as Crossman described them) proved to be a period of revelation.

'First of all,' he wrote, 'I have the prejudice of a Gentile, a discovery which I made in the course of these 120 days, and I discovered that the most dangerous person is a person who says to you, "I don't know what anti-Semitism means." Every Gentile has the virus of anti-Semitism in his veins. You know that we all carry the bacillus of pneumonia inside our system. What happens is that this bacillus is quite harmless unless we get run down, and then it suddenly comes out in a disease. Exactly the same is true of anti-Semitism.'

Attlee rejected the Commission's Report, and told Crossman: I'm disappointed in you, Dick. The Report you have produced is grossly unfair.' When Crossman asked: 'Unfair to the Jews or the Arabs?' Attlee replied crossly: 'No, unfair to Britain, of course. You've let us down by giving way to the Jews and the Americans.'

28

'Everyone to whom I was introduced seemed eager to explain the Palestine situation to me,' wrote Bartley Crum of his appointment to the Anglo-American Committee of Enquiry. 'But it was not until I met Loy Henderson, Chief of the Near East Division of the State Department, that I received my sharpest and clearest briefing. He took me aside and told me, "There is one fact facing both the United States and Great Britain, Mr. Crum. That is the Soviet Union. It would be wise to bear that in mind when you consider the Palestine problem" . . . I was to hear the same view expressed by a representative of the British Foreign Office aboard the *Queen Elizabeth* en route to Europe, and, later again, in Europe itself. It was this same British gentleman who was to unburden himself completely in Lausanne, Switzerland, where we wrote our report, by assuring me that British policy was based on the protection of British interests against Russia, and explaining that it should be in our interests to fall in with that policy.' (*Behind the Silken Curtain*, Victor Gollancz, 1947, p. 16)

At the first meeting aboard ship this warning was repeated more explicitly by Evan Wilson, of the State Department's Near East desk: 'If the committee reaches a decision which could be interpreted as too favourable to the Jews, an aroused Arab world might turn to the Soviet Union for support. That is a matter the committee must consider seriously.' Crum asked him how such a policy could 'square with all the assurances this Government and the Labour Party have made to the Jews?', and Wilson assured him that the State Department's concern was shared by the British Foreign and the British Colonial Office.

This was confirmed by Horace Beeley, the Near East expert who had been assigned to the Committee by the Foreign Office. He told Crum that the Palestine issue had to be seen in the framework of strong Soviet expansionism. The Soviets planned to move down into the Middle East. The United States, therefore, would do well to join Britain in establishing a *cordon sanitaire* of Arab States. If Palestine were declared an Arab State, it would be a strong link in this chain.

On the third day out Crum was handed a document marked, 'Contents of file of confidential communications on Palestine supplied by Division of Near Eastern Affairs for use of Anglo-American Committee of Enquiry'. According to that file, since 15 September 1938, each time a promise had been made to American Jewry regarding Palestine the State Department had promptly sent messages to the Arab rulers discounting it and reassuring them, in effect, that regardless of what was promised publicly to the Jews, nothing would be done to change the situation in Palestine.

Crum has recorded his strong reaction to this disclosure. 'I said, I think I ought to book passage home as soon as we arrive in Southampton. I don't see that there is any purpose in going on with our work ... I made a careful study of this confidential State Department material. It revealed that steadily and successively we had made public promises to the Zionists and private promises to the Arabs ...' (op. cit., pp. 36–37)

During the London sessions Bartley Crum met Foreign Secretary Ernest Bevin at a formal luncheon. '"The British Government," he told us, "would accept your recommendations."' Later, when Crum charged publicly that Bevin had made this promise, the British Foreign Office stated that it had no record of it.

At the conclusion of the London hearings the members of the Committee divided into groups, each assigned to a different area.

Crum went on to Frankfurt (which he insists on referring to as 'Frankfort'), where he made his acquaintance with displaced persons camps and learned a little about the wartime experiences of some of the inmates. Sir Frederick Legget was with him when a group of children broke out in a Hebrew song.

'It was entitled *Hatikvah*, meaning "Hope", and we were told that it was the anthem of the Zionist movement, and had become the Jewish national anthem wherever Jewish national sentiment was alive.

'"You see what I mean," Sir Frederick said to me quietly. "That is nationalism implanted in the hearts of the very young, after the Nazi fashion." I disagreed completely. "Would you feel the same way if you saw a group of British youngsters sing *God Save the King*?" Sir Frederick smiled. "You know that's ridiculous".' (op. cit., pp. 71–72)

In Nuremberg they visited the war trials and were able to examine 'a thick file of documents' which proved to be a record of the ex-Mufti's association with the Nazis and his close involvement in the extermination programme.

'Before we left Nuremberg Army authorities invited us to a private showing of German and American motion-picture films, taken during and after the concentration-camp period. I saw the unexpurgated films of the actual mass murders, of bodies piled like cordwood to feed the crematorium fires: pictures that the Germans had carefully preserved, perhaps with the thought that well-documented files might legalize massacre. I became so ill at the sight that I was unable to remain throughout the entire showing. I could no longer look upon these scenes of victims dying, of victims dead, of piles of dead bodies being pushed by German bulldozers into huge pits dug into the ground . . . As Sir Frederick and I walked back to the hotel we were accosted by a German boy about 14, begging for a cigarette. Sir Frederick said, "We must take care of these young German people. What will their future be?"''

In Vienna, Crum's group, which now included Crossman, asked for an Interim Report recommending that the displaced-persons camps be emptied, but this was rejected by the other British groups on the ground that the Arabs would take this as a political move and a prejudgement.

'Not only was I so discouraged by the decision not to issue an Interim Report, but we were everywhere presented with such evidences of anti-Semitism that it seemed hopeless to continue ... A shocking example of this occurred when Crossman and I had cocktails with one of the British officers in charge of the displaced persons and prisoners of war in the British Zone of Austria. A red-faced, militant figure, he was not hesitant about discussing the problems of the thousands of displaced Jews with whose care he was charged.

'"It is too bad the war didn't last another two or three months," he said, toying with his glass. "They'd all have been done away with by then. We'd have had no problem." Crossman and I stared at him. "Frankly, I'm an anti-Semite," he said. "I honestly hate the Jew bastards. I wish they'd all been burned to death." I'm afraid I gasped a little at this, and he turned his ruddy face to me. He leaned forward and tapped me on the knee. "Ah-ah," he said chidingly. "I wager you have some of them as your clients, eh?"''

In its Report published 20 April 1946, the Committee recommended '(A) that 100,000 certificates be authorised immediately for the admission into Palestine of Jews who have been the victims of Nazi and Fascist persecution; (B) that these certificates be awarded as far as possible in 1946 and that actual immigration be pushed forward as rapidly as conditions will permit.' In a further recommendation the Committee asked 'that the Land Transfers Regulations of 1940 be rescinded and replaced by regulations based on a policy of freedom in the sale, lease or use of land, irrespective of race, community or creed; and providing adequate protection for the interests of small owners and tenant cultivators.'

Crum has described how, during the final discussions in Lausanne,

'some of the British, returning to what they had suggested four months earlier aboard the *Queen Elizabeth*, wished us to recommend the disbanding of the *Haganah* and the withdrawal of recognition of the Jewish Agency ... Sir Frederick Legget sided with Sir John [Singleton] in this ... Lord Morrison had similar convictions, and so, too, did Manningham-Buller ... Judge Hutcheson was particularly firm. Finally he said, "I will not, in any circumstances, be a party to any recommendation which would strip the Jews of Palestine of their right to defend their lives" ... What happened between the time we signed the report and the subsequent actions of the British Government, I do not know, but certainly all the American members of the committee were greatly surprised and disappointed when Mr. Attlee said in the House of Commons that before any immigration into Palestine could be permitted the *Haganah* must be disarmed. The subsequent, and to me almost incredible, statements of Mr. Bevin cannot be explained except in terms of high imperial strategy ...' (op. cit., pp. 203–206)

In addition to supporting the above-mentioned recommendations, Bartley Crum asks, in his book, for the revocation of the British White Paper of 1939, on the ground that the Permanent Mandates Commission of the League of Nations found it in violation of the terms of the Mandate (which was also the finding of the Anglo-American Committee), and also that the United States oppose the admission of Trans-Jordan to the United Nations.

'There is no question,' he wrote, 'that the removal of Trans-Jordan from the terms of the mandate was a violation of its original purpose. All of Palestine, east and west of the Jordan River, was set aside by the framers of the mandate for Jewish immigration and settlement. The setting up of Trans-Jordan as an independent kingdom, moreover, is a violation of Article V of the mandate, which forbids Britain from ceding or placing under the control of any foreign power any Palestine territory.' (op. cit., p. 212)

29

In 1846 the British Foreign Minister was Lord Palmerston (Henry John Temple, 3rd Viscount). The reader will no doubt recall that in 1841 he had written to the British Ambassador in Constantinople 'that the Jews who are scattered throughout other countries should be induced to go and settle in Palestine'. In 1946 Britain's Foreign Minister was Ernest Bevin, a former trade union official dedicated to the belief that Jews should not be encouraged to settle in Palestine, warning them not to 'push to the head of the queue'.

James G. McDonald, who, as a member of the Anglo-American Committee of Enquiry had first met Bevin in 1946, called on him in London while en route to Israel as first U.S. Ambassador to that State. McDonald's diary for Tuesday, 3 August 1948, records his impressions of that meeting.

'Facing Bevin across his broad table, I had to tell myself that this was not Hitler seated before me, but His Majesty's Principal Secretary of State for Foreign Affairs ... What extraordinary demagoguery! Did he believe his own diatribe? ... His bitterness against Mr. Truman was almost pathological: it found its match only in his blazing hatred for his other scapegoats – the Jews, the Israelis, the Israel Government ... Bevin, like Hitler and Mussolini in my interviews with them when I was League of Nations High Commissioner in the 1930s, had impressed me with a complete sense of ruthlessness.' (*My Mission in Israel, 1948–1951*, Gollancz, 1951, pp. 22–24)

Golda Meir, in her autobiographical *My Life* (Weidenfeld and

Nicolson, 1975) records a similar impression.

> 'I don't know' she wrote, '(nor really does it matter any more) whether Bevin was a little insane, or just anti-Semitic, or both. What I do know is that he insisted on pitting the strength of the British Empire against the will of the Jews to live and that by so doing he not only brought great suffering to people who had already suffered enormously, but also forced upon thousands of British soldiers and sailors a role that must have filled them with horror. I remember staring at some of the young Englishmen who guarded the DP detention camps on Cyprus – when I went there myself in 1947 – and wondering how on earth they managed to reconcile themselves to the fact that not so long ago they were liberating from Nazi camps the very same people whom they now kept penned behind barbed wire on Cyprus only because these people found it impossible to go on living anywhere except Palestine. I looked at these nice young English boys and was filled with pity for them. I couldn't help but think that they were no less victims of Bevin's obsession than the men, women and children on whom their guns were now trained night and day.' (pp. 164–65)

Crossman had known Bevin longer than either Meir or McDonald. After Attlee had chided him for 'giving way to the Jews and the Americans',

> 'A few months later,' wrote Crossman, 'Mr. Attlee's irritation had been transformed into a cold anger and Mr. Bevin's into a violent passion. It was the stubborn refusal of the Yishuv to be grateful for his protection and to conform to the plans he had made for them that finally tipped Ernest Bevin into overt anti-Semitism ... Driven by a frightening mixture of anger and violent self-pity, he became convinced that the Jews were organising a world conspiracy against

poor old Britain and, in particular, against poor old Ernie . . . By 1947 British policy in Palestine was largely motivated by one man's determination at almost any cost to teach the Jews a lesson.

'At this stage it is difficult to deny that Mr. Bevin's usually shrewd and far-sighted appreciation of any situation he was handling had become heavily clouded by anti-Semitism. One sign of this was an extraordinary credulity. One day he came and sat down beside me in the House of Commons (throughout the crisis he was always ready to talk to me, I think because he liked a little opposition as long as he was certain he could smash it). "Now I've got something which may finally convince you that you're in the wrong," he started. "The Foreign Office have given me their latest information from the Soviet Union. The Russians have massed an army of Jews at Odessa, ready for the attack!"

'In measuring the personal responsibility of Ernest Bevin for the Palestine catastrophe, it is as well to remember this systematic misinformation to which he was subjected month after month by the Foreign Office and the Service Chiefs . . . He took full responsibility for the successive schemes which his experts hatched in order first to turn Palestine into an Arab state, with a Jewish minority, and then, when the United Nations accepted partition and the Jewish State was born, to expose the infant to a murderous assault. There came a time when these experts were appalled by the obsession which they had induced in the mind of their master. But by then they could not hold him. He was permitted to prosecute his vendetta until the day when five British fighters, which he had personally ordered into combat, were shot down behind the Jewish lines.' (*A Nation Reborn*, 1960, pp. 69–72)

A further instance of this fixation is related in Jon and David

Kimche's *Both Sides of the Hill* (Secker & Warburg, 1960, pp. 115–16). On 22 April 1948, 'Ernest Bevin had called on the Prime Minister in the late afternoon in a state of rare panic. Newspaper reports from the Arab capitals, Bevin told Attlee, had reported that the Jews had massacred 23,000 Arabs in Haifa while British troops, under Major-General Stockwell, had stood by and done nothing about it. Bevin said that the Army had let him down and placed him in an impossible position in his relations with the Arabs. Attlee was impressed and summoned Field-Marshal Montgomery to No. 10. This was at 7.30 p.m. The Minister of Defence, A.V. Alexander, was also present at the meeting. There was a heated discussion; we have Montgomery's evidence that ' "Bevin was very worked up" (*Memoirs*, p. 473) and that Attlee was inclined to support him.' According to Montgomery, the Foreign Office was actually so ill-informed on the morning of 23 April as to have concluded that, in the light of this purely fictitious massacre, world opinion would support a British proposal which would leave the proposed Jewish State without the Negev, without Jerusalem and without Haifa – a kind of greater Tel Aviv.

30

Bevin lost little time in ventilating his rejection of the Anglo-American Report, informing the Labour Party Conference at Bournemouth of 12 June 1946 that admission to Palestine of the 100,000 homeless Jews, recommended in that Report, would necessitate the despatch of yet another division of British troops to Palestine: a measure which he was not prepared to consider. He continued: 'I hope I will not be misunderstood in America if I say that this was proposed with the purest motives. They did not want too many Jews in New York.'

The British Ambassador in New York, Lord Inverchapel, responded to this gibe on the following day, reporting the American reaction to the unrepentant Bevin. (FO 371/52529) When he suggested that Bevin might at least reassure Washington and Truman that Britain had not prejudged the question of admitting the 100,000 Bevin demurred, replying: 'I am not sure that this is a wise thing to do. I am getting upset with this Jewish agitation. We have made our position clear.'

It was being made painfully clear to the American public. On 21 May the *New York Post* printed an article by Ruth Gruber about the Palestine police: 'These men who loathed the idea of fighting their friends, the Nazis, embraced with passion the idea of fighting Jews. They walked around the streets of Jerusalem and Tel Aviv, the city built by Jews, singing the *Horst Wessel* song. They marched into crowded market places giving the Heil Hitler salute.'

In *A Nation Reborn*, Richard Crossman describes the behaviour of troops at Givat Brenner, a Jewish village near Rehovot, on 29 June.

'The troops had been told they were to "occupy" it, and they behaved accordingly. They began to break into the schoolrooms and into a small laboratory which the children use; they broke into the girls' dormitory; pilfered watches, fountain-pens and other trinkets; tore or cut up clothing stored for the use of the *halutzim*, and generally behaved like "conquerors". Characteristic of the whole proceedings here were the slogans used by the "invaders": "What we need is gas-chambers!" "Hitler didn't finish the job!" Swastikas were chalked or painted on walls (and also even on the pavements of Rehovot).' (p. 136)

The impression shared by the Palestinian Jews that all imaginable forces were being mustered against them could only have been reinforced at that juncture by the news that on 9 June the ex-Mufti had succeeded in extricating himself (by all accounts with a minimum of effort) from the custody of the French and had arrived in Damascus. (WO 169 23022) On the same day that British troops were celebrating their triumphant occupation of Givat Brenner, the ex-Mufti was given a public welcome in Cairo by Prime Minister Sidky. In America Congressmen John McCormack and Thomas Lane announced that Haj Amin's fifth miraculous escape had been arranged by Ernest Bevin to forestall Jewish immigration.

The occupation of the Jewish Agency headquarters in Jerusalem on 30 June, together with that of other Jewish premises and 25 Jewish settlements had involved the employment of 100,000 troops and 10,000 police. At the end of that day 2,659 men and 59 women had been detained. (Major R.D. Wilson, the historian of the 6 Airborne Division, gives the numbers as on 1 July as '2,718, which included 56 women. Of that number, 571 were released within a week.') (*Cordon and Search*, 1949, p. 60)

The settlement of Meshek Yagur, near Haifa, was attacked on June 29 by a force consisting of one battalion and a company of

194

the 1st infantry Division. When the troops arrived at the settlement, at 9.30 a.m., they found the entrances blocked. The tear-gas shells they fired were rendered harmless by the settlers, using wet sand and manure bags, and water cannons were then brought into action. Men, women and children then crowded around the central building and refused to move. Eventually the soldiers got into the central dining room, whereupon the women threw dishes and boiling water at them. By 11 a.m., 75 men, 18 women and 11 children were arrested. By 2 p.m. the number of men detained had risen to 250. (WO 168 22957)

That turbulent month of June 1946 was marked also by a markedly different event. For his 70th birthday a group of Dr. Weizmann's American friends had planned the inauguration of a scientific centre which would embrace both organic and physical chemistry in addition to other branches of science. The cornerstone of the main building was laid on 3 June 1946, in the presence of a distinguished gathering of scientists from Harvard, Columbia University, Brooklyn Polytechnic Institute, University College, Cardiff, and other centres of learning. Five weeks later, on 6 July, the Zionist leader called some thirty of the Jewish leaders still at liberty to his house in Rehovot and threatened to resign his presidency of the Zionist Organisation if Haganah would not agree to suspend all activity until the August meeting of the Jewish Agency in Paris. This ultimatum was accepted by the majority of those present.

Weizmann's authority – such as it was: it was never absolute – was not acknowledged by the Irgun and Lehi dissident groups. The Irgun had emerged in 1937 in the form of an underground army which, in the words of Menachem Begin, represented

'a new generation ... which turned its back on fear. It began to fight instead of to plead. For nearly two thousand years, the Jews, as Jews, had not borne arms, and it was on this complete disarmament, as much psychological as

195

physical, that our oppressors calculated. They did not realize that the two phenomena were interdependent: we gave up our arms when we were exiled from our country. With our return to the land of our fathers our strength was restored.' (*The Revolt*, W.H. Allen, n.d. (1951), p. 40)

Earlier on the same page Begin asserted that: 'the officials of the British Foreign Office could not gauge the character of the Jews who came to Eretz Israel. They assumed that the Jews would continue to be timed suppliants for protection. The conduct of the Jews – or rather the attitude of their official leaders, expressed in the well-known policy of self-restraint (*havlagah*) – seemed to justify and confirm this assumption.' A footnote expands on this.

'During the disturbances of 1936–39 the Haganah pursued a policy known as *havlagah*, a Hebrew word meaning self-restraint. It prescribed non-retaliation except under direct attack. As a result of this policy the Arabs were always sure of the initiative and never suffered any counter-attack. Their risks were reduced to what they were liable to suffer during attacks timed to suit themselves and on a battlefield chosen by themselves. It was largely in negation of this policy that the I.Z.L. came into being in 1937.'

On the outbreak of the Second World War in 1939, the dissident groups agreed to call a truce in the activities they had directed against the British Administration forces in Palestine following the publication of the White Paper of that year, which they saw as a death sentence on the prospect of the Jewish National Home, but in January 1944 the Irgun resumed its activities. The British responded vigorously. They caught a pupil of Haifa High School. Asher Tratner, in the act of putting up an anti-British poster on a wall. He was unarmed, but they opened fire on him and wounded him in the hip.

He was not seen by a doctor, nor sent to a hospital, but taken, his wound open and bleeding, to the Acre Jail. 'The wound festered. His jailers tied him to the bed. The boy had to wipe the blood and pus from his wound with strips torn from his shirt. The guards continued to maltreat him.' The prison chaplain, Rabbi Blum, drew the attention of the officials to the critical condition of the boy, but was told that 'Rabbis should concern themselves with the souls of the prisoners, not with their bodies – mind your own business.' Eventually the prison doctor saw the boy, and diagnosed blood poisoning. The boy was removed to the Haifa hospital, where he suffered first amputation and then death.

Bethell relates another incident involving the shooting of an unarmed civilian.

> 'Late one night Captain Davidson and Lieutenant Benjamin Woodworth were walking down Ben Yehuda Street, Tel Aviv, on their way home to the officers' club, when they passed a group of Jews on the pavement. According to the British weekly report, one of the Jews jostled Davidson: "For some time past the citizens of Tel Aviv have been in the habit of barging into British military personnel in the streets." (WO 169 22957) According to the Jewish version, Woodworth pushed his way through the group, while Davidson picked on one member, Avram Rosenberg, calling him a "Jewish bastard" and attempting to trip him up. Anyway, the result was that Woodworth drew his revolver and shot Rosenberg dead. He was subsequently charged with the killing and removed from Palestine, suffering from a nervous breakdown.' (op. cit. p. 242)

In the course of the operations of 30 June, three Jews had been killed by the British and many injured. These and other incidents served to fuel the conflict which was being waged between the military and police forces on the one hand, and the revisionist groups on the other, and which culminated in the destruction by

197

the Irgun of the British Army Command and the Palestine Government Secretariat quarters in the King David Hotel on 22 July 1946. Ninety-one people were killed in that action – 41 Arabs, 28 British, 17 Jews, and five others.

A great deal has been written about this incident. Begin wrote: 'The rules we had laid down for ourselves made the evacuation of the hotel essential. There were many civilians in the hotel whom we wanted, at all costs, to avoid injuring. We were anxious to ensure that they should leave the danger zone in plenty of time for their safety.' Passers-by were to be kept away from the building by the detonation of a small cracker-bomb, 'noisy but harmless'. The timing of the attack was chosen to ensure that the basement Regence restaurant would be empty of customers. Half an hour before the bombs were set to go off there were to be three telephone warnings: the first to the King David Hotel, the second to the *Palestine Post* office, and the third to the French Consulate-General close to the Hotel.

There is ample evidence that Adina Hay-Nissan, the Irgun girl who was deputed to make the warning telephone calls, delivered these on time. The *Middle East Mail*, the British Forces newspaper in the Middle East, reported that at several minutes past twelve the telephone operator in the Hotel heard the voice of a woman warning her that bombs had been placed in the hotel, which should be evacuated without delay. The telephone operator at the *Palestine Post* testified on oath to a police officer that at 12.15 she received the warning and 'at once' passed it on to the duty officer at police headquarters. Begin 'subsequently learned that when the warning to evacuate the hotel reached a high official he exclaimed: ''We are not here to take orders from the Jews. We give *them* orders.''' (op. cit., p. 221)

A 347-page book reviewed at length in the *Sunday Times* of 9 August 1981 appears to have been a full and conscientious investigation of the operation: 'meticulously researched', according to

Peter Wilsher, the reviewer. The author, Thurston Clarke, concluded that the warnings were given in the period between the planting of the bombs and their explosion. 'But the hotel, confused by earlier fighting while the bombs were being smuggled in and often hoaxed by such calls in the past, ignored her [Adina]; the French merely opened their windows to avoid blast; and the newspaper switchboard only got through after fatal delay.' (*By Blood and Fire*, Hutchinson)

Speaking in the House of Lords on Tuesday, 22 May 1979, Lord Janner read a letter from a doctor who was Medical Superintendent of Douglas House Sanatorium in Bournemouth. Prior to taking up that position in 1943, Dr. John Crawford had been Assistant Medical Director of the Emergency Medical Services Hospital at Preston Hall Sanatorium, Maidstone. In the course of his duties there he had been associated with Major-General Dudley Sheraton Skelton, CB, DSO, FRCS, formerly DGMS in India, Hon. Physician to HM the King and to HE the Viceroy of India. When he retired from the forces about 1937 he was given the rank of Brigadier and was ADMS in the SE Command, the area in which he met Dr. Crawford.

In 1946 Skelton was head of a hospital in Palestine near Jerusalem and was a frequent visitor to the King David Hotel. He told Crawford that he was in the Hotel on the day of the explosion and that the warning was passed on to the officers in the bar 'in rather jocular terms, implying it was "Jewish terrorist bluff". But despite advice to "ignore the bluff", he decided to leave and thus was out of the hotel when the explosion took place.'

'But while our Assault Unit in the lion's den had done everything possible to ensure the timely evacuation of the hotel', wrote Begin, 'others had taken a different line. For some reason the hotel was not evacuated, even though from the moment when the warnings had been received there was plenty of time for every living soul to saunter out. Instead, the toll of lives was terrible. More than two hundred people were killed or injured. Among the victims were high British officers. We particularly mourned the alien civilians, among them good friends, who had so tragically fallen. Our satisfaction at the success of the great operation was bitterly marred. Again we went through days of pain and nights of sorrow for the blood that need not have been shed.' (op. cit., p. 220)

Lieut.-General Evelyn Barker, the G.O.C., wrote in a different vein.

'I am determined that they (the Jews) should be punished and made aware of our feelings of contempt and disgust at their behaviour. We must not let ourselves be misled by hypocritical sympathy expressed by their leaders and representative bodies and by the protestations that they are not responsible and cannot curb the terrorists. I repeat that if the Jewish community really wanted to put an end to the crimes it could do so by co-operating with us. I have accordingly decided that as from the receipt of this letter all Jewish places of entertainment, cafés, restaurants, shops and private houses are out of bounds. No British soldier will have any contact with any Jew, and duty contacts will be made as short as possible and will be limited to the duty concerned. I understand that these measures will create difficulties for the troops, but I am certain that if my reasons are explained to them, they will understand their duty and will punish the Jews in the manner this race dislikes as much as any, by hitting them in the pocket, which will demonstrate our disgust for them.'

When the text of this letter came into the hands of the Irgun they lost no time in having copies posted all over the cities of Palestine: in their view it illustrated the venomous anti-Semitism of their adversaries. In America a *Washington Post* editorial saw it as a Nazi line of argument, blaming all Jews for the crimes of the Irgun: 'The whole farrago, with its smears and its intimidation, was written in bile and malice and was the work of a weak rather than a strong man.' Other American newspapers expressed similar views, and letters were sent to the British Embassy. 'Implicit in much of this comment,' reported Ambassador Inverchapel, 'which in some instances links General Barker's remarks to Mr. Bevin's words about Jews not being wanted in New York, is the idea that the British Government is really anti-Semitic.' (FO 371 52548)

31

The British military response to the King David episode was swift and powerful. Major R.D. Wilson described Operation 'Shark' as 'the largest-scale operation of its type ever to take place in Palestine'.

In the early hours of 30 July four army brigades (about 20,000 soldiers), together with police, threw a cordon around Tel Aviv and then proceeded to divide the town into sectors with barbed wire and guard posts. For four days a curfew confined the inhabitants to their houses, permitting two hours each evening for essential shopping. The Divisional Operation Order directed: '6 Airborne Division and attached troops, in conjunction with the Palestine Police, will cordon Tel Aviv and the Jewish quarter of Jaffa, and will thoroughly search every house and building with a view to checking up on all inhabitants and detaining any suspects.' 'The essential feature of the operation,' wrote Wilson, 'was that every house, attic, cellar and basement in Tel Aviv had to be searched, and every inhabitant old or young, healthy or infirm, had to be screened by the police.'

> 'There were three methods of screening. The first was by the searching teams which went methodically up each street. Each household was first assembled in possession of their identity cards, in one room, while the rest of the house was searched, probably in the presence of the householder. Then all except the aged and the children were escorted to the Battalion screening teams. Here they were further segregated, and all doubtful ones (the majority of males between the ages of 15 and 60) were taken to the expert screening teams at Brigade Headquarters ... All

suspects and persons who were unable to give a satisfactory account of themselves were sent to the detention camp at Rafah under military escort . . . In the course of the operation, which was completed without a hitch in four days, approximately one hundred thousand persons were screened at battalion level and about ten thousand at brigade level; 787 were detained and sent to the detention camp at Rafah. There, further thorough screening continued with the object of releasing any innocent persons who had been detained . . .' (op. cit., pp. 70–71)

The 6th Airborne Division had been assigned to Palestine in the late autumn of 1945. Initially their Main Divisional Headquarters were established near Gaza. Before their first clash with the Irgun on the night of 31 October their problems were of a more domestic nature.

'The camps themselves,' wrote Wilson, 'were almost primitive, and the Divisional Engineers worked unceasingly to improve them. The main reason for this state of affairs was that whenever a camp was left vacant (and these were taken over in that condition), the Arabs would descend on it by day and night and carry off every moveable fitting . . . One of the first lessons to be learned was the safeguarding of property. This was almost a science in itself and the battle of wits on either side went on unceasingly. The custody of arms was the main problem. After that came all other articles which could be removed by any number of Arabs working quite noiselessly during the hours of darkness. At this stage the problem was confined to pilferage by Arabs only. The Arab worked by stealth, and very rarely attacked sentries. He was a specialist at penetrating the best defences undetected, and after visiting one or more tents occupied by sleeping soldiers, left silently with his loot. The risk of his being shot in so doing was small deterrent.

'From time to time, and particularly as the end of the Mandate approached, camps would be closed down. Within a few days, not only any fittings which remained, but the very structure of the huts, cookhouses and the ablutions themselves would vanish into the desert, laden on the backs of the Bedouin and his ass. The only signs left which suggested that there had ever been a camp were a few tent hard-standings.

'Instances at first were not rare in which individuals (in one case a Commanding Officer) would wake in the morning to find their bed and the blankets over them were the only articles left in the tent or hut. Pistols could disappear from under pillows, and even tents themselves if unoccupied would vanish without trace on a dark night. These operations would take place while sentries prowled around the camp, and were only curtailed by the installation of perimeter lighting and searchlights.' (op. cit., p. 6)

On 14 November 1945, the 3rd Parachute Brigade was ordered to occupy Tel Aviv, where 30,000 Jews were protesting against Bevin's statement of policy published the previous day. The Brigade was withdrawn on 19 November, after six Jews had been killed and sixty wounded. According to Bethell, many of the Jewish casualties were young and a few were children, which provoked the Hebrew newspaper *Davar* to print a cartoon showing a surgeon in a ward and the caption: 'Good marksmen, these English, not to miss such small targets.' The paper was suspended for this insolence.

For the next two years the 6th Airborne was engaged almost continuously in actions against Jewish settlements suspected of being involved in illegal immigration, or against the ships and crews bringing the immigrants. On the night of 22/23 November a naval patrol vessel boarded a Greek schooner, the S.S. *Demetrius*, after she had landed a number of Jews on the coast about 12 miles north of Tel Aviv. They had escaped into nearby settlements, and the 6th Airborne Division was called in to assist the British Army's searches for the fugitives.

Wilson has listed the detachments employed in these cordon and search operations. To the north of the spot where the *Demetrius* had been boarded were assembled the 1st Battalion The Loyal Regiment, 2nd Battalion The North Staffordshire Regiment (both 2nd Infantry Brigade), 1st Battalion The Argyll and Sutherland Highlanders, 1st Battalion The Royal Ulster Rifles (both 6th Airlanding Brigade), 2nd/7th Battalion The Middlesex Regiment, 1st Reconnaissance Regiment, 6th Battalion The Gordon Highlanders, and one company 1st Battalion The Hertfordshire Regiment. In the south, 8th Parachute Battalion had been reinforced by 3rd Parachute Battalion, and 2nd Battalion The Oxfordshire and Buckinghamshire Light Infantry (placed under command of 3rd Parachute Brigade from 6th Airlanding Brigade). One squadron 3rd The King's Own Hussars was placed under command of each brigade of the Division taking part, and 195 Airlanding Field Ambulance and 224 Parachute Field Ambulance each supported their respective brigades.

In the face of this imposing assemblage the reader will not be surprised to learn that when at '1120 hours (on 26 November) the troops were ordered into the settlements all resistance became passive' (despite the fact that the Jews 'were armed with bricks and clubs'). At Shefayim, to the south, the troops used tear gas and resorted to baton charges to effect an entry into the settlement: 900 of the inhabitants were arrested and placed under guard. At Rishpon the troops felt obliged to open fire on a crowd. The searches at the settlements were completed by 1700 hours, and the troops withdrew, leaving six Jews killed and some 42 wounded. 160 Jews were sent to Athlit for further interrogation.

Operation 'Pintail', carried out by 3rd Parachute Brigade, with 4

Parachute Brigade under command, on 29 December, was launched against Tel Aviv, where 1,500 persons were subjected to a detailed investigation and 59 were taken into custody. A similar raid on Rishon-le-Zion on 8 January 1946 resulted in the detention of 55 suspects. During the two years or so in which the 6th Airborne operated in Palestine, they were involved in more than 70 similar operations, mostly of the 'Cordon and Search' type, but also, in the second half of the term, concerned with the interception and transhipment of 'illegal' immigrants.

The armed clashes in which the troops were involved were in the earlier period, at least, with the two dissident organisations, who distanced themselves from the plea made by Weizmann on 6 July 1946, for a suspension of all activities against the British. On 16 December 1946, he confronted the issue at the Zionist Congress in Geneva, aware of the changes in attitudes which had resulted from British policies on Palestine.

'The frustration of our creative impulses in Palestine,' he wrote, 'with all its demoralizing effects had its repercussions on the Zionist movement everywhere . . . The twenty-second Congress therefore had a special character . . . the absence – among very many delegates – of faith, or even hope, in the British Government, and a tendency to rely on methods never known or encouraged among Zionists before the war. These methods were referred to by different names: "resistance", "defence", "activism". But whatever shades of meaning may have been expressed by these terms – and the distinctions were by no means clear – one feature was common to all of them: the conviction of the need for fighting against British authority in Palestine – or anywhere else, for that matter. My stand on these matters was well known; I made it quite clear at the Congress. I stated my belief that our justified protest against our frustrations, against the injustices we had suffered, could have been made with dignity and force, yet without

trucking to the demoralizing forces in the movement.' (op.
cit., pp. 542–43)

At the conference he had spoken with greater passion,
declaiming:

'If you think of bringing the redemption nearer by un-Jewish
methods, if you lose faith in hard work and better days, then
you commit idolatry and endanger what we have built . . .
Zion shall be redeemed in Judgement – and not by any
other means.'

32

Weizmann's views were rejected by the majority of the delegates at the Congress: in Palestine the conflict between the dissidents and the British Army escalated. Two 16-year-old Irgun boys were convicted in December for carrying arms during a bank raid and were sentenced to 18 years' imprisonment.

These sentences may possibly have reflected a response to the approach by Major-General Montgomery and Commander-in-Chief Miles Dempsey to the Cabinet on 20 November 1946, for harsher measures against the 'terrorists'. (CAB 127/280) Attlee responded by approving a process which would allow the army and the military courts to take sterner measures than had previously been the case. This decision would appear to be in strong contrast to a War Office minute of 23 February 1946, on the subject of the war trials at Nuremberg, pointing out that those who received heavy sentences 'would become martyrs, and those who were given small punishments might come to regard them as an honour.' (WO 32/12208)

Certainly the sentence passed in March 1946 on Paul Heinen, a Nazi found guilty of 'a crime against humanity', of 'two years and one month's penal servitude and three years loss of all civil rights' (FO 371/55771) might seem to be lenient when compared with a British army sentence of 18 years' imprisonment on a 16-year-old for carrying a gun in a bank raid. The judge who imposed this latter penalty could not have been aware of Sir Basil Newton's comment, on 17 June, that 'if sentences err on the side of leniency that is a fault on the right side,' (FO 371/57548) but of course Sir Basil was talking about Nuremberg, not Palestine.

Sir Patrick Dean, however, did not share this view, commenting critically to the War Office on 18 June on the low sentences, often of 'a few months only' for 'particularly atrocious murder'. (FO 371/57671) Of the 177 Nazi criminals found guilty at Nuremberg of crimes against humanity, 12 received death sentences. Of the 1,085 Nazis who were found guilty of war crimes in the British Occupation Zone (which included Belsen), 240 were sentenced to death. But only about half of these sentences were actually carried out.

On 27 December Benjamin Kimche was flogged. Begin had published a warning that if the sentence was carried out 'every officer of the British occupation army in Eretz Israel will be liable to be punished in the same way', and on 29 December Major Brett of the 2nd Parachute Brigade was taken from a hotel lobby in Nathanya to a remote spot, where he was given 18 strokes and then released, about an hour after he had been abducted. Begin later wrote: 'There were no more floggings in this country', but there was retaliation in England, with a synagogue in Dollis Hill, London, broken into and vandalised.

On 30 December the 1st Parachute Brigade, the 8th Parachute Battalion, and the 3rd Hussars descended on the south-east part of Petah Tiqva and, after screening 939 of the inhabitants, detained 19 males; while at the same time the 2nd Parachute Brigade with one Squadron 12th Lancers raided Gevah and Ramat Tiomkin (south of Natanya) and arrested 24 males. For the next four days these raids continued: 18 males were arrested at Rishon-le-Zion on 31 December, and 2,242 persons were screened in Tel Aviv on 1 January and 47 males arrested. During the following two days Rehovot and three other locations received similar attention, resulting in the screening of more than 4,000 persons and the arrest of a further 83 males.

During the rest of the month the 6th Airborne Division was engaged in snap searches and road checks which resulted in the arrest of numerous suspects, while on the nights of 27 and 28 January curfews were imposed on Hadar ha-Carmel and 241 curfew-breakers were arrested. On 6 February the 9th Parachute Battalion descended on a soccer match at Haifa, rounding up 8,000 spectators, detaining 55.

In the light of all this activity it is small wonder that the Cabinet Defence Committee, meeting on 1 January, came to the conclusion 'that to continue this policy in Palestine in present circumstances placed the Armed Forces in an impossible position'. It is not clear whether the 'present circumstances' included the factors introduced into the 'Top Secret' memorandum on Middle East Oil which was circulated to the Cabinet on 7 January by its authors, Ernest Bevin and Emanuel Shinwell (the Minister of Fuel and Power). The memorandum included charts which illustrated 'the vital importance for Great Britain and the British Empire of the oil resources of this area' and stressed the grave risks of offending the Arabs 'by appearing to encourage Jewish settlement and to endorse the Jewish aspiration for a separate State.'

This last was a reference to the Jewish support for the partition solution, which Bevin opposed. 'The certainty of Arab hostility to partition is so clear,' he wrote in a further 'Top Secret' memorandum (dated 14 January) and the consequences of permanently alienating the Arabs would be so serious, that partition must on this ground be regarded as a desperate remedy.' It would 'contribute to the elimination of British influence from the vast Moslem area between Greece and India . . . it would also jeopardize the security of our interests in the increasingly important oil production in the Middle East'. (CAB 129/16) When the Cabinet met on 15 January, the Minister of Defence, A.V. Alexander, submitted that if Britain had to choose between the Arabs and the Jews, 'it was vital for us to retain the goodwill of the Arab world.' (CAB 128/11)

Within the Cabinet both the Colonial Secretary, Arthur Creech

Jones, and the Minister of Health, Aneurin Bevan, expressed their disagreement with these views. At the Cabinet meeting on January 20 Shinwell, too, cast doubts on the reliability of a unitary State with an Arab majority in Britain's Middle East strategy. Finally, on 14 February, Bevin announced that, in view of the deadlock, he would pass the problem to the United Nations. On 27 April the United Kingdom Delegation addressed a letter to the Acting Secretary-General of the United Nations, requesting that the question of Palestine be placed on the agenda of the next regular session of the General Assembly. The letter also indicated that the United Kingdom would submit to the General Assembly an account of their administration of the Palestine Mandate and would ask the Assembly to make recommendations under Article 10 of the Charter, concerning the future Government of Palestine. A Special Committee was appointed by the General Assembly consisting of the representatives of Australia, Canada, Czechoslovakia, Guatemala, India, Iran, Netherlands, Peru, Sweden, Uruguay and Yugoslavia. It held its first meeting at the interim headquarters of the United Nations at Lake Success, New York, on Monday, 26 May 1947, and arrived in Palestine in stages on 14 and 15 June. On Monday 16 June the Committee met at the Y.M.C.A. Building in Jerusalem, and there received a cablegram from the Secretary-General of the United Nations advising the decision of the Arab Higher Committee to abstain from collaboration with the Special Committee. After failing in its attempts to influence a reversal of the Arab Higher Committee's decision, the Special Committee resolved to invite the Arab States to express their views on the question of Palestine, and letters of acceptance were received from Egypt, Iraq, Lebanon, Syria and Saudi Arabia, with the information that Beirut had been designated as the place of meeting.

A few weeks before the arrival in Jerusalem of the Special Committee, four Irgun men had been taken from Jerusalem and hanged in Acre. One of these four was Dov Gruner, who, severely wounded, had been captured after an Irgun raid on the police fortress at Ramat Gan. He was tried and sentenced to death by hanging by a Military Court on 2 January 1947: the sentence had been confirmed on Friday 25 January, and the execution fixed for 29 January.

On Sunday 27 January the Jerusalem detachment of Irgun captured a British Intelligence Officer, Major Collins, and on the following day the Irgun 'arrested' Mr. Justice Windham while he was in the process of trying a court case in Tel Aviv. On the evening of 28 January it was announced that the Commander-in-Chief, General Barker, had consented to postpone indefinitely the execution of the sentence of Don Gruner, ostensibly to enable him to lodge an appeal with the Privy Council, and the Irgun accordingly released their hostages.

An appeal for Gruner's reprieve was submitted to the Privy Council by his uncle, Mr. Frank Gruner of the United States, and rejected. At the end of March Gruner was joined in the condemned cell by Yechiel Drezner, Mordechai Alkoshi and Eliezer Kashani, who had been arrested in December after the flogging of a Brigade Major and three sergeants on 29 December. When the sentence of death was passed on these men, 'Palestine was swept by rumours that these were to be the first of a series of hangings, that the British were preparing to massacre. Barker was supposed to have boasted at one of Katie Antonius's parties: 'I will hang a hundred Jews and there will be peace in Palestine.' He denies that he ever said such a thing, but his generally favourable attitude to the use of the death penalty in that situation is shown by his confirmation of the three latest death sentences two days after they were passed, on the actual day of his departure.' (Bethell, op. cit., p. 302)

Before Drezner was hanged he managed to smuggle out an account of the treatment the three men had received after their capture. They had been travelling in a car when it ran into a

212

barbed-wire barrier, and were immediately surrounded by troops.

'We had no choice but to leave the car with our hands up. Eliezer got a bullet in his back, and Mordechai (the driver) in the shoulder . . . As we came out I got a blow in the back and rolled into the ditch. As I lay I heard a revolver shot and I saw a soldier pointing his revolver at Mordechai. He fired, missed Mordechai, and killed his brother-Britisher. He at once hit Mordechai over the head with his revolver and threw him on to me in the ditch. We both got to our feet while, with their revolvers trained on us, they kicked us. We heard more shots. I thought they would finish us off . . .

'Then began the chapter of beatings which ended only the next day at seventeen hours – about twenty hours consecutively. Amid blows we were taken into a small armoured car, each of us guarded by a soldier. The guards at once emptied our pockets, ordering us to keep our hands up. They took everything: our watches, about fifty pounds in cash, purses and notebooks, pens and pencils, even a handkerchief and a comb. When they had done this they all began to hit us. They aimed particularly at our faces and stomachs. When we doubled up from blows to the stomach they would hit us in the face to straighten us up again. I remember how my nose ran blood like a tap and the soldier called out happily: ''I have broken his nose . . .''

'They began an organized attack for which they had apparently got an officer's permission or orders. They hit each of us in turn and then all together. Four or five soldiers took part in this. When they got tired they were relieved by others. They hit us with their fists in the head and the feet, and they kicked us in all parts of the body not even omitting the testicles This went on until late at night. An officer

213

came in then and ordered them to stop hitting us, to wash us and give us blankets for sleeping . . . But no sooner had we dozed off than the guard came, kicked us awake and pulled off the blankets. We had such visits about every fifteen minutes . . .

'A doctor, a short elderly man, looked at our wounds and asked the soldiers if they wanted to go on "playing" with us. The soldiers replied in the affirmative. "All right, then," said the doctor. "I'll bandage their wounds after-wards" . . . At about nine o'clock they washed us again and gave each of us a pair of trousers. The same doctor came again . . . and had plasters put on two of us. After that a police officer came, accompanied by the Jewish officer Karlick and several detectives. They hardly questioned us, only asked our names and addresses . . .' (Begin, pp. 269– 72)

The Select Committee reported that during their sessions they had received appeals for securing a commutation of death sentences and had reached agreement on two points: that while it was beyond the terms of reference of UNSCOP to interfere with the judicial administration in Palestine, the Committee should take some step to point out that the execution of death sentences might have repercussions on the task entrusted to them. The concern was to be communicated to the Mandatory Power through the Secretary-General of the United Nations.

33

Two days before the Irgun men had been hanged in the Acre prison, three Jews were killed by a Royal Navy boarding party attempting to transport them to Cyprus after their ship, the *Guardian*, with 2,552 'illegal' immigrants aboard, had been intercepted at Haifa. The *Guardian* was one of the many immigrant ships which had sailed for Palestine during 1947. The motor sailing vessel *Mercia*, with 664 immigrants aboard, had been intercepted on the high seas nine miles west of Caesarea by the destroyer *Chieftain*. The passengers attempted to resist the armed boarding party by throwing bottles: the Royal Navy replied first with tear-gas canisters and then with warning small-arms fire. One Jew was wounded by a ricochet bullet and of three others injured by stick blows to the head, one died before the boarding was accomplished. (FO 371 61802)

During the following four weeks 807 immigrants in the *San Miguel*, 1,416 on the *Haim Arlosoroff*, and 601 on the *Abriel*, were similarly intercepted and sent to Cyprus. On 30 March 1,750 immigrants from the *San Felipe* were caught by the Navy and diverted to Cyprus, and in the following two months over four thousand 'illegals' from the *Galata*, the *Trade Winds*, the *Orletta* and the *Anal* suffered the same fate. The conflict between British and Jews on the seas and in the Land grew in intensity and bitterness.

At that time twenty-nine key Irgun men were in the Acre prison. It was a fortress with a place in history. In 1799 it had withstood a siege by the forces of Napoleon. In 1840 it had taken the combined fleets from Britain, Austria and Turkey, under the joint command of Sir Charles Napier, to capture it from the Egyptians.

On 14 April 1947, the British transferred to the safety of this formidable fortress four Irgun men from their condemned cell in Jerusalem.

On 4 May the Irgun carried out one of its most daring and successful operations by breaking into the heavily-guarded fortress and releasing from their captivity forty-one Jewish prisoners in addition to 214 Arab convicts. The 1st Parachute Brigade of the 6 Airborne Division went swiftly into action and were successful in intercepting a truck carrying thirteen Irgun men at a road block. Eight of the Irgun men were killed: the remaining five, severely wounded, were arrested.

Three of these were brought before the Military Court in Jerusalem. At their trial, one of them, Avshalom Haviv, reminded the judges of a letter by Bernard Shaw printed in the *Daily News* of 10 May 1916, referring to the execution of five Irishmen who had fallen into British hands during the Irish rising. Shaw had then written: 'My own view is that the men who were shot in cold blood, after their capture or surrender, were prisoners of war, and that it was, therefore, entirely incorrect to slaughter them. An Irishman resorting to arms to achieve the independence of his country is doing only what Englishmen will do, if it be their misfortune to be invaded and conquered by the Germans. The fact that he knows that his enemies will not respect his rights if they catch him, and that he must, therefore, fight with a rope round his neck, increases his risk, but adds to the same measure to his glory in the eyes of his compatriots and of the disinterested admirers of patriotism throughout the world.'

Another of the three, Yaacov Weiss, who in Hungary had saved hundreds of Jews from the Nazis, warned the judges that the barbarous treatment of the wounded Irgun prisoners at Acre would inevitably result in retaliation. 'And though we shall not compare with you,' he declared, 'in the maltreatment of wounded men and in sadism, you will, for the rest, be paid in full.' On 16 June 1947, the three British officers acting as judges condemned all three defendants to death, and they were hanged on 29 July. Within 48 hours of their execution the Irgun, rejecting Zionist pleas to spare the lives of the hostages they were holding, and the declaration of the Vaad Leumi (the Jewish National Council) that any act of reprisal would be 'a blood-thirsty deed contrary to all human standards', hanged two British sergeants.

This action brought world-wide condemnation. The Zionist writer Jon Kimche declared that the Irgun leaders had proved themselves worthy of the award of a Streicher Medal, if such a thing existed. The *Palestine Post* of 1 August published the Jewish Agency's condemnation of 'the dastardly murder of two innocent men by a set of criminals.' But Begin was unrepentant, writing: 'We repaid our enemy in kind. We had warned him again and again. He had callously disregarded our warnings. He forced us to answer gallows with gallows.' Later he confessed:

> 'It caused great pain in our hearts, but the decision of the high command was unanimous. We had to save our men. We intended to carry on military operations and we knew that some of our men might be taken prisoner by the British. In fact, many men of the Irgun were captured. Eighteen members of Lehi were captured and sentenced to death. But all the sentences were commuted. Why was this possible only after our retaliation? Why was it possible to refrain from executing Irgun and Lehi men for nearly a year after the two sergeants were killed? I think that by what we did we must have saved the lives of several dozen men of the Underground. It was a cruel deed to hang the two sergeants, but it was inescapable.'

Anti-Semitic mobs in England were quick to register their own response to the killing of the two sergeants. The Derby synagogue was burnt down, riots broke out in many of the larger cities, and Jewish premises were attacked in several areas. In Palestine the rioting was much more serious, with gangs of soldiers and policemen descending on Tel Aviv on the evening of 31 July. 'The depredations of these rioters consisted of window smashing, smashing the windows of omnibuses, overturning vehicles and assaulting members of the Jewish community.' (CO 733 477)

At 9 p.m. 12 soldiers beat up a taxi-driver and stole his vehicle. About an hour later six armoured vehicles entered Tel Aviv and started firing indiscriminately. Deputy Superintendent R.S. Hainsworth reported of the attack on a bus, in which one Jew was killed and three others wounded, that: 'This shooting was deliberate, felonious and entirely without justification.' A few minutes later police from an armoured car attacked a café in the Neve Shaanan quarter and then fired at another bus in the Hatikva area, killing three Jews. Five minutes later policemen raided another café. As they left, they exploded a hand grenade: the dead body of a Jew was later found nearby.

Hainsworth made every effort to find those responsible, but ultimately confessed: 'I have been met with little but evasions and untruths . . . The required evidence of identification is in the possession of certain British police personnel and these decline to divulge it.' No criminal charges were brought against the policemen who had caused the five Jewish deaths and committed the other acts of violence which had been listed. In America a former Under-Secretary of State, Sumner Welles, argued in the columns of the *New York Herald Tribune* on 12 August that though the hanging of the two sergeants was morally wrong it should be viewed against the 'judicial murder' of three young Jews who had helped their friends to escape from Acre fortress, the torturing to death by a notorious British strong-arm squad of Alexander Rubowitz, and the simple fact that the British administration in Palestine was 'shot through from top to bottom with anti-Semitism' as shown by the Tel Aviv pogrom on 31 July. If High

Commissioner Cunningham thought that the Tel Aviv retaliation was understandable, Sumner Welles took the view that, given the nature of British rule in Palestine, the murder of the two sergeants was equally understandable.

It was against this background of violence and murder that the United Nations Special Committee on Palestine had to conduct its meetings. Four of its members personally witnessed the arrival in Haifa of the immigrant ship *President Warfield*, renamed *Exodus* by the Jews. They were accompanied to the scene by Aubrey (Abba) Eban, one of the two Jewish liaison officers to the Committee, who has described the 'gruesome operation' which the Committee members were called upon to witness.

'The Jewish refugees,' he wrote, 'had decided not to accept banishment with docility. If any one had wanted to know what Churchill meant by a "squalid war", he would have found out by watching British soldiers using rifle butts, hose pipes and tear gas against the survivors of the death camps. Men, women and children were forcibly taken off to prison ships, locked in cages below decks and sent out of Palestine waters.' The four members of UNSCOP returned to Jerusalem 'pale with shock ... I could see that they were preoccupied with one point alone: if this was the only way the British Mandate could continue, it would be better not to continue at all.'

And, indeed, the first of the 'Recommendations Approved Unanimously' by the Committee in its Report of 31 August 1947, was that 'The Mandate for Palestine shall be terminated at the earliest practical date'. They further recommended that 'Independence shall be granted in Palestine at the earliest practicable date' and that 'Palestine within its present borders, following a transitional period of two years from 1 September 1947, shall be constituted into an independent Arab State, an independent Jewish State, and the City of Jerusalem'; the last to include 'the surrounding villages and towns, the most eastern of which to be Abu Dir; the most southern Bethlehem; the most western Ein Karim and the most northern Shu'fat.'

34

The trauma experienced by Emil Sandstrom and Valado Simic, the UNSCOP delegates from Sweden and Yugoslavia, when they witnessed the arrival in Haifa of the *President Warfield* will have been shared world-wide by those who were able to see the films and the photographs taken at the quayside. After the women and children had disembarked, the stretcher cases were taken to hospital. Two hundred Jews were in urgent need of medical attention. Two more had been killed by the boarding parties; a third, the ship's mate, Bill Bernstein, had been so severely coshed over the head that he was now dying. A medical team under Surgeon-Lieutenant D.C. Bett had found twenty-eight Jews in need of hospitalisation.

When, six days earlier, the *President Warfield* had reached the open sea, Bevin had announced that 'we intended to make an example of this ship by obliging her to return to a French port with all her passengers.' He warned Paul Ramadir, the French Prime Minister, that French indulgence to Jewish 'unauthorized persons and troublemakers' was likely to cause alarm among France's own North African Arabs. 'Was it too much to ask,' he demanded, 'that the French Government should reciprocate in the matter of this illegal traffic, which was in any case largely a financial racket controlled from New York?' (FO 371 61815)

When, on 9 July, the *President Warfield* left the harbour of Sete, some 80 miles or so west of Marseilles, she had been joined first by the Royal Navy frigate *Mermaid* and then by the destroyer *Cheviot*. On 13 July the *Ajax* joined the procession, and on 15 July the *Cheviot* was relieved by the destroyer *Childers*. When the *Chieftain* was further added to this imposing escort, the captain of the *President Warfield* suggested that his ship was enjoying a better naval escort than that of the British King and Queen, at that time on a voyage to South Africa.

At this stage of the operation the Royal Navy was assuming that they would be going through the usual process of interception (once the *President Warfield* had entered territorial waters) and transhipment of the immigrants to Cyprus for internment. They had as yet no knowledge of the Colonial Secretary's decision, which had been communicated to the High Commissioner, Sir Alan Cunningham, that the ship was to be boarded off Palestine and escorted back to France by the Royal Navy, informing him: 'It will be most discouraging to the organizers of this traffic, if the immigrants in the first ship for some weeks to evade the British "blockade" end up returning whence they came.' Few would argue with this presumption.

By 17 July the *Cheviot* had been replaced with the *Cardigan Bay*, and the boarding parties of the four destroyers were undergoing intense physical training for the approaching encounter. Because of the *President Warfield*'s shallow draught, which would permit her to sail in shallow waters which the destroyers could not enter, the warships made their attempt to board the *President Warfield* while she was still 20 miles west of Gaza, and in the early hours of that morning the sailors succeeded in getting aboard and seizing the wheelhouse.

The *President Warfield*'s captain protested that his ship was a long way from territorial waters, and that his assailants were guilty of an act of piracy. But the battle continued while the ship sailed on. The captain of the *Childers*, Lieut.-Commander Tony Bailey, later reported: 'The *PW* certainly presented a fantastic spectacle as she steamed at full speed through the night, keeled under rudder, with two enormous Star of David banners streaming from her mastheads and illuminated by our 20-inch searchlights. Her wailing siren gave the impression of a wounded cow bellowing through the night, as it fled from some unknown terror.'

'Our job was to hurl teargas grenades and fearsome pyrotechnics into every opening in the ship as we drew alongside,' wrote W.J. Williamson, a petty officer on the *Chequers*. 'This was "to wear the buggers out", we were told. I can assure you that I now often cringe at the memory, considering that the below-deck spaces were packed with women and children.' By 4.30 a.m. the captain of the *President Warfield* had surrendered his command, and half an hour later the ship was placed under British control.

'Both sides nevertheless felt that they had won a victory,' wrote Bethell. 'The Royal Navy were glad to have maintained the efficiency of their blockade, overcoming with courage and ingenuity the fierce resistance of the Jewish passengers and crew. Bailey believes that it can be claimed that the arrest of the *President Warfield* was technically the most difficult boarding operation ever carried out in peace or war. Both he and Watson, speaking (they believe) for all the British officers involved, express their admiration for the skill and imaginative approach of Aranne and his crew, as well as for their resolution in defence against the largest and most highly-trained squadron ever employed to arrest a single ship.' (op. cit., p. 332)

As the UNSCOP delegates and crowds of newspaper correspondents watched, the women and children – numbering almost 2,000 – disembarked first. They were followed by over 1,000 teenagers and 1,600 men, and by the early hours of the next morning, 19 July all 4,500 had been consigned to three cage ships. On the next day the *Palestine Post* headed its description of their departure: 'Expected in Cyprus this morning.'

It was not until six hours after the prison ships had sailed that it was revealed to their passengers that they were being taken, not to Cyprus, but back to Europe. Bevin had decided, on 12 July, that they would be returned to Port-de-Bouc, which they had left on 9 July, and on 19 July had informed Paris that 'Guards have been instructed to use whatever force may be required in order to deliver immigrants into French hands.' (FO 371 61817) On the previous day Ambassador Duff Cooper had warned Bevin that

'Forcible removal from British ships at a French port is likely to provide lurid anti-British propaganda, to which French public opinion may well be receptive in view of memories of German persecution of the Jews under occupation. Man in street is totally ignorant of Palestine problems and sees only in these illicit immigrants survivors of a persecuted race seeking refuge in their national home.' (FO 371 61816)

Cunningham had remarked that it was 'most undesirable that any admission should be made that vessel was boarded on high seas', but the New York *P.M.* was quick to claim that, since the ship was seized outside territorial waters, the killing of Bernstein was murder, and on 24 July at a meeting in New York's Madison Square Park attended by 20,000 people there was talk of arresting the British officers involved on charges of piracy. (FO 317 61758) When the prison ships arrived at the French port they were questioned by the Reuters correspondent, Boyd France, and asked whether they intended to land. They answered with shouts of 'No!' and put up flags bearing the Star of David, and one, a British naval ensign, decorated with a black swastika.

Duff Cooper's fears of 'lurid anti-British propaganda' on the part of the French were swiftly realised. *Humanité* described the three ships as 'a floating Auschwitz', and *Combat* as 'cages for wild beasts'. *Franc-Tireur*'s cartoon, with the caption of 'Alert in the Mediterranean', showed eight huge Royal Navy warships with flights of British aircraft converging on a tiny sailing dinghy flying the Star of David. But the Arab press voiced its approval of Britain's firm handling of the 4,500 immigrants, contrasting this show of strength with a former weakness which had permitted swarms of aliens to occupy Arab territories.

By 16 August Bevin had reached deadlock. The refugees had refused to go ashore: they could not be left indefinitely at Port-de-Bouc, and to send them back to Cyprus would be tantamount to admitting defeat. He informed his Washington and Paris ambassadors that the refugees would have to go to the Poppendorf Camp, near Lubeck!

'It seemed,' wrote Bethell, 'an act of calculated inhumanity to send Jewish survivors of concentration camps back to the country where these horrors had been perpetrated and where their relatives had died. Far from ''making an example'' of the *Exodus* and rallying the world against the organizers of illegal immigration, Bevin succeeded only in shocking the world community into deeper sympathy for the Zionist enterprise.' (op. cit., p. 343)

The refugees were halfway to Hamburg when the UNSCOP report of 31 August revealed the Committee's proposal to end the British Mandate for Palestine and the creation of independent Jewish and Arab States. The political committee of the Arab League declared the partition proposal to be a violation of the rights of the Palestine Arabs and a security threat to the Arab countries. On September 18 Bevin wrote that the 'proposal is so manifestly unjust to the Arabs that it is difficult to see how, in Sir Alexander Cadogan's words, we could reconcile it with our conscience.' He could see no response to the UNSCOP proposal other than a complete and unconditional British withdrawal. 'Britain could reconcile the proposed plan neither with her conscience nor with her national interest. She would therefore refuse to enforce it.'

35

On 29 November 1947, the General Assembly of the United Nations voted in favour of the UNSCOP proposals of 31 August by a majority of thirty three votes to thirteen, with ten abstentions (including Britain). A United Nations Palestine Commission of five nations was set up to aid the separate regimes recommended in the UNSCOP Report, but on 4 December a Cabinet meeting confirmed Bevin's policy of non-participation in the UN decision: Britain would not admit the new Commission to Palestine before 1 May; British rule would end on 15 May 1948; and total military withdrawal would be completed by 1 August.

Cadogan announced that Britain would not act against the General Assembly's two-thirds' majority vote, and would not obstruct the formation of militias, shadow Governments, land purchase or immigration recommendations made by the Assembly, but on the other hand would not assent to the setting-up of a new civil administration while the British were still in military occupation. The American delegate pointed out the anomaly involved in this statement, and the Chairman of the Partition Committee expressed the opinion that the British delegate had not helped to clarify the situation and had again caused delay.

On 16 October Crossman had told a Press conference that, if UNO did not act decisively and vigorously, 'Britain will keep her pledge and evacuate Palestine, but in a manner consistent with her imperial policy, which is based on wooing and appeasing the Arabs.' On 13 November Cadogan stated that 'civil administration would come to an end at any time after it became evident that no settlement acceptable to both Jews and Arabs had been reached by the Assembly of the United Nations. The British authorities would not, therefore, exercise administrative responsibilities during the transition period.'

The Arabs, for their part, were not slow to demonstrate their interpretation of Cadogan's statement. On the day following the partition vote at Lake Success they murdered seven Jews near Ramleh while travelling from Tel Aviv to Jerusalem. No attempt was made to apprehend those responsible, and the attacks in the area continued daily. A Jewish Agency request for police escorts for inter-urban convoys was rejected by the official concerned on the grounds that such a measure 'might be interpreted as British implementation of Partition'. Nor would the Government permit the Jewish Agency to use the armoured cars of the Jewish Settlement Police for escorting convoys of inter-urban travellers. When a settlement came under attack the Jewish police had to be rushed to the spot in open tenders, and on 11 December ten were killed in an ambush south of Bethlehem by a band of eighty Arabs armed with machine-guns when the Jews were going to the relief of Kfar Etzion, which had been under continuous attack by a force of over 1,000 Arabs.

The *Palestine Post* published a letter which a Jewish police officer had addressed to the Inspector-General of Police: 'At the funeral of the 10 Jews killed you did send two armoured cars: one in the front, the second to bring up the rear. Had you sent those two cars with the convoy there would probably have been no funeral to escort.'

This reluctance on the part of the Mandatory Government to appear as an agent in the implementation of the UN Assembly's Partition resolution was expressed in its passive submission to the control by Arab gangs of the entire area of the Old City of Jerusalem. Arab snipers established themselves behind the walls of the Great Mosque to keep the Jewish quarter under constant fire, while Jewish pedestrians passing the Jaffa Gate were attacked and killed. By early January the Arabs had established armed guards at the Jaffa, Damascus, New, Zion and St. Stephen's Gates.

This free hand given to the Arabs was not at the same time extended to the Jewish defence units. While hordes of Arab irregulars, in a motley of uniforms and bristling with a variety of weapons, held undisturbed sway in the Old City, the British police were conducting a sustained campaign against the Haganah. On 4 December they arrested fifteen Haganah youngsters, including two girls, in Julian's Way, Jerusalem, for carrying arms; and on 6 December the Haganah sentries who were guarding the Jewish Home for the Blind were likewise arrested. On 7 December, when Haganah was engaged in defending the Hatikva quarter of Tel Aviv against an Arab attack, the police intervened – to confiscate the arms used by the defenders.

On 12 December the Arab premiers met in Cairo and there decided that they would supply the Arab League's Military Committee with 10,000 rifles, together with other weapons and ammunition, and would organise the passage of 3,000 Arab volunteers through Syria into Palestine. One million pounds sterling would be given towards the cost of the 'defence of Palestine', and a technical committee would organise, train and equip the volunteers. Sir Ismail Safwat, an Iraqi General, was appointed Commander-in-Chief and set up his headquarters at el-Qudsieh, near Damascus. The Syrian army's training camp at el-Qatana would be the base for training, equipping and launching the volunteer army into Palestine.

Major R.D. Wilson records one of the earliest ventures on the part of these 'irregulars'. On 9 January 1948, they attacked the settlements of Dan and Kafr Szold. The troops were called in: Wilson's account of the engagements which followed makes quaint reading. 'A troop of armoured cars of 17th/21st Lancers was despatched to the scene of each engagement, where they both came under sporadic small-arms fire from the Arabs.' (Fortuitously, this appeared to be sufficiently good-natured as to avoid any British casualties, in contrast to the fire directed against the Jews, who suffered nine killed and wounded.) 'The troops replied to the Arabs sparingly at first, and more generously as the day lengthened and their patience diminished' (without, however, causing, according to Wilson's report, any known casualties). 'Eventually the heavy armament of the cars was brought into play and their two-pounder shells had a very salutary effect,' although Wilson fails to explain what this may have been, because (in spite of the very salutary effect?) 'In the middle of the morning there was a call for air support on Tel el Qadi, where the Arabs were in a strong position. In response to this request a number of Spitfires arrived soon after and carried out *dummy attacks* (added italics) on the target area. The moral effect even of unarmed fighters was for some time enough to disperse Arabs on occasions such as this. Later in the day troops of 1st Parachute Battalion joined in the battle with 3-in. mortars. The combined effect of the British counter-measures eventually persuaded the Arabs to call off their attacks and retire over the frontier,' leaving the Jews to bury their dead. 'The very successful outcome of the operation was largely due to the manner in which the situation was handled throughout by Lieutenant-Colonel H.C. Blackden, Officer Commanding The Mechanized Regiment, T.J.F.F. . . . For his conduct on this and many other occasions, he was later awarded the Distinguished Service Order.' (op. cit., p. 160)

It soon became obvious that there was to be very little interference with the Arab preparations for a major offensive. On 20 January the first battalion of Arab volunteers crossed the border into Palestine and set up headquarters near Nablus. Other battalions soon followed. Major Wilson has left an account of this 'Arab Liberation Army', as it became known:

'. . . by February, 1948, it was possible to gain some sort of picture of what in fact the A.L.A. then in Palestine, consisted.

'The strength of the "Army" by the end of February had perhaps reached 10,000, but even this figure might have been on the high side. Reinforcements were thought to be arriving from the neighbouring Arab states at the rate of 1,000 a month, so it was going to be some time before the force was likely to achieve spectacular results. All its members were trained up to a reasonable level and carried a firearm of some description, although there was no standardisation in that respect. The heavy equipment was thought to include a small number of pieces of varying calibre, a few armoured cars, perhaps a few tracked vehicles (carriers or light tanks) and no aircraft.

'The "Army" was organized into several "Divisions" which were named after past Arab successes in the field, or notable Arab leaders. The field commander at the time was one Fawzi Kawukji, a colourful guerrilla during the Arab Rebellion, whom the British had placed in exile. He established his headquarters in that part of the country known by the Arabs during their Rebellion as "The Dangerous (or Terror) Triangle" − Nablus-Jenin-Tulkarm − which he hoped to restore to its legendary fame in the forthcoming campaign against the Jews.

'In the "Army" was reported to be a number of skilled Europeans who occupied posts as instructors and commanders, but it is difficult to estimate how many there were . . . The Arab commanders by no means confined their attentions to their troops, but assumed authority over the whole of the Arab population in their areas. They issued edicts from time to time announcing their policy, and it took a strong and possibly foolhardy man to disagree with a "Liberation Army Officer".' (op. cit., pp. 181–82)

It may well be asked how it was possible that in a country garrisoned by tens of thousands of British troops an invading army of, say, 10,000 men, reinforced 'from the neighbouring Arab states at the rate of 1,000 per month' and supported by 'a small number of pieces (of artillery) of varying calibre, a few armoured cars' and perhaps a few tanks, could have in this way been permitted to establish itself for the avowed and well-publicised purpose of annihilating the Jewish population, under the very noses of the British administrators. The majority of the invaders were coming in across the Syrian border, from their training base at Qatana: Wilson recorded that at that time Blackden was 'responsible for the whole of the northern frontier'. The military authorities may have claimed that their resources in manpower were too extended to permit the effective guarding of the frontiers, and that they were powerless to interfere with the constant procession of troops, vehicles and supplies that were pouring across the northern borders, but on 1 January they had succeeded in mustering the 2nd Battalion The Middlesex Regiment, a Company 9th Parachute Battalion, one Battery 1st Royal Horse Artillery, one composite Battery Airborne Royal Artillery and two platoons 8th Parachute Battalion to cordon the town of Nahariya and to arrest 131 Jews on the suspicion of harbouring illegal immigrants. Presumably the Arab invaders were regarded as 'legal' immigrants, and could therefore be spared such intensive action.

A study of Major Wilson's reports may lead one to suspect the existence of a 'gentleman's agreement' between Kaukji and the British. He describes an attack by Kaukji's army on Tirat Tsvi, a Jewish settlement in the Jordan Valley, on the night of 15/16 February. The attackers had first cut the settlement's telephone wires, and the defenders had to send out lamp signals to a neighbouring settlement for help. The British sent in a platoon from the company of 1st Parachute Battalion together with a party of police. Major Wilson continues:

'At the Arab village of As Samariya, three miles west of the besieged settlement, the small British column met the Arab Headquarters and echelon. The situation was tense to start with but was soon brought under control when the British and Arab commanders went into conference. The Arab was instructed to withdraw immediately with the whole of his force, an order which would have been difficult to enforce had the Arabs chosen to ignore it. Fortunately, however, the Arab commander was under clear instructions from his own superior officer to avoid such an impasse, and he agreed to withdraw on one condition: in order not to lose face with the Jews he requested that the British column should simulate a battle by putting down a concentration of mortar and machine gun fire to a flank. This being a harmless request and not worth disputing, the British Commander (Major R. Steele) agreed, and at the appointed time the barrage was produced and the Arabs started to withdraw.

'At 1300 hours the platoon made its way to Tirat Tsvi where it found the Jews engaged in mopping-up operations. There was still firing in progress, and it appeared that either the orders for withdrawal had not reached some of the Arabs, or they were engaged in a protracted rearguard action. An area to the south-west of the settlement was still proving troublesome and the troops put down a concentration of mortar and machine-gun fire to speed the Arabs on their way. When the casualties were reckoned for each side the weight of the Jewish victory became obvious. The Arabs suffered some eighty casualties of which about half were killed, while the Jews lost one killed and two wounded.

'As can well be imagined, this reverse lowered morale somewhat in the ''Dangerous Triangle'' and a period of some six weeks was spent in reorganizing and recovering from the defeat. The Syrian Commander was relieved of his post the following day. Farther afield news of the attack spread through Arab towns and villages with customary speed, but the account became so distorted in the telling that soon the Arabs were convinced that the operation had been a resounding success rather than the miserable failure that it was. This habit of falsification and exaggeration, which was practised to such an extent by the Arabs, rarely affected the British troops one way or the other: when it did the effect could be either amusing or exasperating.

'On 26 February, a reconnaissance patrol of two armoured cars of the 3rd Hussars was ordered to try and find out whether it was possible for armoured vehicles to cross the Plain of Esdraelon from Ramat David to Lajun. The route took the patrol close to the Arab village of Kafr Lidd. When about 200 yards distant from the village, the two cars were engaged with intense small-arms fire by the inhabitants, some thirty of whom advanced from the village towards the patrol, firing as they came. The officer in command and two others of the patrol had been in the process of reconnoitring on foot the River (Brook) Qishon and were a short distance from their cars. Nevertheless, hastened somewhat by the Arabs, and covered with fire from the patrol, they succeeded in regaining their turrets without mishap. In order to avoid inflicting unnecessary casualties on the Arabs the patrol then withdrew.

'The following day the same officer with a small escort returned to Kafr Lidd, this time by the normal track leading to the village, which they reached without incident. Once they were identified as British the Arabs became very friendly. The officer then asked for an account of the shooting which had occurred the previous day. Thereupon he was treated by the Mukhtar to a dramatic account of how the village had been attacked by 300 fully-armed Jews supported by four armoured vehicles. After a bloody engagement in which 100 of the Jews had been killed, the attack had been broken up and the Jews put to flight. Arab casualties had been "very few". The officer had then explained that he had been the object of the Arabs' attacks and he wanted to know the reason why. The Arabs showed a suitable degree of astonishment and were definitely impressed by the harangue which followed, and explained that they must have mistaken the British patrol for Jews; they were most apologetic and the visit ended on a very cordial note with the customary coffee party.' (op. cit., pp. 184–86)

According to Jon Kimche, had the British G.O.C. Palestine, General Sir Gordon Macmillan,

'been authorised to take action against the Liberation Army infiltration or against its commander Fawzi el-Kaukji, he could have cleared them out of Palestine within forty-eight hours, but Macmillan had strict directives from London, signed by the Secretary of State for War, Emanuel Shinwell . . . Macmillan was forced into the humiliating position of negotiating a live-and-let-live understanding with Kaukji, which assured Kaukji of British non-intervention so long as the Liberation Army kept quiet.' (op. cit., p. 86)

The full measure of the understanding which appeared to exist between Kaukji and the British may never become known. Cecily Mackworth, an English journalist who came across him in Palestine in 1948, and then saw him shortly afterwards at the Orient Palace Hotel in Damascus, describes him in her book* as a man with 'a price on his head in Palestine – but I had seen him myself, on the Allenby Bridge, chatting with the customs officers before leading his convoy across the frontier and on to his earlier headquarters in Jericho.'

---

*The Mouth of the Sword, Routledge and Kegan Paul, 1949, p. 233

Cecily Mackworth's Press card enabled her to conduct her investigations in both Jewish and Arab areas, and ultimately to obtain an interview with King Abdullah. After visiting an Arab hospital in Jaffa, where she saw wounded men who had come to the country from Syria, Yugoslavia and other places, together with Germans from their Fundamentalist settlement at Sarona near Tel Aviv, she set out for Ramleh – 'the Arab stronghold, where Fawzi Bey el Kawukji had installed his headquarters'.

At Ramleh she was given a guide, 'an Algerian volunteer' whom she describes as 'homesick and told me that when Tel Aviv was captured and he had received his share of loot, he would use the money to visit Paris, the "gay city".' They were halted on the road out of Ramleh by 'a group of soldiers, wearing the khaki berets of one of the Scottish regiments . . . The soldiers showed no surprise at my presence and explained willingly, in thick Glasgow accents, that the Arabs had mined the road just round the corner, then ambushed a convoy of workers from Neve Jaakov on their way to Jerusalem.'

'"They're just finishing them off now," said one of them with professional indifference. I asked them what they were doing there, and they shrugged their shoulders: "We don't know anything about it." Disinterested, they stared at the hills, where more soldiers scurried about, in apparent meaningless activity, like bands of insects.' After a sudden volley of shots she 'came on a crowd of about a thousand Arabs, pressing around four shattered armoured lorries. The steel-plated walls of the lorries were so riddled with bullets that they looked like sieves. They were beginning to take fire, the flames licking slowly up the sides and little drifts of smoke went fluttering up into the air.

'There were Arabs of every kind – uniformed soldiers, old men with venerable beards, little boys clasping rifles longer than themselves, cloaked villagers. Others were closing in from the hills — isolated little figures, scampering from every direction over the stony ground, shooting into the air as they came. In the background, I could see several British armoured cars drawn up, with groups of soldiers standing by, either uncaring or powerless against the excited crowd

'Suddenly a small, thin figure in uniform had sprung to the roof of one of the British cars . . . The slit-like eyes, the puffed cheeks, the missing chin . . . it was Glubb Pasha. The figure on the roof began to harangue the crowd . . . At my elbow the Algerian translated: "He says: Allah commands you to have mercy on the wounded. For the love of Allah, have pity!" Hoarse cries of protest from the crowd, waving of rifles, a few cries of approval . . . menacing cries of anger . . . then an ambulance moved in . . .

'The lorries were burning brightly now. The Arabs had been scrambling over them, tossing out any objects they found. The possessions of the dead settlers lay in pathetic little heaps — a thermos flask, tin boxes containing sandwiches, books, a pair of girl's shoes. The Arabs snatched them, waving their souvenirs excitedly. Someone pushed a red-covered book, printed in Hebrew, into my hand.

'The British soldiers were dragging the bodies from the last of the cars, tossing them into a heap on the road, from which they were transferred onto one of the waiting Army lorries. I turned, trying to escape from the sight of those broken things, soaked and still dripping with their own blood, but the crowd forced me forward. They were hysterical now, blood-crazy, bending down to soak their hands in blood, then waving their dripping hands above their heads, breaking into dance, bounding and skipping . . .

'Next day, the presence of Glubb Pasha and of a number of high-ranking British officers at the Battle of Ataroth was confirmed in the Hebrew Press. They had been on their way to Ramleh, for a secret conference with Kawukji, when their convoy had been held up by the fighting on the road ... Fawzy Bey el Kawukji is a Syrian who received his education in Germany. Then, when war broke out, he went back to Germany and organized Hitler's paratroops, becoming one of the favourite heroes of young German womanhood and frequently figuring in a variety of becoming uniforms on the front page of the Nazi illustrated review, *Der Signal.*'

At the Orient Palace Hotel in Damascus she saw the 'Grand Mufti', who 'had come from Cairo with his bodyguard of six huge soldiers on a flying visit from seething Ramallah; the Iraqi General, Ishmael Safwad; Emile Ghoury, Chief of the Arab Executive in Palestine, and other political and military chiefs ... Then a little red-bearded man with neurotic eyes, who was Dixon, the British official who had broken out of the Acre fortress and escaped over the border after his condemnation a few months earlier for inciting British troops to desert and sell their arms to the Arabs ... Fawzy Kawukji ... was followed by his blonde German wife, dressed in the height of fashion ...' (pp. 220–30)

There must be an obvious temptation to research further into the mystery of this colourful person. It is only fair to issue a warning that the Colonial Office files of correspondence on 'Participation of Syrian Arabs in the Disturbances' (CO 793/27/75528/48) and 'Activities of Fawzi Kaukji' (CO 793/27/75528/82) are now marked: 'Destroyed Under Statute'. The reader must draw his own conclusions concerning the need for this measure.

A similar enigma embraces the career of the ex-Mufti. We have seen how openly he committed himself to the Nazi cause during the Second World War. There was a price on his head when, on 8 May 1945, he managed to cross the border into Switzerland.

Near Constance he was apprehended by the Swiss police, who drove him back into Germany, where he was captured by the French. With the former Vichy Ambassador De Brinon and others, he was brought to Paris in an American lorry.

A statement was issued that he would be handed over to the British authorities, but this was subsequently described as premature, on the grounds that the Iraqi Government was the authority competent to demand extradition on account of the part he had played in the April 1941 Baghdad pro-Nazi plot. Apparently the Iraq Government preferred not to be involved, and when the Yugoslav Government then requested his extradition as a war criminal they were persuaded by the Egyptian Government to abandon the request.

He was therefore consigned to languish in the luxury of a villa in the fashionable Paris suburb of Rambouillet, undisturbed until the following 26 February, when Mr. Hoy asked the Foreign Secretary in the House of Commons whether his attention had been drawn 'to the material recently produced at the trials of war criminals in Nuremberg about the role played by Haj Amin al-Husseini, former Mufti of Jerusalem, in instigating and encouraging the Nazi plan of exterminating European Jewry.'

The Under-Secretary for Foreign Affairs, Hector McNeill, replied: 'A special inquiry is being held to obtain accurate records of any relevant evidence that may have been given to the International Military Tribunal. The matter will be considered together with any other relevant matters.' While the matter was being 'considered' (nothing further was ever heard about this 'special inquiry'), the ex-Mufti turned up in Damascus. If indeed the British had ever seriously considered his extradition, the reasons for rejecting such a measure may be found in a Cabinet minute (128/2) that 'the balance of advantage was against putting these Palestine renegades on trial.'

In Damascus the ex-Mufti received a hero's welcome. 'The protracted *fantaseeya* in Palestine which commenced with news of his flight from France on 9 June is proof of his popularity,' wrote Martin Charteris. 'During the three-day celebration in his honour, Arab towns and Arab districts were beflagged and plastered with his photograph'. (WO 169 23022) He was in Cairo in September 1947 when the British sent two senior police officials to 'informally' discuss the question of partition with him, and to obtain his views. (FO 371 61835) It is not clear why the British would need to consult him at this stage, and he had made his views on partition abundantly and forcefully clear on a number of occasions, but some days after this meeting he turned up at Beirut.

There he was welcomed by the Prime Minister of Lebanon, who took him into his own home. In Beirut he ventilated his views on partition with greater vigour than he had expended on Giles and Briance, the two policemen, saying that the moment British forces were withdrawn from Palestine the Arabs should unite to ensure the complete annihilation of the Jews. (FO 371 61836) He attended the meeting of the Committee of the Arab League at Aley, in the Lebanon, in the early part of October, and demanded the establishment of a Palestinian Government which would conduct the struggle against the Jews. In this he received the immediate support of the Syrian and Lebanese leaders, who proceeded to organise arms and volunteers for a Palestinian army. Twenty-seven years after the Jerusalem pogrom which he had led, he was preparing, unpunished, to return to the scene of his crimes.

36

On 1 February 1948, the 6th Airborne were relieved of the responsibility for the transhipment of 'illegal' refugees intercepted when attempting to land in Palestine: this task now fell to the Royal Navy. During the previous four months the Army had been successful in transhipping over 20,000 Jews who had been intercepted in eight ships, ranging from 446 to over 7,600 tons. On 4 January 1948, in the last of these operations, they had moved some 15,000 Jewish refugees from the *Pan York* and the *Pan Crescent*. There were few casualties – no British – just one Jew killed and about a dozen wounded.

They were now free to concentrate their efforts elsewhere, and on the very day that the Royal Navy had assumed the transhipment burden the 8th/9th Parachute Battalion completed a successful operation in Haifa, where they arrested nine Jews 'for being in possession of a large quantity of arms.' The Arabs who 12 days previously had killed or wounded 25 Jews in an attack on their settlement, Yechiam, were, presumably, 'likewise in possession of a quantity of arms' to enable them to carry out their successful attack, but were apparently allowed to withdraw, without suffering any casualties or confiscations, after the settlement had been relieved by a platoon of the 2nd Battalion The Middlesex Regiment.

Similarly, when on 2 February military vehicles were attacked in Haifa by crowds of Arabs, they were dispersed by the use of tear gas but apparently permitted to retain their weapons. On 19 February, when a convoy was ambushed by Arabs near Manara and three Jews were killed and eleven wounded, the Arabs were 'driven off by troops of 17th/21st Lancers and 1st

Battalion Irish Guards' and probably took their farewell together with their weapons, which would doubtless come in handy before long.

Kimche has left an account of this state of affairs.

'Throughout the first months of conflict hostilities were largely confined to isolated attacks on the mixed Arab-Jewish cities of Jerusalem and Haifa, and on the quarters of mixed populations which divided Tel Aviv and Jaffa. The British troops who were still stationed in these cities, and in particular in Jerusalem, did nothing to stop these skirmishes. When the Arab mob set fire to the Jewish Commercial Centre in Jerusalem at the outbreak of hostilities, British troops in armoured cars stood by, taking photographs of the scene. When Haganah forces were rushed up to prevent the pillage the armoured cars were moved against them, preventing them from reaching the conflagration. Later, during the nightly attacks on the isolated Jewish quarters in Jerusalem, the British would content themselves with an occasional search party, usually to search the Haganah defenders. During the first weeks of hostilities in Jerusalem the Haganah forces were far more wary of the British than they were of the Arabs, and this feeling was exacerbated when once a British patrol disarmed some Haganah men, took them to the Arab lines in the Old City and set them free. They were immediately killed by the Arabs.' (op. cit., p. 78)

Had the British been willing to confiscate the weapons in Arab hands, they could have reaped a rich harvest. The Arab League's Military Committee reported to the Arab League council on 8 February that it had to that date delivered to the Palestinian Arabs 1,700 rifles together with half a million rounds of ammunition and some pistols and grenades. The Egyptian Government sent their donation to the ex-Mufti, for distribution to his supporters: 1,200 rifles and 700,000 rounds. Soon after this, following Nuri Said's 16 January meeting with Bevin, the Iraqi Government sent a further 1,000 rifles, and the Syrian authorities another 78 machine-guns, 8 mortars and 645 rifles. If this were not enough, the British issued 360 English rifles to Arabs in Upper Galilee, 200 rifles to the Negev Bedu, and 300 to the Arab National Guard at Jaffa.

This last donation could have been put to good use on 14 December, when the Arabs launched an attack on the detached Jewish suburb of Holon, near Jaffa. When they were repulsed by the defenders they felt justified in complaining to the police, who promptly searched the suburb for arms and arrested six of the Jewish defenders. This was by no means an isolated instance of a widespread practice. Four Haganah members were arrested on 19 December while escorting a convoy of the Palestine Potash Company to the Dead Sea. When, on 28 December, the Arabs attacked a children's home in the Katamon quarter of Jerusalem, the police arrived during the battle and arrested ten of the Haganah defenders – but not a single Arab attacker.

On 29 December the *Manchester Guardian* published a cable from Tel Aviv which declared: 'World public opinion must be made aware that Jews here will be unable to submit to systematic disarming by the Government, which is open to only one inter-pretation – namely, to make the Jews defenceless before the growing armed Arab forces.' The casualty lists issued by the Government showed that 80 Jews had been killed and 50 seriously wounded during the first two weeks of December. In the following week a further 37 Jews were killed: by 10 January the official total of Jewish dead amounted to 769.

By that time the road to the Hebrew University on Mount Scopus had been effectively closed by the Arab concentrations at Sheikh Jarrah. On 13 January Haganah mounted a spirited offensive aimed at re-opening the road, and succeeded in capturing Sheikh

Jarrah as well as the Police Training School. After the battle the Jews were ordered by the British to surrender both places. Haganah agreed, on condition that the Arabs would not be permitted to renew their blockade in these areas, and withdrew their forces on receipt of British agreement to their terms. The British promptly handed Sheikh Jarrah back to the Arabs. It was at this time that Nuri Said was on his way to his discussion with Bevin on the question of arms for Iraq.

Five days after the Nuri-Bevin meeting, on 21 January, Cadogan informed the United Nations Palestine Commission: 'The Jewish story that the Arabs are the attackers and the Jews the attacked is not tenable. The Arabs are determined to show that they will not submit tamely to the United Nations Plan of Partition; while the Jews are trying to consolidate the advantages gained at the General Assembly by a succession of drastic operations designed to intimidate and cure the Arabs of any desire for further conflict.'

Cadogan was of course speaking on behalf of the British Government, but it is clear that no Arab spokesman could have done better, and his performance, while it may have been warmly applauded by the Arab nations, brought forth a rebuke on 30 January from the UN Secretary-General Trygve Lie, who said in London: 'It is not only a matter of nations accepting decisions on which they have always agreed: the nations have to show disciplined loyalty on all issues and on all decisions, irrespective of their viewpoints before the decisions were reached.'

The United Nations Palestine Commission had requested the British Government to agree to the opening on 1 February of a major seaport in Palestine to facilitate substantial Jewish immigration: in his 21 January speech Cadogan had said that this was 'not possible'. Yet even while he was speaking, 700 men of the Liberation Army, under a Syrian officer, Safr Bek, were driving across the border into Palestine in 20 trucks with Syrian numberplates. 'The ease with which the Liberation Army had moved into Palestine, and the striking absence of British intervention,' wrote Kimchi, 'began to produce unexpected consequences. The activists in the Liberation Army were greatly encouraged in their conviction that the British army would not or could not intervene.' (op. cit., p. 88)

On 2 February the Jerusalem Military Court dealt with six members of the Haganah unit which had participated in the defence of the Hatikva quarter of Tel Aviv on 7 January. They were each sentenced to five years imprisonment. However severe this sentence may have seemed, it was preferable to the fate which awaited four Haganah youngsters picked up by a squad of British soldiers in the Bet Israel quarter of Jerusalem on 13 February. Instead of handing their charges over to the police, the squad took the youngsters to the Arab quarter near the Damascus Gate and delivered them to the mob. Their bodies were found an hour later.

Extremists among the British, including deserters from the army and the police, were now emerging to play a more active part in the war against the Jews, frequently using British uniforms and equipment. On 1 February the *Palestine Post* building on Hassolel Street was completely destroyed by the explosion of an army-type car filled with dynamite and parked against the building. The Arabs denied responsibility for this outrage – the *Post* was a journal with an established reputation for moderation and represented no useful target – and it was generally accepted that British policemen were responsible.

Nobody was arrested, and on 22 February the same technique was employed, though on a much larger scale, in Ben Yehuda Street, where three trucks loaded with dynamite were exploded, completely destroying multi-storied buildings and burning many others. Fifty-two Jews were killed: 123 were wounded. Here again the Arabs disclaimed any connection with the crime. A handbill, signed by Fascists, acknowledged responsibility. The Jewish Agency held a public inquiry, where they heard the evidence of a number of witnesses who had seen the trucks, which they claimed were British and driven by British drivers. The official casualty figures published at the end of the month gave the total of Jewish dead from 10 January as 200, with 579 wounded, bringing the official death toll since 1 December 1947, to 969.

On 14 April the usual convoy of doctors, nurses and teachers was making its way up to the Hebrew University and the Hadassah Hospital on Mount Scopus. The convoy, which had set off at 9.30 a.m., comprised two ambulances, three armoured buses, three trucks with food and hospital supplies, and two small escort cars. Assurances had been received from both the High Commissioner and the Secretary of State for the Colonies that medical and civilian supplies traffic to Mount Scopus would have the protection of British Army and police forces.

Before the convoy commenced its climb the responsible British police officer had confirmed that the road was clear, but beyond Sheikh Jarrah the convoy struck a mine, which damaged and halted one ambulance and two buses. The rear car managed to turn round and get away while Arab troops concealed in ambush on both sides of the road immediately concentrated small weapons fire accompanied by grenades and Molotov cocktails on the stricken convoy. Less than 200 yards away the British military post enjoyed a grandstand view of the ensuing massacre but made no attempt to intervene: the British commander later explained that he considered the force under his command inadequate for an effective intervention. Nor would British military headquarters permit the Haganah to attempt a rescue, maintaining that the Army had the situation in hand.

At 1 p.m. a British military car came on the scene and was hailed by the Director of the Hadassah, Dr. Chaim Yassky, but failed to stop. An hour later more British army cars came through: these also ignored Yassky's frantic signals. The Arabs had received reinforcements at noon, and the two Haganah cars which attempted to fight their way through were ambushed. Two other cars trying to bring help from Mount Scopus were mined.

At 1.45 p.m. Dr. Judah Magnes, the president of the Hebrew University, telephoned General Macmillan, pleading desperately for help. By 3 p.m. two of the buses were blazing: the passengers who were not already dead were burned alive, while those who attempted to leave the burning vehicles were killed by the Arabs. It was 4.30 p.m. before the Arabs were finally driven off. Of the 28 survivors of the massacre, 20 were wounded. The 77 dead included Dr. Yassky and a host of doctors, scientists and teachers. The Arab Higher Committee described the massacre as an heroic exploit and a great victory.

Two days later the Arabs were able to celebrate another 'great victory'. At Safad, in which dwelt some 3,000 Orthodox Jews and 12,000 Arabs, the British withdrew their forces after handing over to the Arabs the three police stations which dominated the town and which included the great Taggart fortress standing impregnably 150 feet up on the summit of a hill. The saintly scholars of Safad boasted a Palmach garrison of 35 men: the Arab Liberation Army in the town numbered nearly 3,000, under Adib Shishekli, commander on the northern front of the Army.

On the same day the *Manchester Guardian* published the names of some of those killed at Mount Scopus, including Dr. Doljansky, the director of the cancer research, the deputy-administrator of the Cancer Research Department, Dr. Dostrovsky, and Dr. Joseph originally of New Zealand – the surgeon of Hadassah. Of the Hebrew University staff, Professor Bonaventura, the head of the Psychological Department, Dr. Freiman, lecturer in Jewish Law, Dr. Klar, a lecturer in philology, Dr. Ben-David, secretary of the Medical Faculty, who was responsible for the plans of the

Medical School, and Mrs. Cassuto, the daughter-in-law of the Professor of the Bible and herself an assistant in the Department of Bacteriology, were amongst those killed. Such were the victims of 'the heroic exploit and great victory' celebrated by the Arabs and witnessed by those who had claimed to 'have the situation in hand'.

The Taggart fortress which dominated Safad was not the only place of strategic importance to be handed over to the Arabs as the British prepared to leave Palestine. In his *Diary of the War*, General Taha Hashemi, the Iraqi in charge of the training of Arab volunteers in Damascus, relates how Arab leaders were advised by the British of the exact time of their evacuation of the police fortress, not only of Safad, but also at Nebi Yusha in the Galilee. When the British left the main electricity works at Gesher Naharayim it was immediately occupied by the Arab Legion. The fortress at Samakh, together with the nearby army camp, similarly were passed to the Arabs. It appears from Taha's book that in Jerusalem the British Deputy Police Commander kept the Jerusalem Arabs fully informed of the impending moves of the British evacuation.

By 1 May chaos had descended on Jerusalem. On the following day the *Palestine Post* printed a statement by Robert Graves, the Jerusalem council chairman, in which he announced: 'The present state of Jerusalem is untenable. There is no law and order in certain parts of the town. Cars are being stolen daily. The whole of the Municipal fire brigade plant and cars were stolen and they are not likely to be returned. My own car was stolen a few days ago.'

The Central Post Office had closed down completely on 26 April and the British and Arab officials had left. On 5 May Jewish officials took over: when, nine days later, Sir Alan Cunningham drove out of Jerusalem in his bullet-proof Daimler, followed by the last British civilians and troops, the offices and control posts they had evacuated were taken over by Haganah men within minutes. At the same time 500 Arabs in armoured cars and on foot entered El Alamein Camp on the Jerusalem-Bethlehem road immediately after the British had left it. The shelling of the city by the Arab Legion, which had commenced on 20 April, now became sharply intensified. Vital cadres of British officers had stayed behind with the Arab Legion to direct the bombardment of West Jerusalem. The curious lull in the firing for about half an hour every afternoon was attributed to the need on the part of the British artillery experts to have their traditional tea breaks. During the three weeks after 14 May, Jerusalem was hit by more than 10,000 shells.

The bombardment of Jerusalem engendered comment and correspondence in the British press and discussion in the House of Commons. *The Times* of 20 May, 1948, published a letter from John Connell, who had been

'in Palestine within a week of the end of the mandate . . . In Jerusalem, through which I walked on Saturday, 1 May, I saw looting, hate, chaos, and destruction which will stick in my memory until I die. I saw a beautiful city being murdered. And throughout the whole of Palestine the constructive and creative work was by then collapsing in ruin.

'Britain cannot be absolved of responsibility: this ruin has been willed by His Majesty's Government . . . And now, on the day that the Foreign Office issues its statement on aid to Transjordan and on the position of British officers serving in the Arab Legion, the British public may read that one of these officers is in personal command of the artillery bombardment of the Holy City.

'His Majesty's Government may make great play with legal rectitude. But against this ultimate dishonour I, for one, must speak out in personal protest.'

While Mr. Bevin was assuring the House of Commons that no British officers 'are employed in directing the artillery which is bombarding Jerusalem' the dispatches sent by the Special Correspondents of *The Times* and the *Manchester Guardian* told a different story. The Special Correspondent of the *Manchester Guardian* wrote:

'The bombardment of Notre Dame and some neighbouring buildings continues. A British major of the Arab Legion commands this operation, and other British officers are with him.'

An editorial in the *Guardian* of 27 May asked:

'Is there, perhaps, a secret agreement by the Arab States to destroy Israel and divide up Palestine between them? In that case Britain would be more than ever compromised, for we should be directly guilty of supporting a conspiracy. The only sure way to prove our innocence is for Mr. Bevin to make a full statement withdrawing all support for the Arab League, stopping all supplies of arms while the fighting continues, and withdrawing the few British officers still with the Arab Legion. Sooner or later, too, Mr. Bevin must drop his hostility to Israel. Is it not time to remember with pride, as many Jews even now remember with gratitude, that without this country there would be no Jewish Home in Palestine at all? To help to destroy it now would be a strange fulfilment of our promises.'

On the following day the *Manchester Guardian* printed a letter from a 'Missionary in Jerusalem', which protested:

'A few months ago, when no danger existed, there was a great outcry by the Archbishop of York and some other Church leaders concerning the protection of the Holy Places in Jerusalem. Now that that danger actually exists, they are strangely silent.

'Day after day shells are being poured into Jerusalem by Arab League troops. The arms, uniforms, and wages of this force are paid for by British taxpayers, and no one acquainted with the situation in Palestine doubts that these troops are there by the tacit consent of the British Government. The shells from these British 25-pounder guns and mortars are devastating that city and bringing ruin to places both holy and unholy.

'Yet the Church is silent; no outcry is made either by the Archbishop of Canterbury or the Archbishop of York. No meetings of protests have been called by Church leaders; the Church is silent. Are we to judge from this that political expediency means more than veneration? Is the British public aware that those British guns, firing British shells, paid for by British taxpayers, are dug in on the Mount of Olives by the very spot from which our Lord ascended to Heaven? Does it mean nothing to Christian leaders when we read in our paper today that Moslems have already turned the Church of the Holy Sepulchre in the Old City of Jerusalem into a place of worship of Allah?'

In a letter published in *The Times* of 22 May, a Member of Parliament, Mr. Lyall Wilkes, ventured:

'No doubt if British officers and British-supplied tanks and aeroplanes continue the destruction of Jewish settlements and life we shall earn the bitter hatred of the Jews of Palestine. It is a policy choice for the British Government which will determine whether Israel becomes once more an ally, as in the war,' (during which, he had earlier pointed out, 'Haganah was recognised by G.H.Q. as the one reliable local defence force and Palestine the one base whose loyalty was never in doubt for a moment' – in contrast to Iraq, who 'declared war against us', and Egypt, where 'British tanks had to be driven into the Palace yard') 'or an enemy beleaguered by British arms and equipment who must look elsewhere for aid for sheer survival. And may I say that our attitude – that Israel must show itself capable of functioning before being recognised by us – would sound more honest if it were not troops trained and equipped by British military missions, and the British-officered and subsidised Arab Legion, which were at war with Israel to prevent precisely that functioning.

'Does public opinion at home appreciate (as it does abroad) that every tank and aeroplane now being used by the Arabs has been supplied from the United Kingdom; that the British air mission is still functioning in Iraq; that British missions are now working, training, and re-equipping Arab armies in Saudi Arabia and in Iraq; that between 1945 and 1947 we supplied Egypt alone with 40 military aircraft, 38 scout cars and 298 carriers, apart from a great quantity of small arms and light equipment; that the Arab Legion now waging war is wholly subsidised by us with £2,000,000 a year and is commanded by 38 British officers . . . that no word of protest has come from the British Government at the Arab invasions but that the Jews within the boundaries given them by the United Nations partition decision (which still stands) are denied arms by the British?

'Will we never learn that we cannot subsidise aggression in the Middle East and oppose it in Greece and Persia – that to climb now into the grandstand and attempt to wash our hands of responsibility for the slaughter perpetrated by Spit-fires and British trained and officered Arab troops is conduct utterly unworthy of the traditions of a great nation and indi-cates a moral degeneration within the political leadership of this country?'

On 17 April 1948, the Security Council had voted a resolution imposing a general arms embargo and a ban on fighting personnel going into Palestine. When the Council met on 15 May, the day when the Arab armies invaded Palestine, the Egyptian delegate assured the Council that his country was concerned only with preserving law and order. The Council met again on Monday, 17 May, by which date the Egyptians had advanced beyond Gaza, had besieged the Jewish settlement of Yad Mordechai (on the road to Majdal) and were approaching Isdud, on the road to Rehovot, and the United States delegate proposed that, in view of the breach of peace which had taken place, the Council should order an immediate cease-fire.

The British did not attempt to debate this proposal until the following day, when Sir Alexander Cadogan expressed the view that there had not been a breach of the peace or a clear case of aggression. The Arabs were still advancing on all fronts, and it was clear that in the circumstances the British did not wish to countenance any check to their progress, which in fact continued for the next four days.

On 22 May the American delegate returned with the charge that a breach of the peace had indeed taken place and that the sanctions of Article 39 of the UN Charter should be imposed. Once again he was opposed by Cadogan, and the Council adjourned for a further two days. On 24 May the Council received an acceptance of the cease-fire proposed in the American resolution from the Israelis: the Syrians countered this by requesting an extension of the time-limit within which the resolution should be obeyed. Clearly, such an extension would have enabled the Arab forces to maintain their progress, and Cadogan supported the Syrian request. He also opposed, on 29 May, a proposal by the Soviet Union which was supported by the United States and France, to order a 'cease-fire within 36 hours under threat of United Nations Sanctions.'

The Security Council were aware that Britain was able to use her right of veto to block any form of sanction against the Arab

States, and finally its members agreed to accept Cadogan's nomination of Count Bernadotte as United Nations Mediator for Palestine. Bernadotte's diary has revealed some interesting facts attending his nomination. Ashley Clarke, the British Chargé d'Affaires in Paris, received him there on 25 May and informed him 'that the British Government was not prepared for the time being to take any steps against the Arabs.' Furthermore, the British Government would continue to arm the Arabs, and British officers, who had joined the Arab forces as instructors, were taking an active part in the war. The American proposal that the Arab action should be regarded as 'provocation and a flagrant breach on the United Nations Charter' was, Clarke confided to the Count, not acceptable to the British. (Bernadotte, *To Jerusalem*, pp. 6–7)

Bernadotte's truce commenced on 11 June. Its reception by the Arabs was a mixed one. Abdullah was in its favour, but the Arab public had been encouraged by a succession of newspaper headlines to believe that their armies had enjoyed, until the imposition of the truce, a series of glorious victories: the truce alone had robbed them of the final victory. On 8 July they renewed the war.

When, on 8 July, Bernadotte's telegram announcing the resumption of hostilities reached the Security Council, the Syrian delegate disputed the need for any hasty or drastic action on the part of the Council. Cadogan appeared to share this view, and the Council contented itself with cabling messages to both Israelis and Arabs calling for a ten-days' truce to commence on 10 July. Israel responded immediately, accepting the appeal. The Arabs made no reply. In the four weeks preceding 8 July they had increased their forces in Palestine by the addition of some 10,000 troops and had reinforced their armour and aircraft to an extent which encouraged them to face the resumption of the fighting with optimism.

But on 12 July Lydda airport fell to the Israelis. On the following day they captured Beit Nabala, and Cadogan was galvanised into action. He informed the Council that the British view was now that the parties must immediately be *ordered* to desist from any further military action, on pain of sanctions. On 15 July this resolution was voted and agreed, and a truce came into force on 18 July. This held until 5 October, when the Egyptians, after concentrating numbers of reserves in the area of the Negev, sprang a bombing and artillery offensive against the Jewish settlements.

The Israeli counter-attack came on 15 October, covering a wide front and capturing a number of key points. It continued until 22 October, when the towns of Isdud and Majdal fell to the Israelis and the United Nations ordered a cease-fire. On 4 November the British delegation pressed for an order to compel the Israelis to withdraw to the lines they held before 15 October. The Israelis complied with the Acting Mediator's interpretation of the order, and held their operations in the south, but towards the end of the month were forced to break the truce in the north, where Kaukji's reorganised Liberation Army had opened an offensive against the Jewish settlements in the Galilee.

'Operation Hiram' ended on 31 October after the complete defeat of Kaukji's army, and there was once more a truce in Palestine. But fighting broke out again in the south on 23 December, and on 27 December the Egyptian key position at Auja fell to the Israelis. On 28 December the first Israeli troops crossed the international frontier into Egypt, and by 30 December the southern airfield at el-Arish was in their hands. That was as far as they were allowed to go. Great Britain, invoking the long-disputed Anglo-Egyptian Treaty of Friendship of 1936, sent an ultimatum to Israel, calling for her immediate withdrawal from Egyptian territory.

Moshe Sharett, the Israeli Foreign Minister, fearful that non-compliance with this order would immediately bring the British into the war, ordered Alon, who was in charge of the operations, to withdraw his troops from Egyptian territory. Alon, who had seen the entire Sinai peninsula falling into his grasp, for there was no organised Egyptian army between el-Arish and Egypt proper, was obliged to switch his troops from el-Arish to the Rafah front, which he attacked on 3 January. Once the Israelis had captured the heights to the south of the town overlooking the road and the railway the Egyptians, on 6 January, announced their willingness to enter armistice negotiations at UN headquarters.

We may never know why, at this stage, the British decided to send five of their warplanes into the battle zone on the southern front. Crossman wrote unequivocally that Bevin had 'personally ordered them into combat' in the prosecution of his 'vendetta' against the Jews. The *Manchester Guardian*'s Tel Aviv Correspondent's dispatch dated January 9 reported:

'The destruction of five Royal Air Force fighters by Israeli defence forces in the region of the Egyptian-Palestinian border on Friday [7 January], and the reported dispatch of British troops to Aqaba, are regarded here as conclusive evidence that Britain is taking an active part in the Palestine conflict.

'The Israeli Foreign Minister lodged a strong protest with the Deputy Acting Mediator this morning against the "unilateral intervention" by Britain and intends to raise the matter immediately with the Security Council. It is understood that the dispatch of British troops to Transjordan will be regarded as a blow to the prospects of a peaceful settlement and deliberate obstruction of the United Nations attempt at conciliation.

'Early this morning Mr. Cyril Marriott, the British Consul General in Haifa, delivered a memorandum to the Israeli Foreign Ministry representative there, strongly protesting against the shooting down of the five fighters. The memorandum also included a warning that in view of this unprovoked attack the Royal Air Force has been instructed to regard as hostile any "Jewish aircraft" encountered over Egyptian territory.'

The text of the British protest handed to the Jewish representatives at the United Nations on 8 January read:

'His Majesty's Government take a grave view of the events recorded in the attached statement by the Air Ministry, which have resulted in the loss of five British aircraft as a result of unprovoked attacks by Jewish aircraft over Egyptian territory. They have informed the United Nations acting mediator of these events, and wish also to make a strong protest to the Jewish authorities in Tel Aviv and to reserve all their rights both with regard to claims for compensation and to all possible subsequent action.'

The Diplomatic Correspondent of the paper wrote:

'It may well be that when the initial anger against the State of Israel, which is inevitable, has subsided, more serious reflection than has hitherto been apparent will be given to the question, "What were British 'planes doing flying over a combat area and generally reconnoitring in a conflict to which we are not a party?" They were there neither in virtue of Anglo-Egyptian treaty of mutual assistance nor on behalf of the United Nations.

'Perhaps this incident may cause, too, a more critical examination of our whole policy over Palestine – a policy which it is now revealed has brought us close to direct involvement in the conflict. The British Government's decision to send up 'planes, based in the Canal zone, to reconnoitre Israeli troop movements across the Egyptian frontier would presumably be justified on the grounds that it was necessary for us to know the extent of the Israeli incursions in view of the possibility of Britain's having to come to Egypt's assistance under the terms of the 1936 treaty of mutual assistance.

'In London, such action may be thought entirely normal and unprovocative. But how would it seem to the Israeli authorities and troops? They know that on the termination of the mandate last May forces from the neighbouring Arab countries advanced deep into territory which had been awarded to Israel by the United Nations decision and to overthrow the new State which has now been recognised by the United States and Russia and a number of smaller Powers.

'After initial difficulties Jewish armies have succeeded in pushing back her Arab attackers, and in the case of Egyptians have pressed them back across their own frontier. The people of Israel will not readily understand the objections voiced when, in the course of military operations, Israeli forces find themselves on the territory of the army which they have just driven out of their own land.

'They will remember that during the past year the Government and people of Egypt have spent much time in abusing Britain on the grounds that the 1936 treaty has become a dead letter. They can be excused, therefore, if they see as mere hypocrisy our expressions of anxiety at the possibility of our being forced to go to Egypt's assistance as a result of obligations arising from a treaty which Egypt refuses to recognise and cannot be persuaded to invoke. At least one can understand the reaction of the Jews when they found the aircraft of a country with which they were not at war reconnoitring their military positions, passing this information back to London, where the Foreign Office made it immediately public to the world.

'This action, combined with the dispatch of British forces to Aqaba, will strengthen that Israeli contention that the United Kingdom must be regarded as a party to the dispute. If Mr. Bevin seriously felt that the Israeli incursions across the Egyptian frontier constituted a real threat to Egypt and that Britain's strategic interests required that we prevent this, that is a possible point of view. It might justify our sending up a reconnaissance aircraft and our publication of military information. But those that accept this point of view cannot be surprised or shocked if direct retaliation is made by Israel.'

On 26 January Foreign Minister Shertok informed the State Council in Tel Aviv that:

'The Israeli Government has replied to the British Memorandum protesting against the shooting down of the five British planes which, following its non-acceptance in view of its being addressed to the Jewish Authorities, Tel Aviv, was transmitted to the Israeli Delegation at Lake Success by the Secretary General of the United Nations. The reply regrets that the Israeli Government cannot accept the accuracy of the British statement, since the two captured British flyers admitted that the planes flew over Israeli territory. But even if the British statements of fact were correct, the despatch of British aircraft to the battle zone in collaboration with Egyptian forces constitutes a grave breach of neutrality and warrants military counter-action. The reply regrets that the encounter occurred but places responsibility on those who ordered the operation, which cannot but be regarded as illegitimate and ill-considered. It is impossible to reconcile British action with adherence to the Security Council decisions.'

37

'I say to the Mandatory Power: You shall not outrage the
Jewish nation. You shall not play fast and loose with the
Jewish people. Say to us frankly that the National Home
is closed, and we shall know where we stand. But this
trifling with a nation bleeding from a thousand wounds
must not be done by the British whose empire is built on
moral principles – that mighty Empire must not commit
this sin against the People of the Book. Tell us the truth.
This at least we have deserved.' Dr. Chaim Weizmann
on the Report of the Palestine Commission, Zurich 4
August 1937

'In the course of this century the histories of Great Britain
and of the Jewish people have been tragically yet providentially intertwined – and the man chiefly responsible for this
was Chaim Weizmann . . . The fact that he refused to criti-
cise British Imperial policy did not mean that Weizmann
was blind to the difficulties and the dangers of relying on
British Governments . . . There remains the charge that
Weizmann was pro-British . . . Weizmann, as we have seen,
was enamoured of Britain, particularly of the British ruling
class . . . Nevertheless, it is not my impression that in any of
his countless dealings with successive Governments
Weizmann let the British off lightly . . . What is true,
however, is that Weizmann increasingly believed in the
mutual value of the Anglo-Jewish association.' (Richard
Crossman: *A Nation Reborn*)

As we have seen, Weizmann's loyalty to Britain earned him
defeat at the December 1946 Zionist Congress at Zurich. That it

was by no means a blind allegiance is evidenced in a letter he wrote earlier in that year, in which he said:

> 'Palestine today is not merely a police state: it is the worst form of military dictatorship. To all intents and purposes there is no Civil Administration; that has receded entirely into the background, and my impression is that the country is run by military cliques in Jerusalem and/or Cairo. This has been the case for some time now, but has recently, of course, become more obvious, and the present situation is hopeless. Anybody may be arrested by any soldier or officer, without warrant, without reason given; he can be thrown into custody, and kept there until the military choose to bring a charge, institute a trial or enquiry – or at their pleasure release him. He has no redress. In Palestine today the writ of *Habeas Corpus* does not run. There is a severe censorship – both on Press messages abroad and on the local papers, and no freedom of comment in the Press. The prisons and camps are thronged with people arrested on the flimsiest pretexts, some of whom have already languished there for months, and none of whom has any certainty as to when he will be brought to trial or released.

> 'I am informed that the G.O.C. Palestine is credited with having said that he would like to "uproot every Jew in Palestine". This story was, I believe, telegraphed here by the distinguished British journalist who mentioned it to me (he was in Palestine recently), but received no publicity. I believe it to be true; certainly it is supported by the type of "propaganda" known to be current among British troops in Palestine, who are being taught to regard Jews as "the enemy" . . .

> 'It has been stated by the authorities that there was no intention in these searches of damaging the country's economy. It is difficult to believe this in view of the fact

that in many settlements the whole male population has been carried away into detention, and is being kept in custody throughout the period of the harvest. It is my own view that, contrary to the official statements, the deliberate intention in these operations was to destroy as many of the settlements as possible. I believe that the recent operations were intended as the preliminary stage of something much larger. The military cliques expected a violent reaction to their first effort, a reaction such as would have justified the use of artillery, the bombing of Tel Aviv and other centres, and so on' (21 July 1946)

In a statement issued to the press on 25 March 1948, he said:

'I shall never understand how the Mandatory government could allow foreign Arab forces to cross freely by bridge and road into Palestine and prepare, at leisure and with impunity, to make war against the Jews and against the settlement adopted by the United Nations. I have always paid high tribute to the great act of statesmanship of Great Britain in inaugurating the international recognition of our right to nationhood. But in exposing everything and everybody in Palestine to destruction by foreign invaders the Mandatory Government has acted against its own best tradition and left a tragic legacy to the country's future.'

In April he told Creech-Jones, the British Colonial Secretary:

'The British view seemed to be that Arabs and Jews should be left to themselves for an unavoidable period of blood-letting. The British clearly anticipated that the Arabs would make substantial inroads on the territory allotted to the Jews, and on the basis of the situation thus created a new solution would be reached, favourable, both politically and territorially, to the Arabs. It is an astonishing reflection on the relationship of the British to Palestine that they, who

261

have been on the spot for the last 30 years, should have made so false an appraisal of the factors.'

On 15 May, when Weizmann was in New York, recognition of the State of Israel was extended, first by the United States and then the Soviet Union and Poland. Great Britain remained silent, and there were reports that Bevin was bringing pressure to bear on the British Dominions and Western Europe to withhold recognition.

'It had been my original intention', he wrote, 'to go again to England for personal and family reasons. I now felt that I was no longer free to do so. Arab armies were attacking Israel by land and from the air: the spearhead of this aggression was the Arab Legion of Transjordan, trained and commanded by British officers. An atmosphere had been created in which the ideals of the State of Israel, and the policies of Great Britain, under Mr. Bevin's direction, were brought into bloody conflict. I had no place in England at such a time, and I felt it a bitter incongruity that I should not be able to set foot in a country whose people and institutions I held in such high esteem . . .'

THE MIDDLE EAST IN 1956

EPILOGUE

Weizmann never again set foot in the England in which he had spent the greater part of his life. On 16 February 1949, the first elected Parliament of Israel elevated him from the Presidency of the Provisional State Council to the office of the President of the State of Israel.

He died on 9 November 1952, some eight months after the head of the neighbouring state of Jordan, King Abdullah, had been assassinated by a Palestinian Arab as he was about to enter the al-Aqsa Mosque in Jerusalem. Abdullah's grandson Hussein came to the throne of Jordan in the following May. Nearly three years later the young monarch summarily dismissed his Commander-in-Chief of the Arab Legion, Lieutenant-General Sir John Bagot Glubb (Glubb Pasha), who had served the Transjordanian Army since 1930.

This was not the first signal to Britain of the king's flowering independence. In 1955 he had withdrawn his decision to adhere to the Baghdad Pact which Britain, Pakistan and Iraq had joined, and in 1957 he approved the abrogation of the Jordanian Treaty of 1946 (modified in March 1948 to stress Transjordan's independence and the equal status of the two contracting parties). But he did not hesitate to ask Britain to send her troops into Jordan in order to protect his country's independence following the Iraqi *coup d'etat* of 14 July 1958, when Hussein's cousin King Feisal II was murdered together with a number of Iraqi and Jordanian leaders. Britain's prompt compliance with this request failed to restore her previous position of privilege in Jordan. Nor did the circumstances of Glubb Pasha's humiliating dismissal in any way diminish his pro-Arab sympathies, fully expressed in two books he wrote in his retirement: *A Soldier With the Arabs* (1957), and *Peace in the Holy Land* (1971).

Other events during the 1950s marked the acceleration of British loss of influence in the Middle East, including the failure of the Middle East Defence Organization Treaty of October 1951; the Anglo-Persian oil crisis of 1952–53; the abnegation of the 1954 Anglo-Egyptian Treaty in 1956, and the Sudan's self-determination without any treaty relationship with Britain in the same year. Nevertheless, the British continued to behave as though the Arab states were their protégés. After the 1967 ('Six Day') war, when by 5 June the Egyptians had massed seven divisions – nearly 120,000 men – more than 1,000 guns, 9,000 anti-tank guns and nearly 1,000 tanks in Sinai, close to the border with Israel, and Jordanian forces had commenced shelling and carrying out air raids across the Jordan-Israel Armistice Line, while Syria shelled Israeli villages, the British sponsored the UN Resolution 242 which called for a 'withdrawal of Israel armed forces from territories occupied' in the course of the fighting. Foreign Secretary Sir Alec Douglas-Hume, speaking in Harrogate on 31 October 1970, said that Israel should withdraw from occupied Egyptian territory and from the Golan Heights, and should accept the old armistice line with Jordan 'subject to minor changes': in brief, to hand back to the Arabs the territories they had lost in their failed bid to annihilate the Jewish State. As these last lines are being written, this view still represents official British policy.

Appendix I

The Arab Legion

The formation of the Arab Legion dates back to October 1920, when a unit comprising five British officers and 100 Arabs (75 cavalry and 25 mounted machine-gunners) was created to serve in the Transjordanian part of Palestine. This force was augmented a few months later by the addition of another unit based on Kerak, consisting of two British officers and 50 Arabs.

In March 1921, when the mandated territory was divided and the Amirate was established, the Legion's force was increased to about 1,000 men, consisting of two cavalry squadrons and two infantry companies, one machine-gun company, two mountain guns and a signal section. When the existing town police force and prison service was incorporated into the Legion, the total strength reached about 1,300 men. In 1930 its British Commander, Lieutenant-Colonel Peake (Peake Pasha) was joined by Major J.B. Glubb, O.B.E., M.C., and by the outbreak of the Second World War the Legion's strength had increased to 1,600 men.

Peake retired in 1939, and Glubb was promoted to Brigadier in 1942, when, officially known as the Assistant Inspector General of the Palestine Police, he was seconded to Transjordan by the Palestine Administration. At the time of the Legion's attack on Jerusalem on 15 May 1948, he had under him eight British N.C.O.s and 40 British officers commanding the mechanised regiments and filling the higher posts in the Legion. The General Staff was composed of British officers, headed by one who was formerly the Transjordanian Consul to Iraq. One officer, Col. R.J. Broadhurst, who also held a high rank in the Palestine Police, had been officially referred to as the 'Military Adviser to His Excellency King Abdullah'.

It was natural that in the circumstances the British Foreign Secretary should be called upon to define in the House of Commons the position of British officers in the Legion. His reply, that half of them were regular officers who had been seconded, while about one-third were on contract with the Transjordan Government, could only sustain the conviction that the Legion was not the national army of Transjordan but a professional army of mercenaries provided and paid for by the British Government. In March 1948 the British turned over to the Legion mines, artillery stores, anti-tank rifles and mortars from supplies in Egypt. Before the British evacuation from Palestine the Legion had received from the British sixty armoured cars, 3,500 high explosive mortar bombs, 4,500 smoke mortar bombs, 100,000 rounds of 30-calibre ammunition, and 900,000 gallons of petrol and was left in control of principal military camps when the British left.

When the Legion invaded Palestine it comprised a mechanised brigade consisting of three battalions, each with a strength of 800/900 men (apart from small auxiliary units) and about 15 companies of infantry garrison troops and two security companies. Each mechanised battalion consisted of one staff company, one armoured company and two companies of motorised infantry, mounted on trucks and armed partly with automatic weapons (Bren guns) and about six Bren-gun carriers per company. The Bren gun-carriers had armour plate of 8 mm and two Bren guns. The armoured companies each had about six heavy armoured cars with a frontal plate of 20-25 mm, a two-pounder artillery piece and two Browning machine guns (.30). Some armoured cars were adopted for mortar use. There also some heavier armour with six-pounders and 75 mm guns. Each mechanised battalion had an artillery unit armed with a number of 6-pounders, PIAT anti-tank guns and 3-inch mortars.

The infantry units were armed with Enfield rifles, and sub-machine guns in the ratio of 70 to 30. There were at least two machine guns and one 2-inch mortar per infantry platoon. The total strength of the infantry was estimated at 3,500. The officers were trained in Latrun (near Jerusalem) and in other British Army training centres in Palestine and the United Kingdom at the expense of the Palestinian Government.

When the United Nations decided, on 29 November 1947, upon the partition of Palestine, there were two battalions of the mechanised brigade, two infantry battalions and two companies of 'The Security Group' of the Legion in Palestine, numbering between 4,000 and 5,000 Legionaries. According to a Cairo report attributed to the Transjordan Foreign Minister, the Legion went into action against the Jews of Tel Aviv on 5 December. On 14 December they twice attacked Jewish transport at Yazur and Beth Nabalah, killing 14 and wounding 10 – mostly Settlement Policemen – in an incident which was later the subject of a Court of Enquiry. On 20 December a Group Sergeant of the Jewish Settlement Police was shot dead as he walked past the Allenby Barracks of the Transjordan Frontier Force in Jerusalem.

Wilson's *Cordon and Search* reported a 'Day of minor incidents in Haifa in which casualties were suffered on all sides' on 3 February 1948, but on that day five Jews, including a woman passenger, were killed and 20 injured when members of the Legion attacked a Jewish convoy near the Neveh Shaanan quarter, and on 15 December six Jewish passers-by were killed and 12 wounded when they were attacked by Arab Legionaires near Barclays Bank in Haifa. Wilson does report 'Arab Legion in action against Haganah post near Ahuzzat on Mount Carmel' on 17 February, but not the further attacks by the Legion on the 19th in Haifa and Jerusalem when three Jews were killed, or the

Transjordan Frontier Police attack on a Jewish Settlement Police vehicle on 25 February, when two Jewish police were killed and three others wounded.

On 26 April the Transjordan Government declared 'war on Zionism', and units of the Arab Legion stationed east of the River Jordan entered Palestine and occupied Jericho. On April 30 the Legion claimed to have killed 150 Jews at Jisr Mejam, south of Lake Galilee, and on 12 May the survivors of Kfar Etzion were massacred after they had laid down their arms and surrendered to a force estimated at several thousand headed by Arab Legion armour, artillery and infantry, in one of the most shameful incidents of the conflict. But these incidents were but a prelude to the dawn invasion of Palestine by the Legion's main forces on 15 May 1948.

Appendix II

Archives in the Public Records Office, London.

CAB (Cabinet)
CO (Colonial)
FO (Foreign Office)
HO (Home Office)
PREM (Prime Minister's Office)
WO (War Office)

FO/371/3663
371/3749
371/20804
371/20806
371/20818
371/20820
371/20821
371/21635
371/21888
371/23251
371/24078
371/24090
371/24091
371/24094
371/24097
371/24100
371/24388
371/25189
371/25238/274
371/25238/322

371/25239/150
371/25241
371/25242/117
371/25248/331
371/27126
371/27132
371/32661
371/40816/U5266
371/42817/16
371/52548
371/55771
371/57548
371/57671
371/61758
371/61802
371/61815
371/61816
371/61817
371/61835
371/61836
916/90/19

CAB 23-96
24-279
27-651
67-4
95/15/31

95/15/138
127/801
128/11
129/16

CO 733.429
733/430/76021
733/445
733/446
733/477

HO 45/23515
(GEN 200/117/163

PREM 4/51/1/40
4/51/1/87
4/51/2/116

WO 32/12208
168/22957
169/23022

Concise Bibliography

(Unless otherwise stated the place of publication is London.)

Antonius, George: *The Arab Awakening*. The Story of the Arab National Movement, Hamish Hamilton, 1938.

Ashbee, C.R.: *Palestine Notebook*. Heinemann, 1923.

Begin, Menahem: *The Revolt*. Story of the Irgun. W.H. Allen (1931)

Bethell, Nicholàs: *The Palestine Triangle*, Deutsch, 1979.

Cadogan, Sir Alexander: *The Diaries of Sir Alexander Cadogan*, 1938–1945. Cassell, 1971.

Carlson, John Roy: *Cairo to Damascus*. Knopf, New York, 1951.

Correspondence between Sir Henry McMahon and The Sharif Husain. H.M.S.O. (Cmd. 5957) 1939.

Crossman, Richard: *A Nation Reborn*. Hamish Hamilton, 1960.

Crossman, Richard: *Palestine Mission*. Hamish Hamilton, 1947.

Crum, Bartley C.: *Behind the Silken Curtain*. A personal account of Anglo-American Diplomacy in the Middle East. Gollancz, 1947.

Dayan, Moshe: *Story of My Life*. Weidenfeld & Nicholson, 1976.

Documents on German Foreign Policy 1918–1945 Series D, Volume 11. Her Majesty's Stationery Office.

Duff, Douglas: *Palestine Picture*. Hodder & Stoughton, 1936.

Farago, Ladislas: *Palestine on the Eve*. Putnam, 1936.

Friedman, Isaiah: *The Question of Palestine, 1914–1918: British-Jewish-Arab-Relations*. Routledge & Kegan Paul, 1973.

Frischwasser-Ra'anan, H.F.: *The Frontiers of a Nation*. A re-examination of the forces which created the Palestine Mandate and determined its territorial shape. The Batchworth Press, 1955.

Fromkin, David: *A Peace to End All Peace*: Creating the Modern Middle East 1914–1922. Penguin Books, 1989.

Gilbert, Martin: *The Arab Israeli Conflict: Its History in Maps*. Weidenfeld & Nicolson, 1974.

Gilbert, Martin: *Exile and Return*. The emergence of Jewish Stateshood. Weidenfeld & Nicolson, 1978.

Goodman, Paul (Editor): *The Jewish National Home: 1917–1942*. Dent, 1943.

Graves, Philip: *The Land of Three Faiths*. Jonathan Cape, 1923.

Harkabi, Y.: *Palestinians and Israel*. Keter. Jerusalem, 1974.

Jarvis, C.S.: *Arab Command*. Hutchinson, 1942.

Joseph, Bernard: *The Faithful City*. The siege of Jerusalem, 1948. The Hogarth Press, 1962.

Katz, Samuel: *Battleground*: Fact and Fantasy in Palestine. New York, Bantam, 1973.

Kedourie, Elie: *In the Anglo Arab Labyrinth: The McMahon-Husayn Correspondence and its Interpretations 1914–1939*. Cambridge, 1976.

Kimche, Jon and David: *Both Sides of the Hill*. Secker & Warburg, 1960.

Kimche, Jon and David: *The Secret Roads*. 1955.

Kimche, Jon: *The Second Arab Awakening*. Thames & Hudson, 1970.

Koestler, Arthur: *Thieves in the Night*. Macmillan, 1946.

Koestler, Arthur: *Promise and Fulfilment*. Palestine 1917–1949. Macmillan, 1949.

Laqueur, W. and Rubin, B. (Editors): *The Israeli Arab Reader*. Revised and Updated Edition. Penguin Books, 1984.

Lowdermilk, Walter Clay: *Palestine: Land of Promise*. Gollancz, 1945.

Mackinnon, Nancy: *The Background of the London Conference on Palestine 1947*. The British Association for the Jewish National Home in Palestine. n.d.

Mackworth, Cecily: *The Mouth of the Sword*. Routledge & Kegan Paul, 1949.

Marlowe, John: *Rebellion in Palestine*. The Cresset Press, 1946.

Marlowe, John: *The Seat of Pilate*. An Account of the Palestine Mandate. The Cresset Press, 1959.

McDonald, James G.: *My Mission in Israel: 1948–1951*.Gollancz, 1951.

Meinertzhagen, Col. R.: *Middle East Diary*. Cresset Press, 1959.

Meir, Golda: *My Life*. Weidenfeld & Nicolson, 1975.

Monroe, Elizabeth: *Britain's Moment in the Middle East 1914–1956*. Chatto & Windus, 1963.

Mosley, Leonard: *Gideon Goes to War*. Arthur Barker, 1955.

Palestine Royal Commission Report: July 1937. H.M.S.O., 1937.

Parkes, James: *Whose Land?*. Revised Edition, Penguin Books, 1970.

Patterson, Col. J.H.: *With the Judeans in the Palestine Campaign*. Hutchinson, n.d. (1922)

Patterson, Col. J.H.: *With the Zionists in Gallipoli*. 1948.

Philby, H.St.John: *Arabian Days*. Robert Hale, 1948.

Political Dictionary of the Middle East in the Twentieth Century. Edited by Yaacov Shimoni and Evyatar Levine. Weidenfeld & Nicolson, 1972.

Porath, Y.: *The Emergence of the Palestinian Arab National Movement 1918–1929*. 1974.

Progress Report of the United Nations Mediator on Palestine. Rhodes, 16 September, 1948. H.M.S.O. (Cmd.7530)

Report of the Anglo-American Committee of Enquiry Regarding the Problems of European Jewry and Palestine. Lausanne, 20 April, 1946. H.M.S.O. (Cmd.6808)

Report of a Committee set up to consider Certain Correspondence between Sir Henry McMahon and The Sharif of Mecca in 1915 and 1916. H.M.S.O. (Cmd.5974) 1939.

Report by the United Nations Special Committee on Palestine. Geneva, Switzerland. H.M.S.O. 1947.

Samuel, Horace B.: *Unholy Memories of the Holy Land*. Hogarth, 1930.

Samuel, Viscount: *Memoirs*. The Cresset Press, 1945.

Sharef, Zeev: *Three Days*. W.H. Allen, 1962.

Stein, Leonard: *The Balfour Declaration*, Vallentine Mitchell, 1961.

Storrs, Ronald: *Orientations*. Nicholson & Watson, 1947.

Sykes, Christopher: *Cross Roads to Israel*. Collins, 1965.

Sykes, Christopher: *Orde Wingate*. Collins, 1959.

Wasserstein, Bernard: *Britain and the Jews of Europe 1939–1945*. Oxford University Press, 1979.

Wavell, Lord: *The Palestinian Campaigns*. Constable, 1928.

Weizmann, Chaim: *Trial and Error*. Hamish Hamilton, 1949.

Wilson, A.T.: *Loyalties: Mesopotamia 1914–1917*. Oxford University Press, 1930.

Wilson, R.D.: *Cordon and Search*. With the 6th Airborne Division in Palestine. Gale & Polden, 1949.

Index

276